Brother Iron
Sister Steel

A Bodybuilder's Book

Dave Draper

On Target Publications • Santa Cruz, California

**Brother Iron, Sister Steel: A Bodybuilder's Book
by Dave Draper**

Published by:
On Target Publications
P. O. Box 1335
Aptos, CA 95001 USA
(888) 466-9185

Production: Laree Draper
Copyeditor: Cheryl Miller
Cover design: Valarie Howell/Howell Graphics
Cover artwork: Linda Lima

Publisher's Cataloging-in-Publication Data

Draper, Dave
Brother Iron, Sister Steel : a bodybuilder's book / Dave
Draper.
p. 336 cm. 6x9 ill
Includes index and bibliographical referecences (p. 23)
ISBN 1-931046-65-4
1. Draper, Dave 2. Weight training — Handbooks, manuals
3. Bodybuilding history 4. Bodybuilders — United States —
Biography.
I. Title
796.41

00-191851

Contents

Brother Iron, Sister Steel is a saga about you and me, lifting weights and building muscle. The plot is as simple as ABC and 1-2-3, although I never found anything particularly simple about the alphabet or mathematics. To contribute to the book's simplicity I offer in less than a hundred words an outline of the subject matter contained and its sequence. It goes like this:

Disclaimer

The words that compose this book are written with a logic that comes only from experience, with passion and excitement that come only from a long-time love of the iron. The facts of how to train, how to eat, why and when are presented to you clearly, as insight, not cold precepts that bind you like laws and classroom underscores. Here you'll find exactly what you need to get you going and keep you going with knowledge and understanding, spirit and zeal, purpose and ever growing clarity. Bodybuilding, weight training, nutrition, fitness and exercise comprise an engaging diversion, a healthy sport, a rewarding challenge — a robust lifestyle that lifts you higher and higher.

The writing of this book is based upon my personal experiences. Your experiences and results are certain to be different. All medical experts recommend that you see a doctor before starting a diet or exercise program and that you start slowly.

Brother Iron
Sister Steel

A Bodybuilder's Book

1

THE SOAP OPERA

A person can arrive at a place and not be entirely sure how one got there. The Brooklyn Academy of Music, as I recall, was a gothic structure composed of tall shadows, massive gray stone steps, arches, columns and pigeon-crowned portals. It was tightly pressed into a space amongst towering angular buildings, mortar and concrete that had hardened at the turn of the century. The elegance of its gilded and velvet-curtained opera boxes was not lost to me but the center of my attention focused on the dark and dusty backstage closures, the grandness of which was expressed in bewildering height, intricate pulley and cable systems that raised, lowered and controlled vast curtains, backdrops, scenery and props, microphones, lights and speakers. There, where the strings of the Philharmonic once rejoiced and Caruso had pleaded, wept and conquered, I found a corner to drop my gym bag and prepare an ad-lib strategy for the unknown reckoning ahead: the Mr. America Contest, September, 1965.

I wasn't alone. Tough union stagehands, an amateur crew of fledgling assistants and volunteers, a team of Roloflex photographers and a splat of magazine and newspaper writers spilled over the stage and flowed into the theater's front rows as the judges congregated, shared war stories and sharpened their pencils. Pre-judging would start without fanfare when all the contestants seemed to be present. And, of course, there were the contestants, primed, ragtag and mighty — Mr. America and Mr. Universe look-alikes, dressed funny and still a little wet behind the ears. They were a new breed, putting on Man Tan and pumping up with The Samson Twister and Kool-aid.

I stood in the shadows and peered like a wary owl in a thick forest at the slowly growing commotion around me. I don't mingle much and I mingled less then. I took the long, serious road to get to New York, leaving New Jersey in the spring of '63, stopping off in Los Angeles for a few years and arriving at La Guardia International in mid-September of 1965. Gave me a chance to think and see the sights. They've got sunshine out West; The Beach Boys were right.

A sociological fact stands out: You make friends when you're under stress and wearing the same witless outfit. There was a strong showing of primed bodies from the Islands (Puerto Rico, Trinidad, Tobago and Jamaica) and they were jolly-good. We laughed and had fun, and I'll never forget them. It was a time when I thought I'd never laugh — ever.

And then there's the ritual of oil application done with machismo and very particular care. "Pumping up" presents no problem 'cept for the sliding around and the overtraining, dehydration and hypoglycemia. The dapper fellow who brought the bananas, tuna and a water bottle knew what he was doing. He was the only guy who wore slippers, had a towel ever ready and didn't look like he'd been rolled in the back alley as he presented himself before the judges. He even had spray deodorant in his giant gym bag. Big dandelion. The next year I'd be sure to stock my gym bag with similar backstage contest survival gear.

Pre-judging was a mass of confusion which suited me just fine. The more distracted everyone became, the easier it was to relax, observe and enjoy. Self-conscious mistakes the size of a cow went unnoticed. The immediate post-judging challenge was fueling up before the evening show: no fuel, no energy, no pump, no fun. This I accomplished with Freddy Ortiz and his entourage at an authentic New York delicatessen around the corner, the original fast food of the Big Apple.

Crazy Freddy removed his shirt for no particular reason in the middle of an intersection and stopped traffic as I ate a roast beef on sourdough and drank a container of milk. He was warmin' up for the night's performance. I envied his brashness. It took hooks to pull off my clothes and a net to get me on stage. Good grief. Earl Maynard had his shirt off and was trying to pull down Freddy's pants — I was howling, down to a tank top and hitting double over-head biceps shots be-

Photographer unknown

Mr. America, on stage at The Brooklyn Academy Of Music, 1965. History speaks a clear language in this nostalgic picture. Close inspection of the innocent competitors reveals no tattoos or pierced body bangles. I received an 8x10 of this classic personal prize from a popular female bodybuilding champion who dragged it out of a trash heap that collected in the ground level parking garage of Weider Barbell Company in Woodland Hills, California, winter of 1994. "Thought you might like a copy."

fore a cheering yet ever-flowing stream of busy citizenry. It must have been the carbohydrates, the release from the dark scrutiny of the judges or the relief that accompanies a realization of one's finiteness; standing at the foot of skyscrapers amongst zillions of souls is liberating.

As the evening progressed, Larry Scott and I stuck together behind the thick and impenetrable curtains. America's Mr. America, he knew the ropes — he'd been here before. You might say Larry had already ascended the heights of the famed landmark and returned to reminisce — The Dungeon of Santa Monica meets Vince's Gym of North Hollywood. There's gonna' be a party tonight.

Nothing that takes place backstage can compare with what goes on in a New York City audience, especially a bodybuilding audience, especially in 1965. The enthusiasm arrives in carloads, empties from subway stations, buses and taxicabs. Guys with wives and dudes with chicks on Saturday night, and they are looking cool and feeling no pain. But, wait, my friend. It's beyond that; there's something more and you can taste it. There's a tremor, a stir of expectation, a charge in the air, on the street and in the bowels of the elegant auditorium. It's not frightening; yet, it's not exactly without fright. It's an unknown, a mysterious, penetrating feeling.

The trophies awarded in '65 for your achievement as a muscle builder were towering. We who were so fortunate to win the grand prizes struggled till 2 a.m. with wrenches dismantling the things in order to get them out the back door and into waiting taxis.

Photographer unknown

Activity becomes more of a blur as the night goes on. I pump up again and again, smear more oil around, tire of nakedness, conversation and my now-greasy hairstyle gone ugly. Smudged, fat and skinny coetaneously, with nothing more constructive to do, I relent and turn toward the pulse of the crowd and the throb of the night. The audience hasn't missed a beat. They like the dark rippling men from the Islands of the Caribbean. They like the spiffy homeboys and the thick Europeans. Freddy poses in slow motion and shakes the century-old halls of grandeur; he tears down the house as he flexes his biceps and spreads his lats. No one has seen this stuff before tonight and they're going crazy.

I stood behind Larry, Mr. California and the reigning Mr. Universe, as he edged toward the center dais. Excitement was building as the show neared its crowning moments. He was about to be introduced as the overwhelming winner of the Mr. Olympia title and pass the Mr. A. on to me. The backstage grew soundless, the stony veteran stagehands whispering now, captured and suspenseful. Contestants froze in a line. An unnerving silence possessed the spectators, a restless stillness that gripped everyone at once; no one moved as if waiting for a heartbeat. Larry stepped closer to the spotlight and paused as a silent, motionless silhouette. The hush ached in our bones and tightened our jaws. One more teasing step and the man loomed forward, raising his massive arms overhead, and the first and last note of music was heard.

The sound that broke from the crowd was chilling. It was as if from one deep place a long contained emotion was discharged ... a rolling thunder never before expressed in this tarnished and fading opera house; the chorus built upon itself, stunning its maker, an awesome rumble that stopped the heart.

I joined Larry to receive my trophy, the loving-child embrace of the Big City crowd. The spotlight, the applause, the center-stage dais were mine for long, fiery moments like the continuous striking of stick matches, suddenly ablaze, hot, hissing, smoking and gone. Another followed by another, then gone.

I spent the last half of the Twentieth Century pursuing muscle and might; and I am no less involved in the pursuit early on in the Twenty-first Century. Were I given the opportunity to repeat things,

I would, glaring mistakes and all. The urge to edit out a few embarrassments and hurts exists, but who am I to tamper with the work of God? As it is, so let it be.

Serendipitously and coincidentally I have achieved a place of recognition amongst a world of like-minds. I'm persuaded and compelled to write a book to teach, encourage, affirm; to share and compare notes, to clarify, to affect pause and consideration; to brighten mind and spirit and speed one along by slowing one down.

If I'm proud it's because I'm a muscle-building original. I invented, improvised and rooted about along with a small, disconnected band of rebels with a cause: to build solid muscle and might through the austere, hard labor of love — the lifting of iron. Our shirts were not torn to be fashionable; they were shredded by use and outgrowth. We didn't imitate. Who would be the model before us?

The last thing I want to do is dictate your ways, force round pegs into square holes. Yet, I will shout the sober reminder, "Get to work and quit complaining!" to those who need it. A compliment was directed to me recently over the loudspeaker of the Internet: "Draper doesn't tell you what you should do; he tells you what he did himself." I'm grateful for the observation.

And now the project is before me. There are hundreds of books written by professional bodybuilding champions, researchers, doctors, coaches and scholars. Where do I fit in?

I, like everyone else, do not care to be ordinary. Already, a contradiction. I seek to arrange order and logic within my suggestions, both in exercise and menu. I offer you sound facts and establish sturdy landmarks to guide you, affirm you. Mostly, I don't want this to be a textbook but a view of life as seen by me, a person who did, does and always will lift weights as he eats and breathes.

FROM THE GRIPPER TO THE DUNGEON

Time appears to be a cool character: unchanging, forever on the go, showing no favoritism. Yet time, upon which I never impose gender, is healing. Time forgives. My life inches along, and, may I presume, yours does as well. Two steps forward and one step back. The dance of men, women and children doing the best they can.

I can think of few acts more profitable to growing up and becoming more complete, than the honest, hard work of lifting weights and eating right.

I have two objectives as I set out to write this book: to underscore the things you need to know and to encourage you to do them. Get rid of the notion that you need to know more and more. The learning is in the doing.

Muscle and power building are not and need never become brain surgery or astrophysics. Information beyond the ABCs and simple math only leads to confusion, doubt, controversy and frustration. These conditions distract from the wonderful work at hand and confound the basic instincts and investigative courage to discover. Thus limited, one

Chris Lund and his jolly-good camera, pointing our way in the mid-90s. The Venice World Gym is the mirrored backdrop and I weighed 225 pounds eating meat and potatoes. Lou Ferrigno stood to my left as Chris composed the shot and commented that few of the current wave of bodybuilders squat or deadlift. "It's not like the old days, Dave."

Chris Lund

imitates instead of seeks, copies rather than improvises, becomes dull in place of shining. One stops growing in leaf and grows only in knurly root.

There comes a time, sooner or later, when you must listen to yourself and not those around you. You must become the student and teacher at once. Look directly to yourself and your training as the masters. If you enjoy the magazines and science and research, sip on them as one does afternoon tea. Enjoy the aroma, swirl the flavorful liquid about the palate, note the heady summaries but don't expect sustenance. This comes from you, the gym and hard work over and over again. Insight and revelation fall like sweet rain from above on the sunniest days.

I think I can safely say that I am writing to a diverse audience. And though I may not be penning a bestseller, my ramblings might wind up in the hands of beginners of all ages, resolute former enthusiasts, struggling mid-level bodybuilders and even a nip of award-collecting pros curious about what I have to say. With that in mind, and firmly believing the basics cannot be overstated nor simplicity replaced, I'll begin.

I walked into the picture about the middle of the Twentieth Century when I wrapped a skinny, child's hand around a Hercules hand gripper. It lay there with its bright red handles and gleaming chrome coils amidst a heap of crushed display cartons, well-sampled wiry chest expanders and "how to" pamphlets exhibiting sketches of a handsome and rugged he-man with muscles bursting through his T-shirt. WOW. Wide-eyed and transfixed. WOW.

I was seven and in the sports department of Macy's in New York City Christmas shopping with my mother. Mom got off easy. The hand gripper was harmless enough, fit in my back pocket just right and was only a couple of bucks compared to twenty for the rather cumbersome basketball I'd been fondling earlier. Thanks, Ma, for that lovingly cruel steel device and the cable chest expanders to follow, that pinched my nose and tore hair from my head in clumps.

Queeze.Queeze ... Queeze.Queeze. That repetitious grating sound — music to my ears — became like dripping water to the senses of my family, not unlike an ancient Far Eastern torture. We all endured: I, the burn in the forearms and the anxious need to grow, and they, their loving patience and frazzled nerves.

By the time I was ten I had acquired the three-spring chest expander, the five-spring super expander and a wall-mounted bungee-

Photographer unknown

Here's a look at the kid from New Jersey relatively new at the underhand-close grip pulldown. 250 and eating.

pulley contraption that hung conspicuously on the kitchen wall. Dear Mom and Dad and older brothers barely noticed. Privately and uninterrupted, I pressed on when they were elsewhere watching the black and white as TV had just arrived on the American scene. Kitchen chairs back-to-back served as a dipping apparatus and fingertips over the doorway entry-ledge provided a tough chinning structure for a future big back. My home gym non-compare, the only one I imagined.

Vividly I remember one day staring down at a small, immovable pile of metal neatly fixed to a sixteen-inch steel bar. On the barren concrete sidewalk in front of my house in Secaucus, N.J., lay my first set of weights, somewhat rusty and full of gravity. My very own purchase from a neighbor up the street: for five dollars he was released and I was hooked. My brothers each had their own thing, my mom smiled and Dad did a shoulder shrug as he walked off. No one said "no" or "hmph." I was encouraged. Self-inspiration was anonymously planted, took root and grew, freely and unencumbered.

I was just a kid and virtually nobody was pushing iron. Weightlifting and muscle building didn't have wide public appeal or approval and ninety-nine out of a hundred athletic coaches gave it the thumbs down. There wasn't a whole bunch of encouragement or inspiration from a society that considered you either stupid or egotistical, and probably a sissy. The two guys who inspired me to lift in those days were Anthony Petrowski and Tony Napierski, local dockworkers with powerful arms from hard work, meat and potatoes and some knarly badboy weightlifting. Though I never saw his movies, a poster promoting Steve Reeves in *"Hercules"* deeply branded me, setting me aside for a labor of love to last, evidently, a lifetime.

What I did with this pig iron, the tens and fives and three pounders, collars and bar, is vague and unfocused. There were no courses or instructions or peer supervision. No mags in my library. I invented and improvised and wrestled and played — hard. I arranged and rearranged the makeshift set of weights and within a month I was fully hooked, cookin,' bombing and pumping.

By the age of twelve, barbells and dumbbells had become my life. They were my solid steel friends that I could trust. When the going got tough, when I kept missing the baseball, and when girls were far too cute to talk to, the weights were there and they spoke my language. I loved the resistance they offered and without coaching, gymnasiums or teams of players, I could enjoy a basic oneness of the activity where you were in control of being controlled.

I fought with those little monsters for hours on end, pushing and pulling randomly to exhaustion until patterns of exercises formed. Slowly and surely my body took shape and muscle power and size became evident. It's interesting to note that these things took place almost by accident. Simply, the play and pleasure of painfully pressing on was my stimulus. And, too, I admit that the exclusiveness and loneness of the adventure had and still has a quality that reaches to the marrow of my bones. Little did I know the reps and sets, moans and groans that lay before me.

My high school had baseball, football, basketball and wrestling, but no weights. I attended a fine prep school in Connecticut in '58 and '59 and they had a pool and soccer and hockey, but no weights. They allowed me to bring my own little pile and I kept them under my bed, a special privilege. The provost took one look at me and said, "The boy needs his weights." Thank you, sir. Am I sick or what?

Corners of bedrooms, basements and garages provided the common training areas for the rare breed of lifters brewing fifty years ago. I wasn't the only one stumbling around out there popping his veins, although some days it seems like I was as I look back over the muddy waters. The YMCAs across the country, I risk saying, all had classic weight rooms that housed barbells and benches to rival "The Dungeon." These undersized rooms had low ceilings with hot water pipes traveling in every direction and were invariably located in the basement next to a big boiler room.

The "Y" in Elizabeth, N.J., was my first gym beyond the environs of home. A good-looking Italian kid — Joey Dinetta, Mr. New Jersey at the time — invited me to train with him one summer that he might teach me how much fun weightlifting with the boys could be. There I gawked at a seven-foot Olympic bar as if it was an oversized, outdated relic, the preposterous length of which surely must have presented a hazard to early lifters. I discovered how to cram twenty big guys into a room large enough for ten and how to pitch a bar into a corner, load it with weight and do killer rows. I learned how to do inclines and spot incorrectly by dropping a dumbbell on my training partner's head. I didn't learn much, but I learned enough to graduate to the big time.

My first job working for a gym was as the weekend manager at Vic Tanny's on Journal Square in Jersey City, circa 1961. Friday they gave me a key and told me I started Saturday at 9 a.m. Imagine, nineteen years old and I'm already a gym manager. I'm on my way, I'm a cool

Photographer unknown

Mr. New Jersey shakes hands with Joe Weider on stage at the Union City high school auditorium in the spring of 1962. Can I put my pants back on now?

guy. As I finished my workout that Friday evening I felt my lats and triceps assume a permanent, flexed position. It sort of hurt, but it was the price one had to pay. Arriving early Saturday morning to take control of my domain I witnessed a miracle. I unlocked the prominent glass doors at the top of the broad staircase and the gym — my gym — all two thousand square feet, was gone. Overnight. Where did it go? I did a series of 360s with my mouth open and it still didn't appear. Squinting, I imagined a sale: "Going Out Of Business Special. Two memberships for the price of one." Gone to the next county, no doubt. I didn't need no stinkin' gym job anyway.

There was no reason why a guy couldn't lift weights and have a family, too, so I married and bulked up along with my wife, Penny. She gave birth to Jamie, a beautiful baby girl, and I was two hundred thirty-five by the time I was twenty-one and Mr. New Jersey. To support a family and my growing bodyweight, I took a part-time job with the Weider Barbell Company in Union City, an aspiring enterprise fixing a hold on the swelling world of muscle. Leroy Colbert, Joe Weider and I did seated dumbbell alternates in the corner of the small warehouse during lunch break. A kid could amass serious arms that way. I can remember Joe saying, "You guys are always bombing it. When do you ever work? Leroy, I'm going to call Draper 'The Blond Bomber.' What do you think, eh?" A month later it was on the cover of *Mr. America* magazine.

Joe, the Trainer of Champions, had filing cabinets full of timeless pictures of the stars from around the world, which we pawed over and chose for upcoming issues of *Muscle and Power.* I'm learnin' and growin.' Weider Company goes west, and I go with it to live in tranquil Santa Monica on the alluring far edge of the earth.

There at Muscle Beach, as it faded into the stunning California sunset, I met and shared with the last of the true erectors of the body-building foundations: the cornerstones such as Joe Gold, Zabo, George Eifferman, Bill Pearl, Armand Tanny and Hugo Labra. A handful of mighty men — heroes — that formed the heart of bodybuilding and lived those golden, carefree days gone by.

These men with instincts intact felt their way around the weights and equipment, lifting more and intellectualizing less. And to them I attribute a certain quality of creativity in my training and an appreciation of the fundamentals. The late '60s have been referred to as the "Golden Era of Bodybuilding," when big men pressed on curiously, methodically and with great concentration. During those years the various training principles were established and stand distinctly today — sound, tried and true.

My most vivid workout memories are set against the backdrop of the Muscle Beach Gym of the early '60s. This famous, beloved relic, once located on the unspoiled shores of Santa Monica, was relocated by the persuasion of the city council to the underground basement of a collapsing retirement hotel four blocks inland. A very long, steep and unsure staircase took me to a cavernous hole in the ground with crumbling plaster walls and a ceiling that bulged and leaked diluted beer from the old timer's tavern above. Puddles of the stuff added charm to the dim atmosphere where three strategically placed forty-watt light bulbs gave art deco shadows to the rusting barbells, dumbbells, sagging milk crates and splintery handcrafted 2x4 benches. Pulleys and twisted cable from a nearby Venice boatyard, a dozen Olympic bars, bent and rusty, and tons of plates were scattered throughout the twenty-five hundred square foot floor. Dumbbells up to 160s that rattled at broken

Standing on the ramp before the glistening line-up of contestants at the '66 Mr. Universe Contest are my hero, Sergio Oliva, The Master Blaster Joe Weider, muscular (and currently misplaced) Chet Yorton on my left and me in the middle. Thirty minutes later the theater was empty.

Photographer unknown

welds added the final touch that completed what was unquestionably the greatest gym in the world.

You have no idea how proud I am to have had this theater and the real-life plays that unfolded day after day as part of my experience. It's pure gold.

Here bodybuilding began, embryonic: the original, not the imitation. Here exercises were invented, equipment improvised, muscle shape and size imagined and built, and the authentic atmosphere exuded like primal ooze. You were awash in fundamentals and honesty. I loved it then, the memory more now.

The magic didn't come from the pharmacist; it came from the soul, the era, the history in the making, the presence of un-compromised originality yet to be imitated.

Those years, curiously content in getting a head start, I arrived at the gym between 5:30 and 6 a.m. while the city slept. I like the company I keep when I'm alone: I like the sounds of silence; I like the uncluttered space. With a crowd of one there's no one to complain or groan, no self-consciousness, no dividing your attention, no one to impress. By the time I left, perhaps three or four other creatures would descend the lonely steps and dutifully take up arms.

The Dungeon was a refuge from '63 through '66. What kept me going without missing a beat was hope in an era where none permanently resided, bouncing around like a pinball in a jangling machine. There was no glory except a rumor of respect and reputation amongst the weightlifters' underground. People in the real world sincerely frowned at you: a musclehead, a misfit, a bewildered loser who's harming himself and isn't doing us any good either. Man, has that concept taken a spin.

My toughest workouts took place in the middle of those formidable years. I did have training partners from time to time and one in particular, Dick Sweet, pushed me, encouraged and goaded me to otherwise inapproachable limits.

My recollection of a late morning workout, one day amongst many, sets a tone of our workouts in general. There existed on the far end of a caving rack the merciless set of 150-pound dumbbells, awesome in length with pipe handles and suicide welds on the ends. These unwieldy contraptions could be further enlarged by strapping five-pound plates on either end with strips of inner tube. You got it — giant rubber bands. Getting them together took two guys, some muscle and engineering. Getting them overhead took temporary insanity. We won't talk about the sixty-degree incline bench constructed of wood and ten-penny nails wedged against the wall. Never did get a good look at it in the dark.

The first set is a growling dog, biting and snapping at the flesh. I love dogs. The second set goes up like stocks in a bull market, fireworks on the Fourth of July, cheers for the home team. On the third rep of the third set the rubber band snapped and slapped me in the face. Some guy standing in the shadows snickered. Shortly thereafter a five-pounder bounced off my forehead; I saw it coming. This made me serious. I had two sets to go and no more rubber bands. A short length of rope got me through the last two sets.

Did I tell you I was supersetting? Workouts without supersets were not workouts at all. I was doing bent-over lateral raises with 60s. The welds this time were on the inside of the dumbbells, and cracked, not dangerous but sloppy. Every third or fourth rep the web of my left hand between the thumb and the index finger got pinched in the crack. This, too, made me serious. Good thing there's not much nerve ending and the blood flow was light or I'd have never finished my workout.

The ten years between 1960 and 1970 boiled like a witch's brew. They gurgled and steamed and splattered in an interesting and seductive manner. We ran about rejoicing in freedom as one foot was placed carelessly in a bear trap. I was Mr. New Jersey in '63, "David The Gladiator" in '64, Mr. America in '65 and Mr. Universe in '66. I wondered around Hollywood and was fascinated. Remember *Don't Make Waves*, "The Beverly Hillbillies" and "The Monkees"? More fun than an amusement park with Uncle Johnny when you were six years old.

In 1970, after winning Mr. World in New York City, I sensed a shifting of the gears in bodybuilding and stepped out of competition. The sport took off like a rocket to the moon, soaring into the '80s with ever-increasing momentum.

Allow me to sneak within a few thin pages a sufficient discourse of my life out to pasture between the years of 1970 and 1985. The weights never left my side, no more than a good old sheepdog leaves a gritty sheepherder tending the south forty. I trained every morning with fire in my gut before the cock crowed. Got along fine with the bird,

Art Zeller

Somewhere people were no doubt dashing about frantically to accomplish something or another. Artie Zeller and I were absolutely content in our afternoon separation from the rest of the world. No pumping, no oil, no expectations; only the sun and warm breezes off the ocean. Circa '67.

'twas people who presented me minor distress. Or, was it the other way around?

Living in Venice in the '60s was like living in a junkyard with a bunch of junkyard dogs. Biting was allowed and the food wasn't free. I had to make a living, learn and grow. My workouts served to stabilize, fortify and entertain me, but no way could I see training to beat Sergio Oliva a real wise career decision — baby needed shoes. (As if I could have; he's from another planet, you know.)

I found myself making rugged oversized furniture out of old wood, loving it and making enough money to pay the bills. Very cool. Tranquil, alone and natural, woodworking matched my workouts. Someone could say the '70s never happened and I'd believe 'em.

I became, quite by accident (as is commonplace in all my pursuits), a carpenter of sorts. To keep me company as I sawed planks and carved wood into oversized objects of furniture, I drank a little wine and smoked a little dope.

This pattern — smoking, drinking, eating, training, carving and sleeping — kept me busy. The world around me, but for a handful of friends and family, spun on its own familiar axis. Frank, Arnold, Mentzer — whoever — did their thing and I did mine, light years apart. I didn't ignore or neglect, judge or deny competitive bodybuilding. I simply lost interest as one does for racing cars on the boulevard or watching corn grow season after season. My respect and affection for the guys and our experiences were cast in bronze. Creating in wood and trips to Big Sur and Mendocino became my preoccupation.

The bodybuilding world expanded; it appeared to grow tentacles and I found it alien to my perception of muscle and might. I dug the metal then and now: the single-mindedness, the struggle, the intense body feelings, the pump and burn and heat and sweat, the battle, defeat and mostly the victory, the wordless communication and knowing amidst a very small tribe and the muddled or vacant stares I captured from puzzled, stumbling on-lookers — the rest of the world, really. Not so much an ego trip, as an amused ape, comfortably aware of itself.

I came to understand that staying big and muscular and strong was inherent and a chosen function for my new passion to build my large wooden forms. The egocentricity I shared primarily with myself was fulfilling and harmless enough. Far as I could see the world nearby was kicking itself up and down the freeway and maybe I could help it by not participating. Somewhere, halfway through the '70s, my family and I escaped from the expanding yet deteriorating Los Angeles scenery to settle like toadstools in the midst of the Santa Cruz redwoods.

Heaven, one would conclude, a dream come true: a wooden house in the middle of twelve wooded acres, lovingly cultivated by God Almighty.

Not quite. I saw my family depart and my sinister, cynical companions, drugs and alcohol, lead me from my home to a barren gardener's shed in a little orchard on the edge of Nowhere. No power, no running water, no bucks, no buddy.

Hey, I still had the weights, was still lifting, never stopped. Commendable. Add to that: the booze and dope stopped. Suddenly.

However, not until after, at one point in '83, so did my heart. The doctors and staff at the Dominican Critical Care Unit treating me for acute congestive heart failure expected my life to cease as heartbeats strained and failed repeatedly. Three weeks after this bout I was wheeled out the side door to resume my tortuous journey.

My eyes cleared and I looked at the black and white and smoldering landscape around me, silent ashes. If I didn't do one good thing each day, I still plugged into the gym and resuscitated the soul. Two years of one day at a time, sets and reps, iron and woodwork therapy, fear and trembling, prayer and God, and I stood upright. Apples grew in the orchard, grapes on the vine and the bees pollinated as they gathered their makings for honey.

From the earliest day to this, I trained to build muscle and might. As the crazy '60s lengthened, bodybuilding took on critical mass and an acute change of direction. The control gates failed and the flood was sudden. Bodybuilding was about to be exploited, big-time. There was money to be made, accompanied by greed, power and frenzy. Muscle mags resembling catalogs appeared ubiquitously. Merchandise, apparel, miracle supplements for overnight muscle, equipment of every description, gym chains, mondo contests and promoters swamped the fields of green.

Lo and behold, I joined the gold rush. No, not really. I did, however, determine to get out from under the hooves of the stampeding horses. One fine day in September 1989 in the corner of Santa Cruz, California, a small gym opened its doors, freshly painted and filled with new equipment. The banner read "World Gym" in large print, my name in the corner along with the hours of operation. February rolled around and Arnold arrived in a police-escorted limousine followed by Joe Gold and a Hollywood-style Venice entourage. We had a grand opening and I established a long-term relationship with the World Gym gang.

Scotts Valley is nestled five miles away and is home to a second World Gym planted by my partners and me only two years later. One of those partners is Laree, my wife and confidant since the gyms' inception.

A website of prodigious proportion has been created by Laree and me with regular updates and a weekly newsletter going out by email to thousands. IronOnline, an email discussion group composed of hundreds of avid muscle-building fans, provides truckloads of inspiration and real information day-by-day. Oaks and redwoods again surround me; a laptop sits at my desk.

Jesus Christ is our Lord; that Laree and I are Christians we hope is evident in these pages and in our work.

Penny, my wife of years gone by, trains at our gym in town and shares in the plans and schemes of Laree and me. Jamie, my daughter and secret delight, visits now and again with her tender brood (also known as grandchildren), Taylor and Cooper, and her husband, Scott. We're alive.

And today muscle building has continued to gain amazing popularity worldwide, both as a sport and as a way of life. The image associated with muscles has been appropriately lifted and the respect and appreciation a bodybuilder deserves is clear. Big muscles have become big business.

We live in a crowded and intense world where computers spit out information faster that we can use it and the media has us confused as to who we are and what to expect of ourselves. We've arranged a high-tech world and often find ourselves trailing far behind, frantically trying to keep the pace. The world of bodybuilding has not escaped this dilemma. We want results and we want them now: lean, hard bodies from QuickStop bodybuilding and fastfood appetites. And from this hurried attitude the only sure results are stress, injury and frustration.

Powerlifting, Olympic lifting, Strongman competitions, physical culture, fitness and bodybuilding have grown. High performance athletes in every sport lift weights as they strive to become champions. Moms and dads and their moms and dads lift weights for fun and fitness, therapy and diversion. Can't watch CNN for a week without see-

Laree Draper

My daughter, Jamie, and me as we posed for a local periodical encouraging health and fitness. I have a twenty-year head start on the precious girl.

ing a gym full of men and women pressing on as the newsperson cites research commending weightlifting for kids, the aging, the AIDS patient, the arthritic, the overweight, the underweight, the depressed, the pregnant, the diabetic.

The once-obscure, male-dominated peculiarity that raised eyebrows is now practiced by everybody, from primitive settings in basement corners and garages to the glittering, splashy spas stretching sometimes over fifty thousand square feet atop high rises in the big cities. We've become a mob.

There are no secrets. You simply have basic God-given genetics, body chemistry and bone structure. And provided the attributes of discipline and determination, you apply yourself full bore, and your body potential emerges, slow and sure.

2

KEYS AND GUIDEPOSTS

I attempt to present a simple, clear and direct way for you to become involved in muscle building and health through weight training, thoughtful eating and discipline — the process commonly known as bodybuilding. Bodybuilding is not a term to be reserved for the development of champion physiques. It is, as the word implies, the building of one's body healthfully to satisfying muscular proportions. This incomparable sport is for all of us.

I particularly underline the exercises, sets and reps, poundage, protein, other nutrients and factors that have been established and proven over the last half of the last century, the good stuff that has worked for my peers and me and is certain to set you in motion as a beginner or further you as an ongoing or returning enthusiast. Bodybuilding, I promise to remind you, is an exciting, fulfilling and priceless adventure in seeking a good life.

What are we doing here?
How did we get here?
Where are we going?

THE EARLY MOTIVATORS...

The question "To whom am I writing?" begs an answer. The spectrum of motives of the men and women who pursue the iron and steel is as broad and deep as the human mind. There is a throng of seekers that

Mike Neveux

Do I put this here or on the other side? Is it backwards or do I have it right this time? Once it's on there what do you do with it? I thought this stuff was basic and simple.

are broken and need to be repaired. They fret and painfully grumble, "I'm overweight, sluggish, weak, unmuscled, unshapely, ailing and frail. I need help. Fix me."

Others in hot pursuit of the weights gather with smiling hearts and the keen desire to be bigger, stronger and faster. They want to excel in their sport from the fields to the courts, from the mountainside to the poolside, in the air, on the bike, on the horse, board, skates or skis. Some are called "bodybuilders" and seek a muscular and sweeping physique that will stun the beholder.

Weightlifting and its attachments, of course, provide the surest and fastest and sweetest way to accomplish the wonderful mission before them. Some metal-geeks just want to hang out and be cool. Every year a number of men and women buy a membership to a gym under the illusion that ownership alone sustains, heals and builds. Do you exercise? I'm a member of a gym. Really?

SIX KEYS TO BODYBUILDING SUCCESS

To make clear the simplicity of bodybuilding I've arranged a list of six basic keys to successful training. They're nothing new and read like the same stuff in any motivational book on the market today. Yet they are a valuable reminder of the essentials to getting started and sticking to it.

1. Set realistic goals — short and long term.

2. Plan an orderly and thorough routine to train the entire body.

3. Make a commitment to stick to your routine for four to six weeks to realize the changes and benefits, develop perseverance and create a habit.

4. Establish enthusiasm for your training, the driving force to perform successfully.

5. Ease into an appropriate training program with a wholesome, thoughtful nutritional plan: proper foods, amounts and order of consumption.

6. Be confident from the beginning that the application of these sound principles will produce the desired results.

Muscle shape, leanness and a strong, healthy system are the early motivators, worthy and always before us. However, if you expect that the benefits of iron are limited to those goals only, you are in for a grand surprise. The flesh alone is not the reaper of the advances you acquire. Look for — better yet — hunt for and gather the riches along the way that develop solidness, depth and width to the character and mind. Each and every workout provides reward, encouragement and good cheer. The gym experience never fails; the lifting, the straining, the winning and the losing make you stronger.

I mention this hazy thought now and forewarn you that I repeat myself loudly and frequently throughout the book to emphasize concepts I fear might get lost. The simple and commonplace, due to their ordinary nature, are almost always reduced in importance and misplaced. These — the basic things — comprise the ore, the raw material from which the gold and gems we seek are extracted. Every workout is an uncovering of fortitude, the further excavation of patience and persistence and a prosperous mining of discipline and humility. I don't want you to give up because you didn't dig deep enough or long enough and, therefore, missed priceless buried treasure.

The uncomfortable truth is too many of those who venture to the fields of iron and steel give up, quit, abandon the glorious task too soon to realize the sub-surface bounty of exercise, good eating and training. The qualities they lacked to keep them going were amongst the qualities they were about to discover. Strength is a product of strength. One does not become strong unless one is strong. Or as they say in my native language, "No ticky, no shirty."

A charge to your advantage: Be strong and courageous; above all, be wise. Reach, but not too far. Too rigid a menu plan or too ambitious a workout scheme will be discouraging, hinder your progress and shut you down. Commit to memory and recite the following ten spontaneous one-liners to your neighbors and their chidren. They're profound, they're priceless ... well ... they're free. Be careful; be happy and stay happy. Stick to the basics. You're in this for the long haul. Today time is your friend, not your enemy. Be supple, be confident and relax. Learn through your own experience; observe, query and glean. Apply the winsome behavior indicated above and you rule.

Remember, most of what you read in the magazines is filler to surround the outrageous pictures that bring us hysterical advertisements for stuff we don't need, to do what we could never do and be who we could never be, all in thirty days. It's silly.

GOALS ARE FOR KIDS

As a twelve-year-old growing up in Secaucus, N.J., where immigrant farmers raised pigs and New York City dumped its garbage, my weightlifting goals were simple and to the point: survive, build big and strong arms and get tough. That's what motivated me to buy my first set of barbells and set my mind and body on training. Interestingly, I didn't set lofty goals, like becoming a champion or Mr. America. I wasn't a fan and didn't seek heroes. My ambitions were focused on getting better each day, one day at a time.

This is not the kind of goal setting, reaching out and striving encouraged in the '80s and '90s. It's not the kind I necessarily endorse as I look back over the years of avid bodybuilding. Yet my trudging along with dogged determination has its qualities and should not be ignored.

Today's world of bodybuilding is out of the garages, and it's high on the minds of people. The incredible media, television and computers are upon us and have us expecting more of ourselves every day.

Man, by nature, is a goal-oriented creature and goal setting has become more than a primal function. Imagery and visualizing (using our imagination to maximize our performance) have become effective and practical in business, sports and medicine. "I can if I think I can" and "I'm getting better every day in every way" are axioms that seem to work in today's pressing world.

Goal setting is the number-one key to bodybuilding success and can be broken up into two basic categories: long-term goals for the years to come and short-term goals (what you expect to achieve in the next days and weeks). Make no mistake: these need to be addressed thoughtfully to ensure clean and positive action.

We often dream as children, our desires masquerading as our fantasies. This type of dreaming is healthy and keeps our eyes on the horizon. But as adults we sometimes allow the child in us to set goals, and we then mix fantasy with reality. The objective must be realistic, or disappointment is the only thing you're sure to achieve. You'll be more successful if you plan your next short-term goal slightly, but not too much, above your last achievement. That way you'll steadily raise your level of aspiration. Long-term goals should be carefully evaluated before you make a commitment: Is the goal possible at all?

Intelligent self-evaluation is the prerequisite to realistic goal setting. Self-evaluation requires time, careful consideration and honest insight. Determining your strengths and weaknesses and your current position are invaluable to realizing your potential and essential in arranging a productive scheme of action.

Don't panic. We are generalizing, making estimates and practicing. I'll caution you periodically not to be self-critical as it drives one crazy. A few reference points, however, will be helpful.

I've compiled a roving list of twenty guideposts to consider in helping you make an assessment. The material reads like an application for a life insurance policy, but separately and collectively it will give you an overall impression of who you are, how you are and where you are going.

1) Begin with the basics, from age, height, weight, and muscle measurement. Measure your body parts: chest, shoulders, upper arms, forearms, waist, thighs and calves.

2) Determine your bone structure — large bone structure, narrow hips, broad shoulders, thin wrists.

3) Check the tone and condition of your skin, an external indicator of internal health. Poor nutrition, hormonal imbalance, excess bodyfat, toxic overload and fatigue might be determined and corrected. Is your skin thick or thin, healthy in color, and is there acne, redness, flakiness or oiliness?

4) What is your current state of fitness, energy and endurance — flexibility, ability to run or jump, strength based on daily activities or sports participation?

5) Do you have any specific physical attributes and abilities, such as excellence in other sports, outstanding beginning physique or heavy musculature since childhood?

6) Consider your medical history: Have you seen a doctor recently for a physical evaluation? What were the results and how do they relate to your weight training scheme?

7) Be aware of your vital statistics, such as blood pressure, cholesterol count (and its various elements) and resting pulse. Make a habit of checking your resting pulse periodically to monitor your progress and check for a rise, which may indicate either oncoming illness or overtraining.

8) Do you have any current injuries, ailments or physical weaknesses? How about permanent or recurring weaknesses, such as back or shoulder problems, numbing or tingling in the extremities, muscle cramps?

9) Be aware of your body chemistry and body type (endomorph — a preponderance of bodyfat; ectomorph — neither much fat nor much muscle; mesomorph — having well-developed musculature). Do you seem to have a fast or slow metabolism? Have you carried extra fat or been very thin all your life?

10) What is your relative state of mind? Are you relaxed or anxious? Is your attitude positive or negative? Are you comfortable and confident?

11) Review your relative behavioral capacities, your level of discipline, focus, patience, persistence, willingness and ability to commit to projects. Are you passionate about strength or muscle size, speed or flexibility?

12) Analyze your current lifestyle. Do you relax at home? Are you busy? Do you party or eat out often? Do you get enough sleep? Do you plan to alter habits that interfere with your bodybuilding progress, or would you rather not?

13) Note your job demands and description: stress, overtime, physically demanding, doctor, lawyer, Indian chief. How much time is available to dedicate to training each week?

14) What are your current nutritional habits? Are they consistent? Is this a problem? Do you enjoy good, wholesome food or do you need fast foods or sweets to satisfy your hunger? Cravings?

15) How long have you been interested in exercise or bodybuilding? Have you already tested your commitment through plateaus and occasional boredom?

16) Review your knowledge of weightlifting and nutrition. Have you read books on the subject, and do you keep up with the latest nutritional findings? Do you spend time in discussion with people who practice this lifestyle?

17) Take a look at your peer influences both at the gym and away. Will your non-athletic friends influence you to skip your workouts to do other things? At the gym, will your friends gradually influence your goals without you being aware of it?

18) How about your gym — do you train at home with sufficient equipment? Do you train where the attitude is energizing, domineering or wearisome ... dirty, packed and impossible?

19) Is good coaching available? Do you have mentors locally to whom you can go for feedback and support?

20) How about your training partner? Do you train alone or with a partner you can count on? Is your partner committed to the same goals, and if your partner's goals change, will you begin to flounder?

One day Alice came to a fork in the road
and saw a Cheshire cat in a tree.
"Which road do I take?" she asked.
His response was a question: "Where do you want to go?"
"I don't know," Alice answered.
"Then," said the cat, "it doesn't matter."

Lewis Carroll
Alice In Wonderland

Where do you want to go? Determine your long-term goals followed by a short-term plan of action. Be encouraged. Once you decide where you want to go, getting there is an adventure. The Six Keys call for a training routine of appropriate dimension to be fixed in place and approached with resolve. Ah, the starting block, where the rubber hits the tar and anxiety is dispersed like dark shadows in the sunshine.

Alas, I beg your forbearance. Before we list the exercises of your masterful scheme and the nutrients upon which you will feed, let's prepare the perimeter of the non-physical requirements to building muscle and might, the musculature of character, observed in commitment, perseverance and patience. Further, a poke at information overspill might advantageously precede the performance of your first bench press and the ingestion of high-protein meal number one.

BOMBER TIME WARP—RANT AND RAVE

As a lifter of weights and other heavy objects, I tend to playfully exaggerate to impress a point. I speak of "information" as if it were a virus that could infect the whole body. Indeed, there are vaults of knowledge that, like water, are essential to life and its improvement. Too much, however, can drown us or at least leave us soaking wet. Let me outline some fascinating basics that will irrigate our minds and float clear thinking to the surface.

We are all different. How many of us miss this foremost point and insist that our way is the only way? Each of us is a separate world unto itself, with differing genes, historical and environmental influences, physical structure, internal chemistry, mentality, economics and goals. All these variables largely determine who we are, where we are going and how we will get there in our training and in other pursuits in our life, as well. We are a fabric of one piece, tightly woven in some corners and loose as a net in others. Take heart. We are, to a greater or lesser extent, capable in effecting the shape and the weave of the developing goods — the strong, well-muscled, high-performance body — by devotion and hard work.

Who was that masked man and what did he say? In order not to appear stupid and to arrest your concerns about my lack of emphasis on cutting-edge science, let me point out that as I've pursued the trails to a greater muscular structure, I've acquired no insight that added an essential drop to the basics of consistent hard work, heart and common sense. This is not to deny the need for every bit of information that has

London Mr. Universe pre-judging, September of 1970. A time alone. Wires of communication tangled and I arrived late for the line up. Some mistook this as an American arrogance and set a mood I found difficult to escape. I'm not smiling. *George Greenwood*

been discovered, documented, shared and stored. In school and seminars, and particularly over the Internet, I've gained reassurance in regard to the direction I mapped out in the early '60s during my Muscle Beach days. And I've learned some fascinating facts about cellular growth, hormones and fast- and slow-twitch muscle fibers. But, I repeat, I added nothing that would have had me alter my steady course, and nothing that could have accelerated my progress or improved my condition.

I'm tempted and feel obliged to be more scientific, more technical and thereby, perhaps, more persuasive and conclusive, but why? I won't, by doing so, add to your forward motion, lighten your load, improve your possibilities, resolve your apparent dilemmas or clarify ... what? Unless you're a student and not a "muscle freak," the minutia of scientific stuff will only slow you down, confuse you, and distract and distress you.

At the end of these pages I've added a resource list of books, newsletters, organizations and websites that are fun, informative, encouraging and inspiring. You can soak in specificity, ketogenics, periodization percentages and the facts, fallacies, myths and mysteries of hypertrophy all day long. I'll be at the gym if you need me. It's leg day.

THE SECRET IS THERE IS NO SECRET

I can't help myself. Sometimes I, myself, get downright technical and intellectual in my observations. There are basically two types of people who use weight training for fitness: Type A, the driven, and Type B, the not-so-driven. Though the degrees of difference vary, I know that if you're an "A" type, it would be an act of cruelty to keep you from your workout; it would be an absolute impossibility, like stopping the movement of a glacier or the stampede of wild horses.

And then, there are those of the "B" type, neither lazy nor irresponsible, who can't seem to make it to the gym or the garage on a regular basis. If this describes you, you have an impressive file of reasons why you cannot and some of them are even pretty good.

Exercise must be consistent to be effective. This is the first and foremost precept of physical conditioning. If there's a secret, it's consistency. Getting to the gym whether you want to or not, even for a short appearance, a salute or a bow is vitally important to the health of your fitness lifestyle. A break in consistency leads to the erosion of your training foundation, and without a sound foundation, no structure will stand.

How do we train consistently, especially if we don't have a milligram of discipline or an ounce of patience? To be consistent, training must be sweet and desirable; not slavery; not dull, boring and fruitless. It can and should be exciting. I got my first set of weights when I was practically in a stroller, haven't put them down since and still find them fun and fulfilling. "Get a life, Dave." Who said that?

Nurture interest and cultivate your attitude by reviewing your purpose, its integrity and its realness. You should look forward to each workout with enthusiasm and confidence to achieve maximum training productivity. Merely "doing it" doesn't do it. Train with steady pace, moving from set to set, breathing fully to oxygenize and prepare psychologically for the set to follow. Get involved with the flow of your movements, always focused on your immediate task and surroundings. Concentrate on the muscle's action, the burn, the pump, the extensions and contractions. This is not advanced thinking reserved for champions and pros. No time is too soon to think in familiar terms. If you're brand new in the gym, the practicing of your exercises with these novel thoughts in mind will speed your progress. Always keep your eye on your goals, knowing you'll eventually achieve them, and savor the time spent along the way.

Absence is erosive. In fact, your insistent presence in the gym is restoring, will bring you out of depression, solve a problem, crunch stress and may very well inspire you to have the best workout of your life. Try it! Go to the gym when the roads lead elsewhere, maybe nowhere. You'll feel like a million buckaroos.

I've discovered new exercise angles, approaches and combinations on these low-energy, downcast days out of simple instinct and survival. I can't count how many times people have crawled in the front door of our World Gym, slim smile pasted on their face and within thirty dedicated minutes march out, arms and hands stretched overhead, exclaiming, "I made it!" They truly did.

You'll want to settle on a sound exercise program for at least six to eight weeks to equip your mind with order and discipline. This provides time to understand each exercise separately and cooperatively and to afford the healthy overload to the muscles so they respond by growing strong.

When the time comes and you're short of time, distracted by life's ups and downs, achy, slightly fluish or overtrained, try one of my

Artie called one morning and said, "I've got some extra film in my camera, can you get a horse?" I said, "Of course, there's gotta be one around here someplace. I'll meet you at the fields under the LAX runway in twenty minutes." The three of us made a good team. That there's Crazy Legs.

Art Zeller

Slumpbusters, found later in the book. They're not original anymore, but they were thirty years ago when I first put them to use. I've written some short and sweet exercise combos that I've used over and over again for great results when my training has hit the wall.

While we're all alone (an appeal of the sport which makes it most fulfilling), we're also all in this together. And in the gym there's probably nothing you'll go through that we haven't all gone through at one time or another. It's the peaks and valleys, the landscape of life.

Training with weights, given half a chance, will teach you about living and strengthen you in many ways where you may otherwise stumble. I say this with conviction, yet in context and tone it may sound like conceit. Lifting consistently for fifty years, I must be a substantially together and well-rounded person, indeed. Hardly. I can only guess what a mess I'd be without it.

Commitment, the main power switch of your mental mechanism, controls the electricity that starts the engines and keeps them running smoothly. Commitment is your personal promise, your word of honor and resolve to seize your recently defined goal. It is vital to achievement. Its absence reduces a sought-after goal to an embarrassment lost to yesterday and yesterday's boasts. The naturally occurring ingredients of commitment are consistency, persistence and determination. These gut disciplines engaged with patience and faith add height to your stature and sureness to your stride. The work to which you fix your mind is accomplished as certainly as each second in the passing hour. Positive motion toward your muscular goals is guaranteed by commitment just as the Federal Reserve secures cash. It's as good as gold.

Each workout is a unique and separate experience unto itself. Events of the day, mood, energy levels and tensions affect every performance differently. Gather up as much enthusiasm as possible before each workout to ensure that you enter the gym with energy and a positive attitude. Attitude and enthusiasm do not exist apart from your persuasion. They are not variables of life that control you as if you were a visitor of your body tagging along for the bumpy ride. Hello. You're the chief. Apply the charm, a clever strategy, some wit, a little finesse. Don't submit.

You're the engineer responsible for your actions and reactions, your thoughts and imaginings, your decisions, directions and frame of mind. Think with weakness, perform with weakness. A slug acts like a slug; a grouch behaves like a grouch. (How do I know these secret things? I must have read about them in *The Reader's Digest* while waiting for a dental appointment.) Any effort you make toward improving your attitude is noble and the effects are powerful and decisive. No, it's not simple or easy, but it is essential. Your workouts are a perfect venue to practice this art-form. The results are visible and long reaching. Your training must not become drudgery or a chore that has to be done. You don't want this to become a negative setting, producing negative energy; it must be willfully resisted. Cheer up!

Keep your workouts tight and efficient, leaving no room for boredom or idle thought. You should quickly develop a mature training attitude, allowing no interruptions in the flow of exercise from start to finish. This is not to suggest that you hurry in your training. A hurried attitude produces anxiety, nervousness and agitation, resulting in negative performance and loss of concentration. I encourage quite the opposite, a steady lean on your training, setting a vigorous pace that reflects excitement, confidence and determination.

Become totally involved with each workout, each set and each rep. Focus on the performance of the exercise, the muscles involved and the feelings that result. Seek your particular groove, sense the burn and enjoy the pump. Training form is your priority and improves dramatically with diligent practice, workout to workout. Don't be harsh in your self-criticism; rather, be kind. Revel in the stimulating fulfillment that somes with subtle improvements. Lift the weights smoothly and deliberately, sacrificing the poundage used to gain skill in your performance.

Don't be quick to overload your body and struggle to lift more than you can handle. This will create poor style and result in disappointment, two failures you don't need. Your body requires precious time to condition to the novel overload. Unused muscles respond to novel exercise rapidly and often exceed the capacity of tendons and ligaments, resulting in soreness, tendinitis or injury. The nervous system, too, is busy gearing up to speed and refuses to be hustled. Once the basic foundation has settled, good work habits have developed and your groove has been established, you're on your way.

Big arms on the kid. Tell him he could use a haircut. AZ took this in the mid-sixties when everyone was growing hair and very few had arms over fourteen inches. Incline curls at Joe Gold's original muscle factory, new and ready for production.

Art Zeller

4

TRAIN WITH STYLE

Here you are reading my point of view, some clean advice but by no means the last or only word. I'm a bodybuilder. I encourage full ranges of motion with full extension and full contraction for the majority of your repetitions. I prefer moderate to heavy poundage with higher reps — eight to twelve — to maximize the involvement of the entire body and all the fiber types. With moderate weight and a mix of reps I'm able to set a groove and incorporate a solid body-thrust technique that brings more muscle groups into play and creates a rhythm in the repetitions. Though I practice single-set training on occasion, I accent my workouts with supersets and trisets.

Through all this I want you to remember we all have our own training style and yours is developing now as you read this and other training books, websites and magazines, observe others in action and experiment on your own.

I trained with and around Arnold for three or four years in the past and we shared similar training methods, which enhanced us both. Yet, in our arm training we went our separate ways. Arnold gains massive and proportionate biceps and triceps through muscle isolation, pumping and burning. I prefer heavy weight with a full range of motion to involve the body more entirely.

In the late '60s and early '70s, Frank Zane and I met at the gym in the mornings at sunrise to train our midsection and either chest, back or shoulders. Yet our arm and leg workouts didn't match — I have more difficulty and require more work in these areas than Frank.

Franco Columbu and I co-trained successfully though his strength in pressing far exceeded mine and we differed in pace. Tom Platz trains hard, often to the extreme. In his radical performance he often trained to complete failure, sometimes doing a bodypart workout consisting of a single set of fifty or perhaps a hundred excruciating reps.

Dave Johns and I trained in Europe for several weeks and I experienced his awesome power in the bench and squat. As he worked, slow and heavy, I often did three sets while he prepared to do one massive set, moving a mountain to my foothills.

When I met Sergio Oliva in New York City forty years ago he was practicing Olympic lifting to thicken and shape his entire body. Ken Waller did reps with four hundred in the bench and five hundred in the squat, yet for shoulders and arms I've known him to use light weights, angular movements and isolation. Very patient Lee Labrada has similar, highly specialized, concentrated techniques to gain fine muscle detail.

I've known Leroy Colbert to do literally a hundred sets of upper body exercises and watched Zabo and friends spend both morning and afternoon doing as many sets of full squats. At the other end of the spectrum, we saw Mike Mentzer grow and grow on his intense, single-set Heavy Duty System.

I could go on and on with great fun describing the variety of training styles I've shared with my partners and peers over the years and in vastly different training venues. From a converted pigeon coop in Sydney, Australia, to Serge Nubret's subterranean cubicles in Paris, I've sorted my way through a maze of crazy workouts. They all seem to work if one's heart is in there, so suit yourself after appropriate trial and testing.

SUPERSETS REIGN

Much of what I've learned has come from observing people in action on the gym floor, an extraordinary cross-section of people training with purpose and good intentions. Locally, as I look out over the gym's square footage, observe the variety of activity and listen to the range of questions thrown my way, I'm convinced that flow and continuity in training should be encouraged from the very beginning.

Once a new lifter completes the first weeks of introductory exercise and gets a feel for the equipment, muscle resistance and personal level of condition, he or she is ready to practice interesting exercise combinations to piece the workouts together. This style of training is called "supersetting," when two or more exercises that complement each other are performed one after another to enhance lifting output. This multi-set training not only condenses workout time; it also increases productivity considerably.

Single-set training has its place in your workouts and should be retained for strength building. However, a training scheme blended with superset combinations adds excitement and dimension to a daily routine. A highly gratifying and inspiring muscle pump is achieved as blood, laden with oxygen and tissue-building nutrients, fills the individual muscles causing greater muscle growth.

Supersetting is a technique I've applied for more than forty years (gulp) and one I put into use long before reading a muscle magazine or going to a gym. I instinctively gravitated toward a non-stop training style to maintain enthusiasm and momentum. Without the downtime between sets, I become more involved in my training. There's no time for daydreaming, wishing I was somewhere else, or for boredom. In fact, a most desirable attitude of training develops, one that we wrongly think is reserved for athletes on the fringe of competition. This attitude of training is a valuable tool of confidence and provides a very real psychological benefit.

With a little time and a little practice your training becomes more athletic as you move through the gym from one exercise to another. Your heart rate remains higher, you stay warmer as you near the edge of aerobic training, concentration becomes locked and the harmony of movements lures you onward.

MIX MASTERS

I'm often asked why I superset. Why do I perform volume training? Because I like it. Because I like the pace, the rhythm, the flow, the accelerated perfection of form, the athletic feel, the etching repetition, the dance, the busy-ness, the involvement, the pump, the burn, the efficiency, the cardio-respiratory application, the high. I notice I'm able

Chris Lund

Chris Lund arranged the lighting, the composition and the action. Little spray bottles provided sweat and his resolute manner set the tone. You work hard for the man and feel beat up after two or three hours within sight of his lens. There's more to curls than biceps, don't you think?

to add hard muscle as I eat heavily and intelligently. I'm able to employ a more complete percentage of my muscle tissue with a locomotion of sets and reps performed with full range of motion, intensity and zeal. My first rep is thoughtful and deliberate; my last rep is thoughtful, deliberate and "red-zone" intense. The volume delivers maximum-force saturation, maximum muscle involvement. I'm a slave.

Why do I mix in heavy days with deadlifts, squats, power curls and presses throughout the month? 'Cause I like the strain, the mighty exertion, the challenge, the force of will, the aloneness of concentration, the pause and focus and grapple of determination, the gravity and poised iron, the total mind-body execution, the play, the white-light approach to "the single" and the trembling darkness after "the single" is completed. I like the power moves because I like the power, the mass and the thickness they achieve. Call me dumb.

Why do I mix them in my loose fashion? First, why miss any of it if you can have it all? It's like building a house of stones of differing size to accommodate shear-pressure, material availability, rugged appearance and the joy of building. Second, because I like it and because it works for me. We're all different and we all need different methods of training. What works for me may not work for you. Too simplistic? Works for me.

It has something to do with the gravitational pull, I believe.

Chris Lund

A lot of folks grow angry and disappointed when the progress is slow. It's always slow. Now is not soon enough. I remember when I was a little kid, twelve maybe, and I hung from a broomstick chinning bar in my cellar while other kids were playing baseball in the park. Nobody was there saying, "Go, Dave, go. You can do it. You look great. Pull. Pull. One more rep. That'll make your lats scream." When the stick broke and I fell on my back, nobody picked me up. When the red vinyl and chrome kitchen chairs placed back-to-back wobbled as I knocked out dips and accidentally built supplementary muscles as I fought to keep them from tumbling, nobody suggested it was fun or even good for me. Those were the good old days. And the muscles grew.

It's not "You go your way and I'll go mine. See ya." It's not "My way or the highway; your way or no way." We're on the foothills together. Any one of us can get to the mountaintop by desire, faith, trial, logic, failure and persistence. We can all get there by encouragement from one another, spirit and humility.

Someone asked me recently if I supersetted regularly in my early years of training. As I recall I applied solely the classic East Coast approach to building muscle, a style one may very well call "Onslaught Training."

You position yourself roughly before a barbell and with little warning you pounce on it and beat it to the ground. Breathing heavily, crouching and circling, you grab the dumbbells in a power lock, twist, pummel and, as before, slam them down without mercy. Always on the move, sweating and cursing, you hold your rusty pig iron opponent at arm's length before performing an excruciating overhead press, a crushing barbell drop set and, finally, the backbreaking deadlift. No whimpering, no reason, no questions, no excuses, no witnesses. All that stuff came years later.

I moved to California in '63 and refined my moves, put order in my workouts and began to use primarily superset techniques. I got a handle on protein, fats and carbs and bore the yoke like an ox on the threshing floor, season after season. For three years the bulk of my training was hard and heavy and my bodyweight hovered like a blimp at two hundred and forty-five pounds, a significant mound at the time. My workouts went three hours from 6 to 9 in the morning, six days a week times fifty-two weeks a year with the following split:

Monday, Wednesday and Friday:
Chest, shoulders and arms
Tuesday, Thursday and Saturday:
Back and legs
15 to 20 sets per bodypart @ 3 to 4 exercises x 5 sets each

A popular 12, 10, 8, 6, 4 rep scheme was used most frequently on major moves with the six to eight rep standard managing secondary movements and change-of-pace days.

Crunches, leg raises and hyperextensions were done first thing every morning for torso strength and warm-up. No aerobics. (What's that?) I always worked forearms and did maximum weight repetitions of various moves every third week to apply the muscle to the max.

Through the years I've tried every technique and muscle group combination, various splits, high reps and low. Regularly I've come back to beefy workouts with last-rep intensity, providing form is B+ and joints and muscle connections aren't severely compromised. On occasion, of course, one must pay the executioner. I'm constantly moving set-to-set, actively recuperating and psyching or arranging equipment for the next combination. Though I'm driven, I don't rush. I like time to immerse myself in my workout — I average seventy miles per hour in the sixty-five lane. When I'm done, I'm done.

Not much has changed over the years except I train two hours a day in the mid-morning and work each muscle group twice a week. My pulling is as good as ever, but the pressing has taken a dive due to injuries and wear and tear. I'm two hundred twenty-five pounds and more enthusiastic than the wide-eyed Dungeon days.

If we cataloged the essential muscle building information we gained over the years, would it stack to the top of a very tall squat rack? Or would it settle into a pile no higher than an average household's incoming mail, junk excluded. How much have we really learned? What do we know?

What did John Grimek know about building muscle that he didn't invent? What did Steve Reeves know that he didn't acquire from the grains of sand of Muscle Beach? Reg Park — Who taught him in the shadows of his old English garage? Bill Pearl learned all he needed to know about weightlifting in the hull of a Navy ship and on the streets of Oakland. Arnold and Franco pushed heavy weights, ate steak and eggs, and laughed and played without reserve, as sure as the California sun.

The cast of characters above played the starring roles in the original drama of bodybuilding. Today via the colorful muscle magazines, the new wave of eager physical culturists review the barbell soaps, hard-body sitcoms, muscular Sci-Fi's and mostly the "get huge fast" commercials. Confounding questions are posed, each with a dozen equivocal answers. We ponder as we enter the gym, confused, spent and beleaguered. Who am I and what am I doing here?

Ignore for a minute, able as you are, the enormous pressure of information and data. Chances are good, should you be locked in a garage full of weights long enough, you'll come out huge and ripped. Or if you're stranded on an un-inhabited island, you'll look for a place to do chins, dips and rock lifts. Alone, with needs and desire, logic and instincts, you'll build the best body in your corner of the world. The only thing to interrupt the passionate process would be finding a tattered book that told you how to do it. You'd stop and read.

We beg for reports, studies and statistics. Indeed, from this there is at least one magnificent benefit. As I read the journals, muscle mags and prolific master-blaster encyclopedias and as I glean through the stacks of facts to pass on to you, I achive a muscular pump in my traps. With each page I turn, I take a deep breath and slowly shrug my shoulders with a full range of motion, focused and flexed, and say in a Herculean tone, "So what?" Depending on the quantity of reading material and number of pages, the reps can really add up.

FRIENDS OF HYPERTROPHY

I came across a word the other day and thought you might want to know what it means. (I'm just a thoughtful guy who loves to share neat bits of information with his friends.) Cool word — we can exercise later or tomorrow. Okay? Have a another donut, why don't ya? The word is "hypertrophy."

Hypertrophy is the technical term for muscle growth: the bull's eye, Target One of the bodybuilder, my very first and on-going chosen objective. Hypertrophy is the enlargement of the size of existing muscle cells by the thickening of the cell wall (stop quivering) and, therefore, its girth, and by the temporary swelling of the cell due to the presence of fluid-bound energy ingredients necessary for cellular activity. (Theory also entertains the possibility that muscle cells split and increase in number, hence, overall volume.)

Hypertrophy is stimulated by progressively increasing the resistance upon the muscle beyond its minimum threshold under a variety of specific conditions. This is called "muscle overload" or "muscle under tension." These conditions determine the training methods that may be applied accidentally, by careful planning, intuitive choice or scientific coaching.

The methods or principles have their worth and place in a player's regimen at one time or another to meet his or her urges, aspirations, time and equipment limitations, potentials and disabilities, psychological boundaries and convictions.

I've prepared a poor man's list of training methods for hypertrophy and strength building that have kept us busy and constructive for a long, long time. Some are familiar to all of us.

STRONGMAN TRAINING: MILO AND THE BULL AND LATER STRONGMEN

There's the legend of the Italian hero, Milo, who applied the principles of progressive muscle overload in the ancient days when he set out as a young man to grow big and strong by carrying his newborn calf everyday. As it grew into a great beast, so did he. Called a "true bomber" by Western hero worshippers, Milo and his bull lived happily ever after.

Other strongmen followed, lifting heavy stones and tree trunks, train axles and railroad tracks, wagons and platforms mounted by men, women and children. They bent nails and bars and coins. Everybody was in awe of the Strongman and he gained his strength by consistent and persistent application with will and spirit, low reps with slow tempo, muscle under tension for long and strenuous singles in an afternoon at the rail yard, in the fields or on the docks. Later he formed iron into solid hand-held forms to make the lifting uniform and more approachable: dumbbells, kettle bells and bulging barbells filled with shot to make them adjustable so men could compete and win prizes, gain fame and muscular physiques. Sandow and Louis Cyr were staggeringly strong and offer us the early lusts and methods for hypertrophy.

DYNAMIC TENSION

Here we have the grandpa of popular muscle-building techniques introduced through the bestselling comic books. It was Charles Atlas years ago who suggested we resist the bully who kicked sand in our face and shamed us before our bikini-clad girlfriend on that sunny beach. The '40s, '50s and '60s had men (boys, really) sending for their course in "dynamic tension" to make a difference in who they were. Flexing your muscles as you stood before a mirror, you were persuaded to resist muscle against muscle in slow and repetitious contracting movements. Tensing your biceps and extending your triceps steadily and regularly fatigued your muscles and made them sore. Braced against a doorjamb and pushing from side to side made your shoulders burn and ache. Squatting slowly and deliberately, muscles super-tense and your hands extended before you, your heartbeat soared and breathing quickened. Something's happening here. Ever seriously pose between sets to further your muscle contractions? Ever practice posing in preparation of competition? Application of dynamic tension within this self-contained, fully equipped "gym on legs" will certainly contribute to the process of getting in shape and improving or maintaining tone. A tough-willed person can develop a tough program and a tough body. Throw in push-ups, dips and chins, some crunches, a jog and ... look out!

Have gym, will travel.

The Russians have researched the clinical depths of this type of resistance training and gave it an A. They gave it a name of their own as well: load-less training. Don't remember seeing that one in *Spiderman*.

ISOMETRICS

This method of increasing a muscle's activity is directed toward strength building with little dependence upon increase of overall muscle mass. Hypertrophy or muscle growth is not the object of this static muscular contraction. We are visiting a major technique expounded by

Bob Hoffman's York, P.A., camp of elite Olympic lifters and their coaches in the mid-Twentieth Century. It was incorporated in the training schemes of the powerful lifters competing mightily in the world games against the Eastern Bloc countries.

We engage in isometrics more by accident than by program as we hold unmoving contractions in a lift that refuses to go up as we refuse to let it go down. This is a mean crossroad. Though no external activity is taking place the muscle cells are severely shortened and a chemistry that demands adaptation is hard at work. This sought after increase in strength may very well be reflected in muscle growth down the line.

HYBRID EXERCISE TECHNIQUES

Combination moves like the clean and press, pullover and press, dumbbell curls from floor to shoulders and press — these are examples of hybrid exercises. They're multi-joint movements recruiting a wide variety of muscle groups through a full range of motion in short order.

I can't resist bringing your attention to this rather obscure technique as it pleads for creativity. There are no particular guidelines in arranging the combination movements providing you carefully consider safety, logic and training skills. You are inventing one big exercise that will encompass two or three in a single repetition. Try the close-grip, bent-arm pullover and press, an old timer representing true hybrid possibilities — or another, the hang clean and push press. Try a variation that allows you to rack the weight between reps to change grip or position. Wide-grip bench press for four reps followed by close-grip for four reps or bench press followed by bent-over row from a standing-on-bench position are all fierce versions of hybrid exercises.

The variations are endless and they afford interesting advantages to the muscle builder, the multi-sport cross trainer and the peak-performing martial artist. Smart combinations will develop healthy joint action, increase systemic blood flow, expand your training boundaries, sharpen your speed, skill and functional strength and provide you with the fulfillment and confidence that comes from invention. And this training will give you an opportunity to look around with pause and take a few deep breaths.

VOLUME TRAINING vs. HEAVY–DUTY TRAINING vs. HIGH–INTENSITY TRAINING

Standing amidst the world of iron and steel it appears there are offshoots of muscle and strength-building techniques that collide. This is not the case should the spectator take a closer look. The techniques expounded and practiced are wide and varied, solid and worthy; they have their purpose and direction and all do a good job. It's the extreme proponents of the techniques who collide. The narrow thinker who believes his way is the only way is obtuse and non-constructive. I implore you to beware of adhering to one principle exclusive of the other. All have merit, each is worth experiencing and, may I remind you again, we differ one from another.

Muscle growth is affected by four predominant training factors:

Volume — sets and reps of work over a given time period
Frequency — how often a muscle is worked over a micro-cycle
Intensity — level of work within a given period of time
Recovery — the ability of the body to restore and replenish itself

It is by these four factors that techniques are defined. The method of training frequently utilizing many sets of many reps of many exercises is noted as "volume training." Training infrequently (perhaps one day in ten) with few sets of varying low reps to extreme failure is Heavy-Duty Training (HD). High-Intensity Training (HIT) is a variation of HD that is practiced two or three times weekly and demands complete effort ending in total failure in either a low or high rep range after appropriate warm up. Hardgainer, made popular by Stuart McRobert, is another offshoot of abbreviated training that encourages the utilization of basic, multi-joint movements to near muscular fatigue without compromising form, endangering the body or miscalculating recovery time.

PERIODIZATION

Periodization is the principle whereby we vary our training methods periodically or cyclically to accomplish a predetermined goal over a predetermined time span. These methods can be simple and logical, or scientific and highly developed.

Based on an intelligent and specific long-term goal (for instance a season, six months, to gain ten pounds of lean muscle, lose twenty pounds of bodyfat, increase bench press by twenty pounds) pre-plan your training cycles to include varied yet complementary methodology to target and achieve the goal. This mixed training is evident in bodybuilders who train hard and heavy and eat substantially during the contest off-season and then rearrange their routines to match forthcoming competitions: supersetting, volume training and calorie-conscious eating.

Track and triathletes may for months train hard in the gym with progressive resistance and heavy systemic exercises for muscle power and maximizing oxygen uptake. Later, as their season nears, they back off their gym workouts, performing higher reps at a faster pace while they substantially pick up their events training.

Periodization, a grab bag of methodology, assures us (by accident, if not by scientific coaching) that all muscles, all fibers, all resources are maximized and not overtrained. The cycles go on and improve in quality as they are practiced and individualized.

OLYMPIC LIFTING

There are currently two lifts performed in Olympic competition: the snatch and the clean and jerk. These electric movements demonstrate the brilliant synchronicity of technique and power. Training to qualify as a recognized competitor is extraordinary and highly sophisticated, two years of diligent practice to acquire the skills alone.

The focus of the snatch is to get the weight from the floor to an arm-extended, overhead position in one continuous movement. Rules are broad, styles are unique and a variety of grip, leg positioning and explosive body movement are permitted. It's a breath-taking and dynamic event.

The clean and jerk is a two-part action. The weight is pulled from the floor to the shoulders, or "cleaned," where it settles briefly. It is then thrust overhead in one steady movement by any of a variety of confounding techniques. Timing, skill, structure durability, explosive power and mental dynamics determine the action.

No exercise movement demands as much muscle, core power, joint performance and range of motion in so short a time frame as the two Olympic lifts. For this reason the clean and jerk and the clean and push press are modified to fit the regimens of serious and tough body-builders, football players and track and field athletes. The advantages are enormous in sports. Stop, look and listen. Smile.

POWERLIFTING

There hovers, like a tenth planet in the universe of iron and steel, the world of powerlifting. This rugged and colorful sphere, populated by its own brawny culture, survives within its own refreshing atmosphere. Pockets of lifters practice their three chief competitive movements (the squat, deadlift and bench press) with unparalleled zeal and internal sup-port. Powerlifters are men and women whose brute-force belies their sensitive and loving brotherhood. They're independent and self-per-petuating with a network of newsletters and contest journals linking them together and apprising them of upcoming events and the drama of the latest records held and broken.

Weight classes determine competition levels and muscle power precedes muscle symmetry. Straps, belts, wraps, power shirts, chalk, smelling salts, the pungency of liniment and looming thick muscle de-fines a scene of gathering powerlifters preparing for action. Powerlifters have heart. They rumble.

It's not uncommon for a powerlifter and bodybuilder to blend training methods to enhance personal productivity. A healthier athlete may very well emerge, as the demands on the system of muscle fibers and hormonal activity are more complete. Periodized overload might reduce joint, ligament and muscle injury. I have always enjoyed body-building with a hint of powerlifting for flavor, like adding just enough garlic to give a meaty dish robust body.

TRAINING PRINCIPLES AND TERMINOLOGY

I forego the heady explanations of the oft-complex relationship between the above methods in achieving a championship body. Each has its loyal proponents, each fill volumes when defined and the collected experimental and experiential data are recorded and compared. Add to these findings differing genes, structures, mentalities, motivations, diets, hormones and other weird variables and what do you have? Don't look at me. I just work here. There are some excellent resources I list in the appendix that dissect the subject matter and in doing so may carry you on to perfection in the years to come. Briefly, I must say that some of the most heated arguments and small wars have been fought over "volume training" versus "high-intensity training" versus "heavy-duty training." My dad's bigger than your dad. I prefer playing marbles.

I know this: For me to grow or improve muscle I must maximize the intensity of resistance within the target muscle for a sufficient period of time through the application of intelligently prescribed exercise without overloading or overtraining. That is, I must up the weight, the sets, the reps; slow the rep tempo or increase the pace or combine some agreeable combination of the aforementioned while considering bodyweight, food intake, rest and choice of exercises. Throughout a workout or cycle of workouts this will be a circuitous process as degrees of resistance will vary continually and irregularly, and set and rep numbers will vary accordingly, as will exercise ranges of motion and body positions to manipulate resistance and further saturate the muscle.

Sounds like a mess, yet it is a most meticulous scheme and prevails on skill, intuition and … er … feeling. Ultimately, as the chapters are written and the books are read, I propose that the latter are the factors upon which we may rest our most successful muscle- and power-building principles. Curiously, till very recently as I prepared to write these pages by reading background material and intelligent training resources, I've never been confused. The confusion came with the reading. It's back to the iron for me.

This looks like Tommy Munichello's Gym in Manhattan at the Mr. World pre-judging in 1970. Three weeks of travel; L.A. to London to N.Y.C. to Ohio to France and Germany to N.Y.C. without a workout had me looking for my club.

Al Antuck

POWER TRAINING

Bill Pearl taught me many years ago that you have to get out of shape to get into shape. You can't maintain excellent definition and tone year-round. The muscular system and nervous system can't accept the stress of intense weight training in combination with low bodyfat for extended periods of time. The mind and the emotions don't fare too well, either. Bill didn't mean that you can't continue to pursue muscle-building excellence with all your might, though a well-timed layoff offers copious revival advantages. He meant modifications in your training would be wise to ensure continued progress and interest.

Routines and diets to maintain peak condition do not encourage muscle growth. You need an abundance of nutrients for high performance and the consequential demand for energy expenditure and muscle repair. Furthermore, dieting and intense workout routines tax the immune system, lowering the resistance to illnesses of all shapes and sizes.

When the timing is right, alter your training methodology to match a weight gain program. Here you can apply an abbreviated "periodization" technique in the form of some good old-fashioned "bulk up training." (This doesn't indicate good old- fashioned "pigging out" unless that's on your training table by wise choice.)

Controlled force-feeding is not an unknown procedure to this professional eater in his past delirium. My contention has always been to hold a few extra pounds (five to ten) to support the hard-working body, to enable it to work harder, heavier and longer in fact, by its bulky presence. The long, cold winter months accommodate this splendid muscle-building approach. Hide the hide while you insulate the body and provide a gratifying strength increase, an abundance of recovery ingredients and an ever-ready energy supply.

Cut back on your aerobic work, decrease the number of repetitions from the eight to twelve per set of bodybuilding to the six to eight per set of power training. Squats, deadlifts and other heavy basic moves with doubles and triples through the months will allow you to handle more weight and put the stress of the weight on different components of the muscle fibers that are not overloaded during the higher reps of peak bodybuilding.

Unless you plan to compete as a powerlifter, it's rarely worth the risk of damage to the tendons and ligaments to perform single maximum reps. It's dangerous to tempt injury and you won't gain more size doing singles than you will doing sets of three's to five's. Be smart.

The overload of bulk or power training will pull your body out of slumps and stabilized periods caused by routine bodybuilding. Expect benefits also as your mind relaxes and you enjoy the challenge of the heavy stuff. Treat yourself to an XXL T-shirt. You deserve it.

Late summer, 1970, with Venice and Marina Del Rey, California, behind me and Artie Z. before me. 235 and anticipating the string of contests ahead. A warm and windy day that filled us with hope, promise and wonder.

Art Zeller

5

MIGHTY WARRIORS

I'm just a guy from Jersey who likes to work out and happened to win Mr. America and stuff doin' weightlifting. I started with pushups, chins and dips like scrawny kids do, scavenged some weights when I was twelve and messed around with 'em till I was outta high school. Then I joined a YMCA, learned a few tricks, moved to California and learned a few more. I trained regularly, grew, ate, trained hard, grew some more, trained harder, ate more protein and sorta got cut. Bingo, won a few contests.

People want to know how I did it, what'd I do, what'd I eat, what's the secret. Fact is, I just answered all the questions in the above paragraph.

Eventually, the essential questions are answered and all that remains is the training. Not that we'll ever know all there is to know, but there comes a time when we know enough to put aside doubt, guesswork and controversy. A time to quiet our minds, collect our energies and train.

Here's a statement worth memorizing: Training with confidence is the only way to train. Enthusiasm and determination will follow like boxcars on a freight train. Confidence — the absence of doubt — is a distillation of hope, faith and knowing.

Confidence by its nature is smart and hardworking. It shovels fuel into the furnace. It is not cocky, conceited or arrogant. It's not stubborn or filled with boasting. These are characteristics of something quite the opposite. Confidence is secure.

Doubt, by contrast, is a stop sign in the middle of a flowing river. It's the brakes to the floor before your car gets moving. The only thing to follow doubt is hesitation and apathy — twelve-inch arms and a spare tire.

Confidence is a friendly and contagious spirit that enjoys the company of wonder. Unlike question, which proposes doubt, wonder is something to be graciously fulfilled. Thoughtful training, concentrated and undistracted, satisfies the wonder. You may never know a thing, but you begin to understand.

Weeks of training are miserably lost if you vacillate, wonderfully invested if you trust. Whether your techniques are worthy or not, you are. Trust your efforts and you'll grow. Your footsteps will not be wasted. Persist, practice form and focus, observe and note for future reference and examination. The process is called molding.

To you who are disappointed in your progress, I'd be glib to say, "Don't be," or "Join the club." I only recommend you accept disappointment until you're able, by dauntless training, to replace it with the joy of another workout completed, another purchase of understanding, another grateful step forward.

NOTHING MUCH HAS CHANGED

In preparation of an earlier segment, I hastily outlined my mass-building workouts of 1962 to reflect changes I would make applying the experience and knowledge I've gained over the nutty years gone by. Two things stand out immediately as I recall those years, my habits, disciplines and goals. First of all, it doesn't seem like such a very long time: thirty-eight years, the lifespan of a man or woman whose concern of turning forty is nibbling at their heels. Second, nothing has changed. I'm still me in an older body practicing the same basic combinations to fulfill the same basic needs, eating the same basic menu to sustain the same basic muscle. And it's not because I'm old-fashioned, stubborn, conservative or unaware. It's because the wheel is round and I like it that way. It works best when it's round.

Weight training for me has always been a need. Working through the stages of growth has not always been fun. There were times when it was a dog and I doubted and moaned and it was miserable. Those

Mike Neveux

A quiz to see if you're awake: What gym do I represent, where was the picture taken, who was the cameraman and what is the name of the recording artist singing in the background? Send in your answers plus a hundred dollars and you'll be considered in the finals.

times were some of the best seasons, where growth was of the spirit and soul. My only company was me and I learned to listen to myself and understand; one learns to like one's self in spite of it all. Heck, everybody else might just as well be looking the other way or in the mirror. Life's like that. Today, I absolutely love to train and, like most of our gym members, must train. Know what I mean?

Within every workout there is room for flex. I like to know where
I'm going each day, aware that I'm not strictly bound. Early on in the
'60s I trained each muscle group three times in a six-day workout week.
I suggest today that more rest is healthier and more productive. I prefer
a five-day week hitting the muscle groups two times. A three-on and
one-off, two-on and one-off with maximum intensity and determined
pace sounds just about right.

There are months and years ahead of us to observe, alter, grow,
revise and grow again. Therein lies the hope and fascination. Too
often, may I mention, many trainees of varying stages of development
change routines or techniques before growth has fully incubated and
muscles are able to hatch. They're capricious. They switch programs
because they're impatient and hunting for the fast track or someone
said to or they're bored or think they've hit a plateau or they simply lack
steely confidence or raw perseverance. Blast on, brothers and sisters.
Blast on.

INSISTENCE ON PERSISTENCE

Present company excluded ...

People are getting fatter and more out of shape every day. Sorry.
The statement sounds rude and insensitive. Is there an excuse or reason
for the failure, thus? Is it emotional, cultural, temporal, technical, chemical? Will it diminish, this condition, or will it increase? The fix is not an
unknown. It's not lost, locked up or in the hands of the enemy. It's not
extraordinarily expensive or rare. Science doesn't propose a "cure for
the disease" in the undetermined future. Corrections can be made by
us, now, independent of one another, quietly, privately, painlessly and
freely. Apply within.

Most days the only thing of significance I have to offer you is my
insistence on persistence. Add the variables "long-term performance"
and a "focused, undying spirit" to the above and most folks, the great
deconditioned masses, have a problem. Big time. Yet it is within the
energy of these prime factors that a resolution to the problem is discovered; they alone supply the answer needed for improvement.

Allow me to repeat the prime factors: long-term performance and
focused undying spirit.

The difficulty is not exercise or smart eating. These are as simple as a dimple and twice as cute. It's not the all-too-familiar scapegoats, time and priorities, although we're getting close. Can we intelligently argue that our daily obligations are more important than our health? It is our health, ultimately, about which we speak: body, mind and soul.

How can I help? It eludes us that practice is the most direct way to establish this inspiring and self-perpetuating habit, this marvelous life-giving, life-sustaining venture. Our exercise must grow into a thing of substance as alive and endearing as a best friend, a discipline that builds momentum like a roller-blader in hillside San Francisco. Sadly, the high road to our freedom takes our breath away before the fragrance of the fresh air is enjoyed; we lose heart as a cooling kettle loses steam and direction as the wind in a retreating storm.

Why isn't physical culture number one on our list of priorities? Why isn't it in the top ten or twenty? Are we lazy, are we glutinous, are we spoiled rotten, are we just plain dumb? A little of everything? I think we're scared. Scared to go to the gym, to meet the challenge, to expose ourself to ourselves and others, to work hard, to compromise, to listen to our needs instinctively, to stray from the societal norm, to be alone without numbing sight-and-sound distraction, to be alone … at all, to trust ourselves, to trust … at all, to stand tall without conceit, to admit shortcomings without self-destruction, to accept help without submission, to hope.

Been there, still am — the human condition, ever ready for service and repair. Take the gym away from the people I know and the road is treacherous. We can't make it up the hills, handle the curves, the stop and go and the speed and the heat and the endless stretch ahead. A good gym is a way-station, a refuge, a safe place where you can lick your wounds or prepare for the good race tomorrow. The field, the track, your garage or the health club downtown, your training is where you cleanse, restructure, restore inside and out: no miracles, no magic, no kidding. You forgive, you forget and remove the thorns, you ease the pain and count your blessings like reps and sets. You become re-united with yourself as a friend who's worthy. Those around you know you better and enjoy you more and life is good for a long time.

You still there? Somethin' else is buggin' me. About gyms: If it's not the right gym, if it's a zoo and the animals are ferocious and too

Backstage at the London Mr. Universe pre-judging late summer, 1970. The anticipation abates and the pandemonium is replaced with yielding, hard work and grime.

George Greenwood

cool, if the operators collect money with a grin and stash it in their shirt, if the personal trainers are about sixteen — this could hold you back. If the music is heavier than a loaded dumpster and the trendiness makes you want to lose your protein, if the on-going fashion show looks like The Oscars and the ever-loving sales team has cheerleaders, perhaps you need to seek another refuge. If the chalk is flying and the dumbbells don't come in pairs and guys in cutoffs are sitting on the equipment with their babes in mini-wear, this is probably not good either.

I know some guys and gals who train at home with limited room and equipment and they are supremely content. They've narrowed their needs to the essentials (typically a bench, an Olympic bar and plates, two or three pairs of appropriate or adjustable dumbbells and a rack that facilitates squats, chins and dips) and they added atmosphere, personality and desire — There are no limits. It's the basic-ness and plainness, the austerity, the lack of distraction that establishes and magnifies the intensity and meaningfulness of each muscle-bound workout.

I first started training in a shared bedroom, moved to the basement and eventually a garage, all the time knowing whatever there was, it was enough, but not for long. A good gym is "where it's at" for me. I'm not fancy, but I'm particular. I like space in all directions, order, cleanliness, fresh air, equipment availability and a handful of cool, hardworking people with whom to share it. This provides the environment with energy, uninterrupted pace and focus, encouragement and assistance when you need it, hope and promise always.

I know some pros who want the scene — lots of attention, glitz and big sound; they are stars in the spotlight. If it's too mild, the weights tend to be heavy and uninteresting. Too much aerobic energy and high-sound performance and you feel like a slug. Too posh, you feel rude and funky like a monkey.

If the gym is big, capital "B," I get lost in a corner, get the job done and get out ... get real.

Find a gym that suits you. Atmosphere is everything. Unless you think you're being robbed, don't fret over price. A good gym is worth it. Finally had to build my own.

AEROBICS IS THE WIND, WEIGHTLIFTING IS THE FIRE

Weightlifting does not stand alone. Knowledgeable coaches compare the achievement of fitness to a stool of three legs: weight training, diet and aerobic exercise. Each leg must bear its fair share of the load to assure balance. Who am I to disagree? I just accentuate the thickness of the weight training support, establish a sturdy dietary leg and use aerobics as a balancing pole to maintain an upright, on-target position. I prefer to lean on hard, well-paced lifting and consistent clean, high-protein, low-carb eating to set and control my muscle building, fat burning, cardio-respiratory health and metabolism with a stray side order of intense cardio to zero in on my course. Here I stray from the crowd. Physical fitness is vitally important. Aerobic exercise to achieve it, I fear, is over-rated, over-consumed and over-worshipped. This doesn't make it bad. The "iron" is better, that's all ... honest.

Aerobics come in all shapes and sizes from an early morning brisk walk to an all-out interval indoor cycling class. Make your choice based on time, needs, goals, equipment availability and desire. Some folks love the high, the rhythm, the demand, the discipline, the socializing and the results. Jump in. But, please, don't let the activity become excessive or it may eat you up. There are, of course, those who absolutely hate the thought of running in place, the stationary bike and classes. If aerobics keeps you from the gym, forget it. Maybe some other time.

Trying to get lean? Too much cardio will cut into your precious time, available energy, desire and training focus. The model for aerobic efficiency is three or four, fifteen to twenty minute sessions of treadmill, stair, bike or road work at varying levels of intensity each week: interval training. Here, the choice of modality is up to you according to desire, effect and convenience.

The amp in our fuel-burning system engendered by aerobics continues to burn calories for hours. Herein lies the real benefit of aerobics: ongoing fat burning via the chemistry change brought about by the exercise, when appropriate and smartly practiced. The calories burned during the actual running and jumping, kicking and screaming are minor. It's during this activity, over time, that the body creates fat-burning enzymes that carry on their delightful role long after our aerobic exercise has ceased for the day.

Cardio? Years ago in the '60s amongst lifters there was none. Hard, heavy, volume training, supersetting and long hours, the kind of training some instructors refer to as sure-fire overtraining, secured our cardio-respiratory needs. As hard bodies and exercise took off in the '70s and the fitness industry erupted, money drove the market to preposterous proportions. The sheep followed. Extensive scientific and pseudo-scientific research in physiology and mechanics presented our urgent need for treadmills, stair-steppers, stationary bikes, climbers, gliders, recumbents, et al. Cardio equipment in all its glory emerged in the '80s and like the car, snappy new styles and new features are offered year after year.

I love barbells.

Something else. Excessive aerobics causes your body to shift its chemistry, calling on muscle protein to provide energy. Have mercy. Throw me in the swamps, lock me in a dungeon, but don't take away my muscle protein.

Cardio activity alone should consist of twenty to thirty percent of your total training investment, depending upon the goals you seek. Your emphasis should be on resistance training to build valuable muscle size, muscle-based metabolism, strength and bone density. This exercise ratio plus your good eating strategy provide a reasonably straight line from A to Z.

DISCIPLINE—MY MAIN MAN

I have something to say about discipline. I go nowhere good without it. It's tough, it's austere and I treasure it as if it were a loving family member. That is, I welcome discipline always and I long for it when it's not present. It has the dimension and life we give it and it resides deep within. Discipline is not mean and self-centered, or at least no meaner or more self-centered than its host. Rarely do people perceive of this vital ingredient without a nagging discomfort as if it were an alien force that is troublesome, a nuisance between them and happiness, a punishment in pursuit of freedom and success. To the contrary, discipline, self-regulation — practiced habit — is a loyal, hand-picked partner that trudges beside us to share the load with calm energy and enabling might.

Are you heading somewhere, going someplace other than the general direction of the far side of your nose? Don't expect to get there too soon, or at all, without the big enforcer: discipline. You may complete half the journey by chance but it'll be a lopsided and forgettable mess. Wouldn't be surprised if you lost your way, forgot where you were going and complained the whole time doing it. You looking for "bigger, stronger, faster"? They're just ahead, beyond the curve. You can't miss them with your discipline intact.

Development of your muscular mass, shape and strength are directly proportionate to the development of your discipline. Or, as it has been observed by the Bomber Research Clinic, as one powerful feature develops, so does the other. Amazing co-adaptation.

NOTHING HAPPENS 'TIL IT HAPPENS

Exercise, working out, weight training, lifting. The routines, the programs, the outlines, the schemes, the workouts. Let's do the thing we talk about. No down-playing the important role of nutrition, attitude, environment and life-style but the center about which our muscle and strength building revolves is exercise, period. Nothing happens until it happens.

Exercise is a meager word for the act of lifting weights, don't you think? It's the iron in motion, the steel in hand and on the back, the weight on the bar and suspended from cable, pushed, pulled and cleverly, forcefully made to move from one place to another. And, you know who eventually becomes the teacher, the coach, the personal trainer to be relied upon? You, whose hands are grasping tightly the equipment before you.

Early on, did your mom and dad tell you how to walk? I'll bet you figured it out on your own, hot shot. Desire, eager pursuit, practice, trial and error are built-in learning systems upon which we heavily depend. As with infant walking, nine out of ten of us will have a similar experience with weight training, provided basic guidance, an outline, a demonstration and an encouraging word of confidence. Given the truth we can take this activity, hobby, sport, diversion — this exhilarating playfulness — a long way with our own common sense, simple motives and driving forces.

Try it, trust it, do it. The routines outlined in the next pages will be accompanied with a scattering of tips and hints to give them personality and remind you of their simplicity. They are a start, sure-fire primers and elementary walkers to get beginners and returning enthusiasts on their feet and back in action. The schemes become bigger and stronger to suit your stability and needs. They become loaded essays pitched with funk, unshaven and gritty.

You want percentages, charted increments of resistance, the science of progression and meticulous calculations one workout to the next? They're available in marvelous publications in brilliant detail. I have a list of recommended reading by highly esteemed, hard-working, science-minded practitioners: good stuff intelligently presented for all of us. They have assured me of the worth of my own insights and training approach, fascinating me with the chemistry, physics and physiology of the processes we practice here today. Fred Hatfield, Ken Leistner, Siff and Strossen, champions of thought and performance. Me? I mostly do this stuff, wonder and do it again.

Let's fly!

Photographer unknown

Mr. America posing routine, the fourth shot I managed in a series of twenty. Inspired by Bill Pearl and Jerry Winick.

5

PUSH THAT IRON

Exercise, sweet exercise, the backbone to achieving a fit and appealing body — and who, may I inquire, doesn't want a fit and appealing body: a healthy, vital and energetic system to carry on the business of living efficiently, joyfully and worry-free? The reason people around the world don't embrace exercise and fitness more fully or at all is because they don't understand it. It's lost in our culture, it's fading or it's reserved for the elite. Hardy physical fitness is absent in schools everywhere and we are, entire societies, getting fat and weak. The great human being, God's creation, in all man's cleverness, appears to be diminishing.

Good morning, friend, and get outta bed,
Run 'round the block, you've got fat to shed.

Push that iron and lift that steel,
Who you are is how you feel.

Exercise is life's surprise,
Within its hold longevity lies.

We're not to say, "Some other time,"
To procrastinate is a sad human crime.

Consider the loss in vitality and desire,
As the body fails and systems misfire.

Sets times reps with focus and pace,
Intensity with sweat should you embrace.

This isn't a hardship, a pain to resist,
It's the thing of life upon which we subsist,

No nuisance is this, no curse to retire,
It's a thing of life upon which we aspire.

Give up the couch some time each week,
Walk, run, lift weights these goals to seek.

You're not alone and need not despair,
The fun's ahead and the game is a dare.

The passages above are particularly moving when read by James Earl Jones to the theme of "Rocky." Hold on to the seat of your pants.

There are as many ways to train as there are thumb prints. And, at any given time they will all work. Some better than others, some forever and some only as a short experience to record that they are not valid for you or even for a gorilla. One of the sterling truths that cannot be repeated too often is "We are not all the same. Different things work for different people at different times in workout and in diet." Another excerpt from the archives of *"The Profound Teachings"* by The Bomber.

There's a previous segment where I drag you through the ABCs of self-evaluation. Read it over as a prep for your first workouts. Get the psyche, the mood, the involvement and commitment engaged. Get your doc's okay. Don't hurt yourself. Be alert. The learning and habit starts now.

You'll find that workouts from the onset can be "touchy" or "iffy." Be happy. A few minutes past "Go" and a well-being and purposefulness surface, and you're on your merry way. Count on the aerobic exercise of your choice to warm you up and set you in motion.

LET'S GET AT IT ... GETTING STARTED

Here's some advice from a former garagehead for those getting started at home with limited equipment. Everything within the pages of this book applies to you except the range of exercises. You, with the right attitude and plan, can reach an exciting level of fitness, no doubt about it. You can build bigger, stronger muscles; you can trim down an overweight body, shape it and tone it. It just takes time, persistence and a keen personal agreement to do it. Do you have these elements? Absolutely.

For starters, define your workout area: garage, bedroom, basement — whatever. Give yourself enough room to move freely, breathe and grow. A cramped area will work against you. A private area will work for you.

Neatly and concisely set up your equipment. Let's assume you have the basics: a bar, enough weight, a pair of adjustable dumbbells, a bench with racks, a couple of sturdy high-backed chairs and a lot of heart. Be a happy bodybuilder; hang a couple of posters and tune your radio to your favorite sounds for some cool background music. Atmosphere and a little company are always welcome. You're in charge and you're getting close.

Give yourself sixty to ninety minutes, three or four days a week, to work out and, most importantly, set a regular time for this special occasion. Regularity is essential in establishing a mental identification, a "mindset," and in creating a physical pattern. Applying order from the very beginning will help you develop the power of habit and give substance and discipline to your new undertaking, this matchless and terrific sport.

Do things haphazardly and you get haphazard results. You'll miss the fun and fulfillment of completing a tough, focused and intelligent workout. You won't pump, burn, sweat, or thoroughly overload. No endorphins, no natural chemistry improvement. Sooner than later, without foundation your inspired endeavor will fade to a guilty memory. Sounds grouchy, doesn't it?

In the early stages your job is basic. Practice, get to know your muscles, which are working in each exercise, what are the factors of resistance, pump and burn. This requires and develops patience, focus and concentration, super qualities to add to your list of accomplishments. You might make notations of the weights you use, the reps and sets and a comment or two on a pad as a quick reference from workout to workout. This weightlifting stuff is pure and simple, bearing your personality and standards; it becomes a vital extension and reflection of you.

You're a home trainer and we're ready to go. Seriously. You've got your water bottle at hand. Hydrate and keep hydrated. You're fully fueled for blast off, of course, with your pre-workout carbs and protein to provide pump, energy and muscle restoration. Begin your routine by working your midsection for five minutes before hitting the weights. This will not only strengthen and define the trunk muscles, but also raise your heart rate and core temperature, stretch your muscles and prepare your focus for the intense workout ahead. Several sets of floor crunches and leg raises to maximum reps should do it for now.

So much for the potatoes, now for the meat: the fun stuff, the major muscle builders, the big guns. There is no fast way to build muscle, get strong and lose fat; only hard work, good food and a lot of time will do that. Right? Right. There are no secrets. There are fifty exercises, maybe a hundred that we can choose. I've chosen the best to do the job for you. More is not better. Different is not better. Not today.

HOME TRAINER ROUTINE # ONE — BUSYBODY

You've got one solid hour, three alternate days a week. Give yourself loads of time for your start-up workouts to determine your level of condition, familiarize yourself with your surroundings and exercises, and enjoy the novelty and substance of your new endeavor. Ease into your first workouts with one or two sets of each exercise. Increase the number of sets to three by the end of the first month, with your eye on four.

Exercises 1 and 2, done together:
Bench Press (1-4 sets x 12, 10, 10, 8 repetitions)
  supersetted with
Stiff-arm Dumbbell Pullover (1-4x10)

Exercise 3:
Bent-over Barbell Row (1-4x8-10)

Exercises 4 and 5, done together:
Barbell Curl (1-4x8-10)
  supersetted with
Dips Between Chairs (1-4x10-12 or maximum)

Exercises 6 and 7, done together:
Light Bar Squats (2-4x15)
  supersetted with
Toe Raise off block (2-4x15-20)

This beginning program uses the superset technique; that is, doing one exercise followed by a second complementary exercise. For example, exercise one immediately followed by exercise two, pause for a weight adjustment and a thirty to sixty second rest (rest times will vary), repeat exercise one followed by exercise two and so on for two to four supersets. We'll spend more time on this discussion later. There's no rush; practice your movements at an agreeable pace with confidence.

HOME TRAINER ROUTINE # TWO — TOUGH FIT

Use the same abdominal warm-up. This function will gain in its priority as you continue with your progress and discern your needs. You've got one hour, four days a week, an extra day with extra interest and willingness. The Tough Fit is a likely next step from Busybody Routine. You can now apply the split routine technique: upper body (torso) on Day One, arms and legs on Day Two, Day Three is a rest day, upper body on Day Four, arms and legs on Day Five, Days Six and Seven off, and repeat the following week.

DAY ONE (Upper Body — Torso)

Bench Press (2-4x12, 10, 10, 8)
  supersetted with
Supine Chin — Wide-grip (2-4x8-10)

One-arm Dumbbell Row (2-4x6-8)
  supersetted with
Stiff-arm Pullover (2-4x12)

Steep Dumbbell Incline Press (2-4x8)
  supersetted with
Bent-over Lateral Raise (2-4x8)

DAY TWO (Arms and Legs)

Seated Dumbbell Alternate Curl (2-4x8)
  supersetted with
Lying Triceps Extension (2-4x12)

Wrist Curl (3x12-15)
  supersetted with
Chair Dips (3xMax)

Squat (2-4x15-20)
supersetted with
Toe Raise (2-4x15-20)

Deadlift (2-4x8)

You'll find the exercise descriptions and a list of routine variations in the upcoming pages.

REASSURANCE

As you get familiar with your routine and workout area it will flow and become comfortable. Be attentive and confident. There's nothing to doubt. You're doing absolutely the right thing for this time. Stick to your outlined routine for at least six weeks with intensity and assurance. Only then will your body adapt to the consistent overload and build muscle. During these days you'll practice, develop form and learn a hundred things I can't describe, things you'll discover that will add to your life more than you ever expected.

If you don't play hard and work hard, plan to add aerobic activity to your schedule three days a week for fifteen to twenty minutes. Try a selection of walking and jogging intervals, steady vigorous bike riding, hiking or swimming. This will increase your fat-burning, muscle-building metabolism and improve the health of your heart, lungs and vascular system. All this combines to enhance your energy and endurance to train more effectively.

With a month invested in your home workouts you'll be familiar with the elements of training and the muscles' responses. You'll be conditioned and ready to increase your resistance output. These routines, with gradual weight and repetition upgrades, can serve you successfully for six to eight months. Does it appeal to you? Stick with it. Are you ready for a change? Move on.

Reminder: I say this again — early trainees are often impulsive and impatient. They change routines too soon, too often, before either good habits or good muscle have a chance to develop from consistent and thoughtful overload. Beware that you don't succumb to premature training changes due to improper assessment, or no assessment at all. Hang in there.

Art Zeller

Artie found this tree in someone's backyard behind Joe's gym. The yard was empty, no one was home, the gate was unlocked and we were there.

4

LIFT THAT STEEL

Introductory Program
Intro — Step Two
Draper All-Time Favorite
Upper/Lower Split
Push/Pull Routine
Four-Day Burner
Advanced Daily Routine
Two-Day Full Body Time Crunch
Full Body Strength Workout
Lean Legs for Women
Quick Fit Program
Rotation Training
Leg Priority Training
Upper Chest Training
Back and Lats and More
I'll be Back
Back for More
Back Again
Shoulder Pump and Burn
Arm Priority Training
Forearm Training and Unassociated Topics
Abdominal Training
Tricks of the Trade
Slumpbusters

The following are sample workouts for you to adapt to suit your preferences and your gym's equipment list. Unless otherwise indicated, I recommend that you change your routine every six to eight weeks. Pick and choose among these — they're in no particular order — or make up your own. Be tough. You're alone with yourself. Become an encouraging and sympathetic and upbeat training partner. No slouches allowed. Be tolerant yet aggressive. Three workouts and the wheels are turning. Don't you dare stop now; it's a good ride.

INTRODUCTORY PROGRAM

Complete one or two sets of each exercise the first two weeks and three sets of each the remaining weeks of the four-week cycle. Be easy; during the first set, warm up and practice the groove of the movement, the track in which the weight safely, effectively and naturally travels. Increase the resistance with each successive set.

MONDAY/WEDNESDAY/FRIDAY

MIDSECTION AND AEROBIC WORK
10 minutes of cardio first, followed by Crunches and Leg Raises

CHEST
Incline Dumbbell Chest Press (1x12)
Dumbbell Pullovers (1x12)

BACK
Wide-grip Pulldown (1x12)
Row Machine (1x12)

TRICEPS
Triceps Press Machine (1x12)

BICEPS
Standing Dumbbell Curls (1x12)

LEGS
Leg Press (1x15)
Leg Extension (1x15)
Leg Curl (1x15)

Focus, form and deliberate motion. Work hard, but don't strain ... yet.

INTRO — STEP TWO

A few additions and a little shifting of exercises give this routine more variety and volume. You're up to two to three sets per exercise, twelve different exercises total; more time-consuming, but you'll be able to move more confidently, more surely and with less rest as your understanding and condition improve.

MONDAY/WEDNESDAY/FRIDAY

MIDSECTION AND AEROBIC WORK
10 minutes of interval cardio
Crunches, Leg Raises, Hyperextensions

CHEST
Dumbbell Chest Press (2x10-12)
Cable Crossovers, Pec Dec or Incline Flys (2x10-12)

BACK
Wide-grip Pulldown (2x12)
Seated Lat Row (2x10-12)

SHOULDERS
Dumbbell Shoulder Press (2x10-12)

BICEPS
Barbell Curls (2x10-12)

TRICEPS
Triceps Press Machine or Bench Dips (2x12)
Pulley Pushdown (2x12)

LEGS
Leg Press or Squats (2x15)
Semi-stiff-legged Deadlifts (2x15)
Leg Curl (2x10-12)
Calf Raises (2x20)

Some activists will scream that this is too much volume, but you're not yet blasting the sets and need the activity and practice. Volume is good (reps x sets x exercises per workout equals exercise volume). Your last rep of each set should feel just right, near-perfect form and concentrated muscular action. Muscle burn — the sting within the muscle being worked — increases with each successive rep. It's a good pain which, when endured, allows greater muscle overload and subsequent increased muscle adaptation. Hence, muscle growth. Give me five, Mama.

Look for the pump, the full muscular feeling that is evident in immediate muscle increase during exercise as blood fills the muscle cells under demand of systemic support. The pump is a mighty good feeling.

This is another routine to be done following a four-week cycle.

DRAPER ALL–TIME FAVORITE

After all is said and done, my favorite training routine is based on a seven-day week, three on — one off, two on — one off, reaching a six-week stretch with enough daily wiggle room for comfort.

MIDSECTION — TORSO

Your favorite variation of Crunches (incline and weighted), Leg Raises, Hyperextensions, Hanging Leg Raises

MONDAY — CHEST AND SHOULDERS AND BACK

Seated Front Press (3-5x12, 10, 8, 8, 6)
tri-setted with
Wide-grip Pulldowns (3-5x12, 10, 8, 8, 8)
and
Standing Bent-over Lateral Raises (3-5x6-8)

Dumbbell Press (4-5x12, 10, 8, 8, 6)
tri-setted with
Dumbbell Pullovers (4-5x12, 10, 8, 8, 6)
and
Seated Lat Row (4-5x12, 10, 8, 8, 6)

TUESDAY — LEGS

Leg Extensions (3-5x10-12)
tri-setted with
Leg Curls (3-5x8-12)
and
Calf Raises (3-5x15-20)

Squats (5-7x15, 15, 12, 10, 8, 6, 6)

Deadlifts (5x10, 8, 6, 6, 6)

WEDNESDAY — ARMS

Rubber tubing rotator cuff work, 5x adductor, 5x abductor

Wrist Curls (3-5x20, 15, 15, 15, 15)
tri-setted with
Thumbs-up Curl (3-5x10, 8, 8, 8, 6)
and
Pulley Pushdowns (3-5x12-15)

Bent Bar Curls (3-5x6-8)
supersetted with
Dips (3-5x12-15)

Dumbbell Alternate Curls (3-5x6-8)
supersetted with
Overhead or Lying Triceps Extensions (3-5x12, 10, 8, 8, 8)

THURSDAY — OFF

FRIDAY — UPPER BODY

Front Press (4x12, 10, 8, 6)
supersetted with
Pulldowns (4x12, 10, 8, 6)

Dumbbell Inclines (4x12, 10, 8, 6)
supersetted with
Pullovers (4x12, 10, 8, 6)

Dumbbell Rows (4x8)

Dumbbell Alternate Curls (4x12, 10, 8, 6)
tri-setted with
Dips (4x maximum)
and
Pulley Pushdowns (4x12)

SATURDAY — LEGS

Same as earlier leg day, with this change:

Light Deadlifts (5x8)
supersetted with
Rope Tucks (5x25)

Ideal conditions are for an ideal world. Still, sticking to the prescribed plan laid out by these orderly routines is very desirable. The body will respond to the consistent overload, the chemistry of the system (hormones, enzymes, metabolism, immune system) becomes more defined and healthier, and your psychological health and mental toughness improves big time. You're invested. You're cleaning out the attic and the junk in the trunk.

By now you should feel like a million bucks: stronger, energized, lighter and more toned, smiling and more certain.

UPPER/LOWER SPLIT

Time to split your routine; that is, divide your routine into two parts done on separate days. Easy to do and gives you more focus on each muscle group: upper body on one day, lower body on the next. This split can be done by alternating upper body and lower body over two equally spaced days a week or working out four days a week, upper/lower, day off, upper/lower, two days off. Here's where you can make the call based on your training needs as they are becoming evident. A little trial and error will give you clues as you choose the suitable path.

DAILY

MIDSECTION AND AEROBIC WORK

10-15 minutes of intense cardio
Crunches, Leg Raises, Hyperextensions

DAY ONE — UPPER BODY

CHEST
Bench Press (3-4x12,10,8)
Flys (3-4x12,10,8)

BACK
Chins or Wide-grip Pulldowns (3-4x10-12)
One-arm Dumbbell Row (3-4x8-10)

SHOULDERS
Steep Incline Dumbbell Press (3x8-10)
Lateral Raise (3x8-10)

BICEPS
Bent Bar Curls (3-4x8-10)

TRICEPS
Dips or Triceps Press Machine (3-4x12)

DAY TWO — LOWER BODY

LEGS
Squat (4x12, 10, 8, 6)
Stiff-legged Deadlifts (3x10)

Leg Extensions (3-4x12)
   supersetted with
Leg Curls (3-4x10-12)

Standing and/or Seated Calf Raises (4xMax)

Long ago, when man was groping about the misty and craggy surface of the earth, he stumbled across superset training, an intense and energetic style that broke away from the stale, single-set Strongman methodology. I was an early proponent who carried forth the principles with resolution and today I center my workouts on them as I perceive them as unfailing. The accommodating exercises can be adjusted in weight, performance intensity, pace, tempo and volume to achieve different goals and satisfy varying physiologies. Huh? I said — read my lips — they're a roller coaster with highs, curves, speed and dips that leave you exhilarated. Stabilize the superset sequences with a single-set base and you have the secret formula. Guard this with your life.

Deadlifts should make an appearance at least two or three times a month if they are not specifically listed in the prescribed schemes. Always keep them in the action to delight in their proud full-body benefits. Three or four stimulating sets of six to ten reps at the end of your leg day without overload can be fulfilling and productive. Be orderly and disciplined without loss of creativity and freedom.

PUSH/PULL ROUTINE

Pushing on one day and pulling on the next is a popular way to split up muscle groups to ensure maximum like-muscle action with a minimum liability of overtraining. Logical, but never my favorite. I resist separating biceps and triceps in my training schemes. They are, in fact, most commonly worked connectively in superset/tri-set fashion. Here's where personal desire or training appeal rule, allowing you to chuckle and train compatibly. This is a nice training outline to follow and, if you choose, beef up with additional pushing or pulling moves that ... er ... move you.

DAILY

MIDSECTION AND AEROBIC WORK
10-15 minutes of intense cardio
Crunches, Leg Raises, Rope Tuck, Hyperextensions

MONDAY/THURSDAY

CHEST AND TRICEPS
Dumbbell Chest Press (3-4x8-10)
Incline Dumbbell Press (3-4x8-10)
Cable Crossovers (3-4x10-12)
Triceps Press Machine (3-4x12)
Pulley Pushdowns (3-4x12)

TUESDAY/FRIDAY

BACK AND BICEPS
Close-grip Chins or Close-grip Pulldowns (3-4x10-12)
Wide-grip Pulldowns (3-4x10-12)
One-arm Dumbbell Row (3-4x6-8)
Barbell Curls (3-4x8-10)
Biceps Machine Curls (3-4x8-10)

WEDNESDAY

LEGS
Squats or Leg Press (3-4x12, 10, 8, 6)
Lunges (3-4x12)

Leg Extension (3-4x15)
   supersetted with
Leg Curls (3-4x10-12)

Calf Raises (3-4x20)

Some fun suggestions, now that we're past the "toddler" stages — You're feeling good, fired up and "ordinary" is repulsive. Today or this week, choose a weight that provides a low to moderate load for ten reps in each listed exercise and perform each exercise one at a time consecutively. This is to be done without haste, but also without pause between exercises. Upon completion of the five movements on Day 1 (or Day 2 or Day 3) take a one-minute breather and continue for a total of four or five or six multi-sets. You're flying and done pronto with mucho pumpo. This is very effective training to rev the spirits and shock the system — long term, a burn out. If you ask me to give you scientific background on this methodology, have a seat while I confer with my crystal ball. Sure is fun and feels great. Does that count?

FOUR–DAY BURNER

This is a mixed bag of pressing and pulling with no serious dense muscle growth targeted. It's a pleasing routine that can whirl you into hard output simply because it's simple. You don't feel threatened by its ominous-ness and thereby willingly blast it with all you've got before it's over and done. Any higher rep range will be suitable. Heavier resistance will slow you down. What animal are you today?

DAILY

MIDSECTION AND AEROBIC WORK
Crunches, Leg Raises, Rope Tuck, Hyperextensions
20 minutes of intense cardio

MONDAY/THURSDAY

UPPER BODY
Dumbbell Chest Press (3x8-12)
Wide-grip Pulldown (3x8-12)
Dumbbell Incline Press (3x8-12)
Seated Lat Row (3x8-12)
Dumbbell Shoulder Press (3x8-12)
Dumbbell Incline Curls (3x8-12)
Triceps Press Machine (3x8-12)
Pulley Pushdown (3x8-12)

TUESDAY/FRIDAY

LOWER BODY
Squats or Leg Press (4x12, 10, 8, 6)
Stiff-legged Deadlifts (4x10-12)

Leg Extension (4x12)
   supersetted with
Leg Curl (4x10-12)

Calf Raise (4x15)

Every workout can be transformed into a progressive-resistance challenge. You can break out your log and calculate your pounds-per-set and your reps-per-set increments with most any scheme, this four-day split notwithstanding. Work between six to eight reps for these pursuits and add a set here and there where overload approach requires it.

If you're backing off the heavier resistance on your upper body to allow some elbow or shoulder tendon to rest, or feel like charging about the gym floor in a high-rep, light-weight manner for any number of legitimate and undetermined reasons, stay in touch with the earth's surface by slugging it out with some good old-fashioned heavy deadlifts. Very constructive. Very peaceful.

ADVANCED DAILY TRAINING

The three-day split with supersets, three on — one off, followed by three on — two off is my most common workout arrangement.

DAILY
Crunches, Leg Raises, Rope Tuck, Hyperextensions
15 minutes of intense cardio

DAY ONE

CHEST AND BACK SUPERSET
Bench or Dumbbell Press (3-4x12, 10, 8, 6)
  supersetted with
Wide-grip Pulldown or Chins (3-4x12, 10, 8, 6)

Dumbbell Incline Press (3-4x12, 10, 8, 6)
  tri-setted with
Dumbbell Pullover (4x10)
  and
Seated Lat Row (4x10)

Cable Crossovers (3-4x12)
  supersetted with
One-arm Dumbbell Row (3-4x12)

Optional:
Deadlifts (3x10)

DAY TWO

SHOULDERS
Overhead Press (3-4x8)
  supersetted with
Side-arm Lateral Raise (3-4x12)

BICEPS AND TRICEPS TRI-SETS

Bent Bar Curl (3-4x8-12)
   tri-setted with
Close-grip Bench Press (3-4x10-12)
   and
Lying Triceps Extension (3-4x10-12)

Zottman Dumbbell Curl (3-4x8-10)
   tri-setted with
Dips or Triceps Press Machine (4x12)
   and
Pulley Pushdowns (4x12)

DAY THREE

LEGS

Standing Calf Raise (4xMax)
   supersetted with
Seated Calf Raise (4xMax)

Leg Extension (4x12)
   supersetted with
Leg Curl (4x10-12)

Squat (4x12, 10, 8, 6)
Stiff-legged Deadlifts (4x10)

I periodize my training in an effective, individualized method according to the season and expected or unexpected urges. This apparent looseness in approach is the smartest working plan for anyone after a hundred years of the iron dance. Sometimes you lead and sometimes you've got to follow. In the earlier years, as I pressed on to competitive successes, I was more regulated in set, rep and weight incrementing with the logical progressive resistance formulas — until I could stand upright. I became brittle at an early age. I crave order and discipline, but too much regimen and I crack. Weird. I can blast it and I don't crack. Go figure.

TWO-DAY PER WEEK FULL BODY — TIME CRUNCH
(Or three-day, continually alternating)

This is a pair of cute, little, cuddly workouts; cute like a rhino and cuddly as a shark. Truth is, if you're planning to go heavy with rigid expectations, yes, we have ugly. However, in the manner of heavy locomotion at a ninety percent output of effort on your last rep (you be the judge, it's your body), this is sweet. You've got to be well-fed, before and after, for this bombardment. Are you drinking plenty of water? Hey, I'm not your baby-sitter.

DAY ONE

Bench Press (4-5x15, 12, 10, 8, 6)
supersetted with
Pulldowns (4-5x12, 10, 10, 8, 8)

Dumbbell Incline Press (4-5x10, 8, 6, 6, 6)
supersetted with
Pullovers (4-5x10, 8, 8, 6, 6)

Deadlifts (4-5x12, 10, 8, 6, 6)

DAY TWO

Barbell Curls (4-5x10, 8, 8, 6, 6)
supersetted with
Dips (4-5x10-12)

Squat (5x15, 12, 12, 12, 10, 8)
tri-setted with
Leg Curls (5x 12, 10, 8, 8, 8)
and
Calf Raises (5x15-20)

I'm giving this routine an "A." Hit it two, three or four times a week, alternating continually. Choose some days to go heavy on certain body parts that lag and some to go light and quick for the happy pump. The pump may not build muscle, but it sure is delicious. I hereby declare that it's a sign of a healthy vascular and cellular system.

FULL BODY STRENGTH WORKOUT

Here's my version of an abbreviated strength workout, similar, I believe, to anything you might find in a Hardgainer or HITer's repertoire.

Always do warm-up sets first x15 reps

MONDAY

Squats (5x6)
Chins (4xMax)
Bent-over Rows (4x8)

WEDNESDAY

Bench Press (5x5)
Cleans and Presses (4x6)

Extended torso work: weighted Hyperextensions, Roman Chair Abdominal Situps, Hanging Leg Raises, Rope Tucks

FRIDAY

Deadlifts (5x5)
Barbell Curls (4x6)
Dips (4xMax)

Grip and Forearm Work:
Bar Hangs (3xMax)

Wrist Curls (3x15-20)
  supersetted with
Reverse Wrist Curls (3xMax)

Take a break from this every couple of months with some higher rep workouts to enjoy the pump you've been missing and give your joints a rest.

LEAN LEGS FOR WOMEN
Six-week program, alternating Week One with Week Two

Warm-up legs and shoulders with deep knee bends and rotator cuff work with rubber tubing. The workouts are fast-paced, sixty seconds maximum rest between sets, supersets or tri-sets. This is designed to prioritize the shaping of the leg and demand the burning of fat while maintaining upper body muscularity. Six weeks is the maximum this workout should be used without the addition of more upper body training. If a fourth day can be added, do your favorite upper body workout.

WEEK ONE — MONDAY/WEDNESDAY/FRIDAY

Front Squats (5x15, 12, 10, 10, 10)

Stiff-legged Deadlifts (3x12)
  tri-setted with
Leg Curls (3x12)
  and
Calf Raises (3x20)

Incline Dumbbell Press (4x10)
  supersetted with
Wide-grip Pulldowns (4x10)

Optional, if time and energy permits, no rest between supersets:

Dumbbell Pullovers (4x12)
  supersetted with
Crunches (4x25)

WEEK TWO — MONDAY/WEDNESDAY/FRIDAY

Wide-stance Squat (Sumo Squat) on Smith Press (5x10)

Raised Lunges on block or step (3x10)
  supersetted with
Leg Curls (3x10)

Dumbbell Pullovers (3x12)
  supersetted with
Seated Lat Rows (3x12)

Dumbbell Shoulder Presses (3x12)
  tri-setted with
Dumbbell Curls (3x12)
  and
Triceps Pushdowns (3x12)

Optional, if time and energy permits, no rest between supersets:

Crunches (3x15)
  supersetted with
Calf Raises (3xMax)

QUICK FIT PROGRAM

Here's a fifty-minute "Quick Fit" workout routine put together mainly for the in-a-hurry crowd ripping up and down the malls, highways and workplace. It's clean and neat, and with thoughtful periodic exercise replacement this outline has the concise and efficient appeal to last a long time. It's like dessert.

15- 20 minutes of aerobic work
5 minutes of torso work (superset)
Crunches and Leg Raises (2xMax)

Chest Press — dumbbell, bench or machine (3-4 sets x 8-12)
  tri-setted with
Stiff-arm Dumbbell Pullover (3-4 sets x 8-12)
  and
Row — any type of cable machine (3-4 sets x 8-12)

Fixed Bar Curl (3-4x8-12)
  supersetted with
Triceps Press — dips/dip machine (3-4x8-12)

Leg Press (3-4x15-20)

ROTATION TRAINING

Rotation training provides freedom with control, order without conformity. It's as advanced as you want it to be, yet suits a healthy beginner if presented knowingly and patiently by an experienced partner or personal trainer. Like stepping up to home plate and hitting doubles and triples your first day at bat.

DAY ONE

Aerobic exercise 15 minutes
Midsection work 10 minutes

CHEST AND BACK AND SHOULDERS

Bench (3-4x8-12)
  supersetted with
Wide-grip Pulldown (3-4x10-12)
  or
Hammer Chest (3-4x8-12)
  supersetted with
Hammer High-low Lat Row (3-4x10-12)

Dumbbell Incline (3-4x8-12)
  tri-setted with
Dumbbell Pullover (3-4x10-12)
  and
Seated Lat Row (3-4x8-12)

Dumbbell Row (3-4x8-10)
  superset with
Single Cable Crossover (3-4x10-12)

DAY TWO

Aerobic exercise 15 minutes
Midsection work 10 minutes

ARMS AND LEGS

Barbell Curl (3-4x6-12)
superset with
Triceps Press (3-4x10-12)

and/or

Alternating Dumbbell Curls (3-4x6-12)
superset with
Pulley Pushdowns (3-4x12-15)

Leg Extensions (3x15)
tri-setted with
Leg Curls (3x8-12)
and
Calf Raises (3x20)

Squats or Leg Press (4x10-12)

Deadlifts (4x12, 10, 8, 6)

Day One Notes

Aerobics are most effective when done harder rather than longer. As your conditioning improves, hit your favorite cardio hard and move directly to your crunches and leg raises with little rest between supersets. Twice a week throw in two sets of rope tucks and hanging leg raises. This fast-paced abdominal work maintains a high heart rate, thereby extending aerobic uptake. A great advantage, a gift.

Pick one superset of the first two listed. The third combination is a tri-set that'll flow like lava.

Dumbbell rows are power moves; left side followed by right, pause and restore, again, left followed by right as you go up the rack. The single-cable crossover allows you to focus resistance to the target area and gain total pectoral contraction. This exercise requires finesse, as do all the moves, and concentrated practice is the master.

Day Two Notes

Bent bar curls are comfortable and safe for the grip and wrist, yet a straight bar provides an unusual total biceps action and peak overload. Experiment, compare and creatively mix these two. Start from a full arm-hanging position and powerfully pull the bar toward your chin. A controlled body thrust is cool in the heavier or fatigued concentric action with a medium to slow lowering to the original straight-arm position for completion. A mighty movement that puts an advantageous demand on the whole upper torso — erectors to traps — it's a great multiple investment to complement Day One output.

Before I get side-tracked here, let me pause to remind you that I'll spend a lot more time on exercise descriptions in the next section.

Triceps Press (Dip) Machine — lower seat, expand handles, grab the ends and slide down to a stiff arm starting position. Lean thirty percent forward into the exercise and allow the bars to rise up to a full-range position, leaning in as you forcibly lock out the triceps. This exercise performed with forward-body position recruits back, pecs and shoulders. Another grateful multi-muscle advantage to add to Day One. We're rich.

To perform dumbbell alternate curls — standing or seated, doesn't matter — bring the right dumbbell from a palms-forward, fully hanging position tight to the shoulder with a medium to slow return to the straight hanging start. Add a mini-second pause and repeat with left. A little rocking, a little thrust, a little growling and you're in there. Follow this by your standard pulley pushdown done with might and form.

Leg extensions, leg curls and calves are tri-set counterparts. Deliberate, clean, piston-action reps get you through some painful lactic acid blues. Leg presses are safe, sound and productive if you don't roll your lower back by going too deep — tough on the knees and lower back. High reps (15-20) are most productive for leg health and performance.

Add high rep deadlifts for a strong back — a classic favorite of hardcore lifters with a generous heart. This is an excellent addition to a mundane routine. Gives it guts and charm.

Warm up and stay warm. Fuel up and stay fueled. Drink lots of water. You'll perform far better, stronger and longer, inspired by an awesome pump and high spirits with less chance of injury. Feed your hungry muscular system plenty of protein and carbs within forty-five minutes of your workout, before and after.

LEG PRIORITY TRAINING

Let's give legs priority once in a while. It's not unusual for men and women alike to undertrain their legs, assuming that running, biking or the Stairmaster will be sufficient. Leg training ranks low on the popularity scale amongst early trainees; the fact is, it's very hard work. Legs, the body's largest muscle group, put the greatest demands on the heart, lungs and vascular system. Not only exhausting, leg exercises are rather dull, limited in variation and cause a nasty burn from major lactic acid accumulation. Frightening. Besides, young bodybuilders often wear pants and are too busy looking at their biceps or chest, anyway. Can't see them, why bother?

Inevitably, men and women do look down and great legs are most desirable. They're exciting. Ask an older person and they'll tell that if you lose your leg strength you lose your ability to get around, to be free — independent. Legs are the foremost transporters: hikers, runners, dancers and peddlers. They represent strength and impart power. They burn calories like crazy and make handy clothes hangers.

Last and most interesting, they are responsible for the growth of the rest of the muscles of the body, especially when squatting. The abdominals and trunk, back and shoulders bear the strain and balance of the weighted bar and develop accordingly. Furthermore, with the body's largest muscles under overload, a message is sent to the brain that it must prepare itself for this increase of resistance by building proportionately the muscles of the whole system. This process — this systemic action — was the final incentive noticed years ago by early bodybuilders before researchers noticed or cared. If you want to exceed in this sport you must squat.

Are you ready? The leg routine you've been waiting for — Leg Priority — designed to improve form, function and power of the whole body.

Cardio warm-up, Crunches and Leg Raises

Leg Extensions (4x12-15)
  tri-setted with
Leg Curls (4x8-12)
  and
Calf Raises (4x20)

Squats — Warm-up then 4x12 reps
You can use other set and rep variations another time. We're here for life.

Lunges (3x15)
  fast-paced superset with
Stiff-legged Deadlifts (3x15)

Standing Calf Raise (4-5x15-25)
  superset with
Seated Calf Raise (4-5x15-25)

Volume plus Volume equals Volumes

Begin with an aerobic warm-up followed by crunches and leg raises. This is essential to energize the core muscles and joints, ready the trunk, raise the heart rate, dispel distracting thoughts and focus on the critical work ahead.

Start light to protect the joints and add weight each succeeding set working up to a moderate effort on the leg extensions. The powerful quad can too easily overload the knee, a joint already in a compromised position; a slow tempo will accomplish more in the extension with less risk, two seconds up, contract without hyper-extending for a sweet split-second and return over two seconds to the start. No squealing. Once you're in condition, you can power into the leg curl; a more explosive concentric with a slow eccentric. It's a matter of twitch and fiber. These combined exercises increase circulation favorably, shape the quads, hamstrings, glutes and calves while further preparing for the squats.

Squats deserve respect and require total concentration. Balance is critical with the knees and low back at risk. Practice strict form and proceed slowly with the weight you choose and you will be drawn to the whole-body work they provide. If possible, set up a rack and relax. For the first time squatter, safety bars can be placed at six or eight inches to allow short yet effective range of movement until strength and control are achieved. The bars can be lowered as confidence is raised.

Stand upright with the bar across your traps. Look forward and up a few degrees and squat down as if sitting on an imaginary chair, concentrating to push through your heels (as opposed to your toes) to ensure that the upper legs carry the workload. The more one descends, the more one tends to lean forward and force the resistance onto the lower back. Danger. Stay as upright as you can, continually holding the load on the quads. Do partial movements and in time you'll achieve a full squat position with the thighs parallel to the floor, or deeper. Practice sessions should be performed with light weight, of course, yet too light a weight and you'll find it hard to maintain balance and locate a groove. Don't be shy.

Performed twice a week this program has a long life span. The first day should be reserved for a heavy workout, with the second workout consisting of higher reps, less weight and increased pace to afford functional variety without overtraining.

UPPER CHEST TRAINING

The legs we stand on, that synchronized pair of odd-shaped wheels that move us about at varying speeds over diverse terrain, have had their moment of blitz. Let's move up and forward and talk about our chests.

Upper chest development depends largely on skeletal structure (rib cage) and the pectoral attachments to that structure. Continue to do your favorite medium-grip bench press and dumbbell presses of varying degrees of incline with an emphasis on the fifty-five to sixty-five degree range. Focus on the target area by keeping your elbows out and pressing straight overhead, plus a few notches to the rear: elbows-in position delivers triceps predominance.

Incidentally, barbell inclines scare me. The rigid bar is tough on the shoulder rotation for most body structures, eventually leading to chronic pain, whereas the individual dumbbells allow a more forgiving range of motion and more accurate targeting.

With this in mind, and considering I'm mad about antagonistic supersets, here are my favorite chest combinations:

Medium-grip Bench Press (4-5x12, 10, 10, 8, 6)
  superset with
Wide-grip Pulldown to the front (4-5x10+/-)

Dumbbell Incline - 55-65 degree (4-5x12, 10, 10, 8, 6)
  superset with
Stiff-arm Pullover (4-5x10+/-)

One-arm Cable Crossover (4x10-12)

It's worthwhile to note that the pressing motions engage an integrated mass of torso muscle not limited to chest, front shoulder and triceps. Thus, the effective combining of pullovers and pulldowns, each a specific lat exercise which nicely encourages pectoral recruitment as well as shoulder, serratus, biceps and grip activity. Note this blending of resistance and exercise compatibility. I intrinsically insist on and delight in training the body as a functioning, working system: full range of motion, appropriate body thrust, tightly engaged body positioning and rhythmic, machine-like locomotion one set to the next. These multi-set combinations provide field for this training style.

Stiff-arm pullovers, suggested in my favorite superset above, will effect perimeter pectoral development, especially when you extend the positive return motion of the pullover to a forward position toward your knees some forty-five degrees. Every bit of concentrated action adds to the cause. Even close-grip overhead pulldowns and seated lat rows at some point of contraction will recruit the muscles of this often-shallow area and contribute to the mass refining process if we focus, capital F.

Exercise without focus will get part of the job done, like gathering berries while wearing boxing gloves. If you want to get in shape and enjoy your new diversion, begin to center attention on the exercise, its performance and the muscles worked. Make the connection and watch your appreciation for lifting weights grow as will your strength and musculature. Concentration is at first a mental process and an act of discipline, a basic yet elusive element of thinking that you chase about and fumble to catch, here one moment, gone the next. Some folks don't try. To be particularly good at this muscle-building stuff, sufficient mental energy will be required and eventually accomplished. The accomplished violinist, the chess player of honors and the champion weightlifter know focus to have momentum, texture and heat.

The ability to concentrate in one area enables a person to apply the quality in another. This is an invaluable tool not confined to building a strong and healthy body alone. You carry and use this power everywhere you go. Experience it.

Let's pause and consider the following side notes as we probe our resources to develop high-inner pectoral mass and muscularity.

Barbell Curl (4-5x6-10)
superset with
Tucked Dips (4-5x10+/-)

For instance, look at medium-grip dips, deep execution with knees and thighs tucked tightly forward. This posture positions the torso for high pec resistance and works well in a superset of biceps and triceps on your non-chest day.

Smith Press Behind Neck (4-5x6-8)
   superset with
Dumbbell Shrug (4-5x12, 10, 8, 6)

Or how about shrugs with dumbbells to work upper pec? A neat benefit added to trap and shoulder girdle work, a cool second part of a pressing superset. Standing erect with shoulders back will emphasize upper pec engagement. Tough 'n' tight.

Cable Crossover (3-4x10-12) at the completion of your chest workout

Cable crossovers drawn high across the pec recruit upper chest muscles near the clavicle, tying them into the front deltoid. I prefer single cable crossovers to further the range of motion and direct the resistance more accurately and with greater muscle building contraction.
Dumbbell Flys (4x8-10)

When doing flys, grasp the dumbbells in a palms-forward grip for upper chest targeting (palms inward for whole chest recruitment), extend outward slowly and deliberately, arms slightly bent. Upon the positive return, the thumbs will lead the action, placing greater resistance on the upper and inner pec. Complete the movement with the weights high over the forehead.

Plate Raise (4x12, 10, 8, 6) as you increase plate poundage: i.e., 1@10 lbs x12 reps, 1@20 lbs x10, 1@25 lbs x8, 1@35 lbs x6

The plate raise works. Grip a ten-pound plate in both hands. Standing upright but not rigid, bring the plate forward from a hanging position to a position some forty-five degrees above a horizontal plane. Lower slowly with focus on the negative action. At all times, stay tight with hands pressing deliberately inward to maintain control and enhance pectoral contraction.

Minor body thrust will enable you to continue your set and rep intensity and achieve a tight front delt, high inner pec overload, with healthy rotator cuff activity and diverse torso involvement: erectors, traps and more. I do this plate raise regularly at the end of my midsection work just before shoulders, supersetting the move with hanging leg raises. Nice pacemaker. Maintains high heart rate, trims wasted time, keeps me busy and focused and prepares me for the killer shoulder workout ahead.

Throughout our weekly cycle of training, body parts overlap and important bits and pieces of each are being worked, often without our realizing it. Be alert and master the direction of these subtle muscle building and shaping potentials crouched in our workouts. Engage the whole system.

BACK AND LATS AND MORE

The grapevine has it that you want to build a broad, powerful, deeply-muscled back. Heavy rows and weighted chins are the two primary exercises for a thick and wide back. In fact, here's a list of major movers that should be included in your workouts as you continue on

There's a guy named Steve Cepello who roams the streets of Venice, California. He's 6'4", weighs 260 and easily sits back and observes the life going on around him. He's an artist who's compelled by love to paint and sketch what and whom he sees; and with remarkable detail often exaggerated to express a message we — you and I — too often miss. A.k.a. Steve Strong, this mighty man shared the pro-wrestling stage with tag team partner Jessie Ventura, tossing bodies out of the ring like they were dead fish. I thank him (in both his personalities) for being my friend and composing this cool drawing, now the label of The Bomber Blend.

Steve Cepello

your big-back journey. I've taken into consideration that there are many readers of different training levels who will value exercise descriptions, which you'll find later in the book.

These are the bombers:

Weighted Wide-grip Chins
Chins Behind the Neck
Close-grip Pulldowns
Seated Lat Rows
Bent-over Rows
Stiff-arm Pullover
Reverse Grip Barbell Rows
One-arm Dumbbell Rows

There are a variety of one-arm cable exercises that can be brought into play for pumping and creatively working the lats. They target specific areas of the sweeping musculature and engender a pump, a burn and a provocation that stirs muscle growth. They provide let-up and a welcome change of pace. They are sweet desserts, tasty hors d'oeuvres, tender burning-pumping morsels. They go down like smooth honey from the honeycomb.

From this block and tackle repertoire you can form your workouts over the years ahead. Here are some random suggestions for reference:

• Work the back two times per week.

• Choose three or four movements per workout, four if you're a gorilla and if you are prioritizing your back; that is, working your back exclusively on one day twice a week or emphasizing it throughout your current cycle.

• Five sets per exercise using a 15, 12, 10, 8, 6 sequence is the standard of application I prefer. A smart and appealing mix of high reps for blood-gorging, form and groove developing and low reps for power-intense advantages, until you design your scheme more specifically for set, rep and weight resistance progression. I'm not always geared for the exacting set and rep approaches.

• Recognize primary and secondary muscle involvement. Back work is primarily pulling: muscle extension under fire — meaning a big demand on biceps insertions. Take this into consideration.

• Work with intensity, instinctively maxing weight or reps, keeping your eyes on the clear line defining excess and overtraining, know your moods and motivators. Coax yourself into heavy workouts, but don't plunder your stores. Back off every other workout, save doubles or singles for every third or fourth week.

• Remember deadlifts as a supportive exercise, performing four sets of eight to ten constructive, therapeutic reps. One or two work-

You can pause but never look back. Press on to the task before you.
Art Zeller

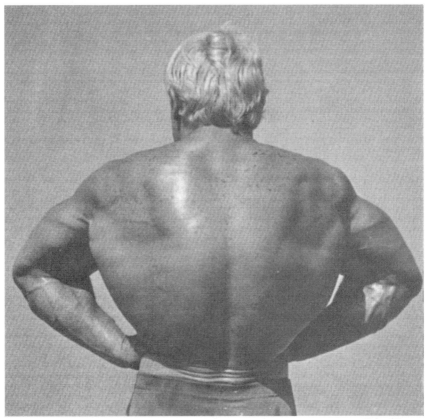

Russ Warner

Seen one back, ya seen 'em all.

outs per week after legs, or six to eight workouts per month for torso protection, resistance and much, much more. Deadlifts are, along with squats and barbell curls, among my favorite exercises. I'm reluctant to include them in a workout with an accent on power because of the already heavy load on the lower back, considering bent-over rows as king. As training goals get reorganized, deadlift workouts can be accentuated. Heavy deadlifts are systemic muscle builders, but they can drain the body for days.

This is what I'm considering for my next back workout: The Superset Junkie Guzzle. After my usual warm-up, I'm gonna do some weighted chins, then go into wide-grip bent-over rows, supersetted with pullovers, followed by seated lat rows, supersetted with moderate dumbbell shrugs. The rest is up to you. Get crazy.

I'LL BE BACK

Moving on to keep us invested, I offer you two worthy routines for building the back, that broad part of the anatomy that so bravely bears the burdens of the world. Let us put before us that trusted region unseen by our own eyes yet follows us everywhere we go. The back, the place upon which we sleep and dream, and, with a yawning stretch of the imagination, the three-word promise about which Arnold spoke so decisively in his interpretation of *The Terminator*.

A strong back, broad and deeply muscled, sounds good to me but may not be the goal of every female bodybuilder-athlete. Not so fast. The exercises listed here and performed as indicated will achieve an awesome power and appealing shape that radiates inborn sureness and physical control, a basic human bearing which has become as remote as our instincts, and looks particularly cool on the female of the species.

To stimulate muscular might throughout the body, the torso or midsection should be worked regularly and preferably at the onset of your workout. Three supersets of crunches and hyperextensions to maximum reps with minimum rest is a cool pre-back midsection routine. This will warm up your muscles, mind and spirit, sculpt your abs, protect your lower back and prepare you for high performance in your back training.

BACK FOR MORE

Let's start with hanging wide-grip chins to the chest/chin area, elbows in line and back arched (4x8-12 reps — if you're able to do more than twelve, add some weight via a harness and drop to eight).

The accomplishment of the chin with bodyweight is a worthy goal. If you are unable to do this, you are not alone. We'll work on it together. Perform wide-grip pulldowns in a fashion similar to the chins to continue your building. However, as a productive challenge make three solid attempts each back workout to complete your chins until you have one, two, three and more. Only direct and consistent "chinning tries" bring success. Have someone assist you from behind or lever your feet off a bench to get the range of motion, the benefit of the neural motor activity and the confident feel. No doubt that if you're overweight you're attending to that, as you are attending to your strength and muscle work. Chins are not a pee-wee exercise, lest you thought otherwise.

Medium-grip Bent-over Barbell Row (5x10, 8, 6, 6, 4)

Seated Lat Row (5x12, 10, 8, 6, 6)
   supersetted with
Pullover, stiff-arm or bent-arm — your choice depending on shoulder structure and health (5x12, 10, 8, 6, 6)

This routine, performed twice a week with a touch of priority, is certain to add sweep, muscle mass and power to your body.

Oops, almost forgot. Once a week at the end of your heavy leg workout, add power deadlifts (warm-up x15, then 5x10, 8, 6, 4 reps), incrementing each set enough to make it tough, but don't draw blood.

BACK AGAIN

We want mass with style. The heavy bulldozers have moved the groundwork. Time to replace the tools and reshape the surface. Muscularizing is our goal and we intend to keep the pace keen and the reps tight. Moderate weight is our choice as focus, form and feel are in our sights.

Pulldowns (4x12)
supersetted with
Wide-grip Machine Dips (4x8-12)
This pull-push combination is not listed in Vogue but with a grain of imagination and concentration you'll get the picture. Dig in.

One-arm Dumbbell Row (4x10)
supersetted with
Reverse Pec Dec (4x8)

One-arm Overhead Cable Pull (4x12)
One of those custom, trick cable pulls that isolate and etch. See exercise description section for more thoughts.

Deadlifts:
Continue power-style deads on your leg day of choice. 4x8-10 reps — medium weight for a healthy pace. A smile; mean yet serene.

This routine also is done twice a week.

SHOULDER PUMP AND BURN

I don't know about you, but sometimes I need a jolt. I need to go to the gym, get slammed around and deliberately remind myself of why I'm there. Time to purchase some pain and endure the sore. This happens to me seasonally, and I know I'm not alone.

By all means, let's keep going with spark and enthusiasm, nothing less. Try this shoulder, back and lat combination that taps into the bis and tris as well. It's a giant set of five movements done as if they were one. This doesn't imply hurry or haste. This is not a complex, frantic, unconnected scramble. These carefully chosen exercises are cooperative and can be performed fluidly and powerfully if you know them and yourself well. Walk through the sequence in your mind to determine your path, to approximate the weight to be used and understand the logic of the muscular flow and reinforcement.

Choose a weight where ten reps per set can be performed on the first cycle. No rest between sets, only the comfortable time it takes to move from place to place, secure a grip, a deep breath, focus and go. Between each giant set take a gulp of water, three deep breaths and move. Chances are you'll be energized, warmed up and psyched, and ten reps per set will sustain through set two. Subsequent sets will see the reps drop as you soldier on. That's okay. It's all okay as long as you persist one-hundred percent, seek intensity to near failure without sacrificing form — always form — and gratefully embrace the pump, scorn the burn.

Exercise sequence, 4 giant sets x 10, 10, 8, 6 :

Press-Behind-Neck
Pulldowns
Shrug
Pullover
Bent-over Lateral Raise

Seated press-behind-neck, performed on a Smith machine using a back support bench and belt, is another favorite shoulder builder and muscularizer. (We're self-publishing; I can make up words as I go along.)

Though tough on the rotator cuffs, it's one of my standards. Position a utility bench so the bar will come down and just graze the hair on the back of your head. Warm up, don't go deep and don't go heavy. This is strictly an exercise, not a powerlifting movement like the bench press. Shoulder mechanics in the press-behind-neck are too precarious for heavy weight. Go heavy and deep and you pay the devil's price. Isolate deltoid with your determined focus — fifteen, twelve, ten and eight repetitions. Light, well-formed, bent-over lateral raises or pulldowns behind the neck are good secondary superset movements, eight to ten reps.

Big breath, big psyche. This is tough: for men and women wearing hardhats only. No sheep, no turkeys. Surely a combination with such depth of character and shades of personality is well worth knowing.

The picture is a little blurry and so is my memory. I have no idea where or when this was taken, although Laree suggests it was taken during the madcap trip to Hawaii with Arnold. That would be Mits' Gym in Honolulu in the background.

Photographer unknown

ARM PRIORITY TRAINING

Standing Bent-bar Curl (3-4x8-12)
  superset with
Lying Triceps Extensions (3-4x8-12)

Hammer Curl (3x4x10-12)
  superset with
Overhead Triceps Extensions (3-4x10-12)

Here I am captured doing some weird dumbbell thing, perhaps thumbs-up curls, in the Venice World Gym. Chris Lund behind the camera. 1995 and all's well.
Chris Lund

Wrist Curl (3x15)
  tri-set with
Thumbs-up Curl (3x8-12)
  and
Pulley Pushdown (3x12-15)

Here you have in simple language the three most effective, most enjoyable and most reliable arm combos I've ever used. They go back to the '60s and will go on and on as long as the grass grows. Sorry they're not more startling, but the truth when recognized seldom is. "Old-fashioned" exercise combinations are, in fact, today's cutting edge — but only when sharpened and tempered with persistence, patience, confidence and desire. And remember, time is our companion, not our enemy, and deserves, rather, demands our respect.

Choose any one, two or all three combos — one or two times a week, depending on your goals, potential, time allowance, ability to recover and resistance to burnout. Continue your training with commitment for at least six weeks. This will give you time to develop pace, form, strength and understanding. Make slow and thoughtful set, rep and weight changes, dutifully logging each workout for best results.

Pay close attention to the details of your movements, focusing on all the muscle groups involved. You'll be amazed at how one or two of these combos when performed with diligence and intensity will work the entire upper body.

In curling, we bring the weight forward and up, putting a counter balance demand on our torso, requiring hard work from our thighs, glutes, erectors, traps, upper back, pec minor and deltoids. A lot of blood flow, heart demand and maximum pump are additional benefits enjoyed by this action. Lats are brought in when doing our triceps extensions, and other muscle groups less specifically if we wish to recruit them with full range of motion and muscle extension and contraction.

Arm priority training fortified with squats, deadlifts and a chest press and lat row superset will set you in motion. Be bold — persist — let your workout intensity build momentum with this unorthodox training approach and you'll grow.

FOREARM TRAINING
AND UNASSOCIATED TOPICS

This is as good a time as any to talk about forearm training and silly training tricks. Help us get a grip on ourselves. There are those rare days when you absolutely don't want to be in the gym. You've been there; it's a common experience we all share. Excuses abound; it's crowded, it's Wednesday, it's empty, it's Tuesday, it's hot, it's cold, I forgot my rubber ducky. Unless you're overtrained, you're being just plain lazy, downhearted and undisciplined. An ugly combination and missing a workout will not help. I'm telling ya I'm lookin' out for ya, kid. Next it'll be pizza and beerskies.

My strategy to overcome this cowardly enemy is to sneak up on it and play dead. Nonchalantly as if I don't really care, I apply myself to my favorite exercise, keeping in mind I can leave whenever I choose. No big deal. Just a few wrist curls to get a quick pump, get a little blood goin' and I'm outta there. Better than nothing, right? Little do I know that this is just a trick, a clever distraction from the truth I have conjured up. This is really going to be a mean, nasty, very cool workout to surpass all workouts of the most recently inspired past. Stand back, guns. No pressure of a predetermined workout, no heavy poundage to disappoint my expectations, no repetition and no limitations. Just invention, improvising and honesty. Freedom. For a moment I feel like Van Gough or Mozart. I could paint a fence or move a piano. I could paint a piano.

I commence with wrist curls. Straddling a bench with a precision Olympic bar in my grasp, forearms supported on the thighs, I slowly lower the weight to a full extension and return to a tight contraction. The appeal? A nifty, pocket-sized muscle tool, a lever of sorts, to get the stubborn ball rolling ... a minor movement demanding little of my energy stores and willpower yet vast sums of attention as the burn and the pump are swift. The notion that I'm fully engaged floods my mind. I yelp, I'm alive.

With the inertia overcome and momentum building, I move directly to the thumbs-up curl. Starting out with dumbbells hanging at my side, palms inward, feet close together, knees slightly bent, back and shoulders erect, I draw the dumbbells up as if the flat of the plates were to whack me in the cheekbones. I reverse and slowly lower the dumbbells to the starting position — full extension, lats flexed, chest out and repeat. Another rep, focusing on the outer forearm, lower biceps. Tug up and lower slowly, the negative rep being the critical action. Fight the dumbbell going down, locating and determining the resistance. Full extension, deep breath and repeat. Heading for eight or ten reps, fight fatigue with an appropriate body thrust to bring the dumbbells to position and again lower with accent on the negative.

This exercise gets to be quite an upper body workout if you should ascend the dumbbell rack. The exaggerated reps on heavy days resemble almighty dumbbell cleans. Not a bad transaction. This engages back, erectors, deltoids, pecs, traps, heart and lungs. Serious movement.

Wild, yet still in control, I proceed to the jungle for pulley pushdowns — I've been using a rope handle since Muscle Beach, allowing me a variety of body positions to pinpoint different parts of the triceps and engage accommodating muscle groups. I position myself a foot or so beyond the overhead pulley, crouch slightly, and as if my elbows were pinned to my ribcage, I extend the gripped rope fully, recruiting the triceps. A lean forward, a bit of minor thrusting, focusing on the eccentric and finesse all assist me in fully involving the upper torso.

Three to four circuits of this compound set will give you an entire upper body pump with the major focus on biceps, triceps, forearm and grip. At this point I could leave the gym fully satisfied that I almost worked out. I don't, you know.

During normal weeks when I don't need to call on my silly training tricks, I train forearms twice. Three to five sets of wrist curls and reverse wrist curls at the end of my arm day keeps my forearms relatively pumped.

Art Zeller

Furiously doing crunches with no one caring but me. I like my heels hooked on a support for a more intense contraction and control. Thirty-five years later I do more, more fervently, on an incline and holding a 10- or 25-pound plate behind my head. Who said you can't teach an old dog new tricks? I also eat Purina Puppy Chow.

ABDOMINAL TRAINING

Your abdominal and oblique area will definitely improve as you continue to apply yourself. My midsection has become stronger and more muscular in the most recent years. First, I stopped thinking of the all-too-illusive abdominals and began thinking of trunk development — for stability and full-body power. This change of perception gave me more purpose to train the midsection. The stretching, focus and athletic warm-up added to my motivation; the constant and intense movement afforded legitimate aerobic value.

Considering all these benefits, I came to enjoy the movements, improvising bench angles and body stabilizing positions, contraction and extension, rhythm and exercise combinations. Soon I brought in weighted exercises for warm-ups to prepare me for my forthcoming bodypart workout. The whole blend of movements over the seasons — the pump, the burn, the ability to locate, isolate and contract specific areas (oblique, intercostals and abdominal ranges) gave me more-than-agreeable results.

I like weighted crunches mixed with high rep un-weighted crunches, all within one set of a hundred and fifty to two hundred on a ten- to twenty-degree angle. I arrange a bench appropriately before the Smith Press and hook my heels over the bar for stability. I assume a suitable position and breathe in. From a fully extended torso position, hands behind the head, I exhale and intensely contract the abs, rolling up into a C position, without momentum and without the flat of the back coming off the bench thereby risking lower back health. Twenty-five reps to the front, twenty-five slightly to the right, twenty-five slightly to the left, engaging abs, intercostals and obliques in the process. I then put the flat of my foot on the bar and repeat the count, this time raising my hips by foot pressure to meet the rolling contraction. Intense muscle activity accomplished, I include the final reps with a ten or twenty-five pound plate.

These reps, when performed with rhythm and beat, build momentum and can be borderline meditative. They are not done fast as I see some do them; fast is abusive, agitating and shallow. Work the midsection as you would work your biceps or any other part with concentration, depth and interest — almost curiosity.

Train, of course, according to your own physical condition. You might try the incline at the height of a four-inch block, ten reps to the front, left and right, a shift of foot position, and do the crunch for the same sequence. Practice with an agreeable weight, a five or ten pound plate. It takes some time to get to know the elaboration of the standard crunch action, yet it's worth the time and practice.

Try these combinations:

Swing around and put your hands on the end of the bench, backside comfortably on your hands to ease low back stress. Do leg raises to near failure, twenty to twenty-five — whatever — and repeat for three or four sets. Magnificent.

Hanging leg raises using Brad Harris' AbOriginal straps are dynamite for the lower ab region, groin-hip flexor area, 4x15-25 reps, no swinging.

Another thought: rope tucks are super torso builders. There are so many variations of body positioning to get the whole upper body warmed up, pumped and thoroughly conditioned. Be inventive, using 4x25-35 reps of mixed positions. No lunging with your bodyweight to ease the work; use the muscle.

Hyperextensions for the erectors, spinalis, hamstrings and glutes make a nice addition twice a week, three to four sets, 15-20 reps. Muscle up with no momentum.

A final note: This is extensive torso muscle building to accommodate your training and practical daily activities.

TRICKS OF THE TRADE

Changes of pace add spice to your life. If on one day I'm comfortable and confident but routine is getting me down, I consider a slow, heavy workout to meet my mood. This is good timing for a power workout, with low reps in mind — a gentle pyramid followed by some psyched singles. This brings on growth and challenge that turns a puny training session into a dominant goal-setter. I've also noticed it's beneficial to test myself at recognized periods in my training to continuously probe my level of strength. Note: I apply to the appropriate occasion a legitimate trick to best a weary attitude, a methodology only as sound as one's instincts and determination.

Tricks are for imposters. I will therefore refer to them as tactics, strategies, schemes and unique plans. Outlined below is a list of schemes that are credible, but are not encouraged to regularly fashion your training. Don't make a habit of gimmicks and gadgets in your workouts. Beware of broad margins that allow sloppiness and laziness and excuses. Remember: Design your routine and stick to it for at least six to eight weeks to gain the most from your trips to the gym.

You may enter the gym discouraged, but you don't want to leave that way. These tactics ease you into a workout that becomes solid, bold and mighty; well-worn strategies to enable and enhance a dubious gym experience:

• Check out the territory (simultaneously aided by clever and inspiring conversation with yourself). What will it be today, Bucko? The only sane way out of here is across the gym floor, through a workout and into the shower. What doesn't hurt, what looks appetizing? Don't hesitate. Don't falter. Keep moving. Smile. Hi, gang. I feel like a million and I'm ready to rock. How about you?

• Ease into your workout with a mild midsection warm-up. Let the momentum build. It always does. Release the tension and doubt as you count the reps and invest the ticking seconds. This has got to be done.

- Make an exception and put aside routine. Choose a favorite exercise and body part to break the pervasive numbness of the spirit and flesh. Seek the pump, burn and heat.

- Abbreviate and stimulate. Training intensity might be approachable if you sidle up to a lightweight exercise with massage-like high repetitions. The rhythm and blood flow are appealing and non-threatening. They often preface a pounding beat and a full pump. Ignore the count, focus on action.

- Consolidate and rearrange. A fake-out strategy, which if successful will have the rest of the gym in awe and wonder. "You're on fire. Where'd you pick up the exotic routine? Cool." Haven't you heard? I'm an impervious metal warrior, the real steel deal.

- Create through experimenting. These are the wonderful times to improvise and play. These are not the times to be serious, the precursor to depression and defeat. Spare the child. Whatever dumb movement you concoct, perform it with knowing professionalism. Somebody's always taking notes. The best inventions grow from need.

- Perform supersets, tri-sets, extended sets and circuit training. Order out of chaos. Momentum out of inertia.

- Train against the clock: sets and reps against minutes, quarter-hours, half-hours and sixty minutes. A race for pace without sacrificing form. The distraction becomes an attraction for self-competition, invigorating, and you always win.

- Try a power workout. Just don't ask me to join you, not tonight.

- Cycle or do aerobics or color.

Excuse me, kind reader. I, or, that is, we are in the midst of an article I offered to Julian Schmidt, long time friend and writer for *Flex Magazine*. The words come from a taped phone conversation we had one afternoon in the fall of 1993. I was at the gym in Santa Cruz and

Julian was at his desk at Weider's in Woodland Hills, California. I talked for over an hour with as much coherency and continuity as one can with his ear pressed against a hunk of plastic and the world spinning out of control around him. Here are the results of the spatial conversation eventually recorded in *Flex* sometime later, ironically titled "*Tricks Of The Trade.*" I tried to upgrade the faltering, babbling structure of the tome only to distort its message. I gave up, frustrated, and decided to present the heap as is, in hopes to amuse you, the reader, and give further insight into the behind-the-scenes bodybuilding world. The info, though mumbly, is real, true and clear enough. Check out some pictures as you read to minimize the inconsistencies. Team spirit.

The body is designed to work wholly and interactively and function as a system — different muscle groups working together in a coordinated fashion, rather than separately in stunted, isolated motion. A wholesomely arranged training routine subscribes to this notion.

Give me your ear for ten minutes and let me jabber about multi-set training as if it were the latest flash of lightening in the vast unexplored bodybuilding universe.

I want to be attracted to working out, not forced to enter the gym as part of day-to-day regimen. Anyone who trains should have something that builds the enthusiasm and keeps successive workouts interesting so there is positive anticipation.

A variety of antagonistic supersets does all this for me. Antagonistic supersets provide a constant, rapid pulse to your training in which little time is spent between sets. You do not prepare extensively for the next set. You work at restoring your breath without letting the blood subside from the muscle area, or allowing the burn to diminish or waiting for your heartbeat to go down. The variety keeps you eager.

I want to spend a few pages here developing and explaining this superset technique, which has for many years defined my training life.

I sometimes train six days a week, with chest and back on the first day, shoulders and arms on the second day, legs on the third day, tackling two of these cycles before taking a day off. Often, I'll change the variety of exercises, but no matter what the exercises are, workout days overlap with movements that hit the same body part. Admittedly, there's some conflict there in terms of recuperation, but as long as you keep in mind good nutrition and timely rest, it remains a valid concept.

Realistically, two out of four weeks will find me backing off, in that I will detect the hints of overtraining. Mondays, Tuesdays and Wednesdays in those weeks will be very intense, but the next three days will diminish in intensity, or I might sustain intensity until Friday, when I may condense the last two workouts and have two days to rest instead of one. There is a scheme to it but I'll never know what Friday I'll condense my workout into a Friday-Saturday session or continue to push on into Saturday. It has to be played by all my feelings depending on my eating habits, the stress in my life, the intensity of my workouts or what I'm looking for that time of year. I find that because of my longevity in the sport I'm able to detect these factors more intuitively.

For chest and back day, one of my favorite superset combinations is a tri-set of dumbbell inclines, dumbbell pullovers and seated lat rows. The antagonistic principle illustrated here is the pushing movement for the chest and higher angle of the inclines on the chest and shoulders, combined with additional triceps work and the stretching movement of the pullovers (which also get the upper back, deltoids and triceps again), all complemented by the pulling motion from the seated lat row (which hits the rhomboids, spinatus, rear deltoids, spinalis, erectors, the full length of the lats, mid-back and upper back).

Incline dumbbell presses are done conventionally, but pullovers are from a longitudinal position on the bench, stiff-armed to get a good stretch as far back as possible, then pulling upward and forward, sometimes bringing the dumbbell down over my abdominal region to work my upper back and front deltoids. It's a very complete, full-range movement.

For seated lat rows, I lean far forward, arch my back, throw out my chest and bring the cable all the way into my midsection, tugging it in tight, really contracting the rhomboids, until I can feel it throughout my entire torso. The high reps make this tri-set tough; it's not a race but more like a locomotive, very steady with plenty of concentration.

For my next combination, I break away from supersetting momentarily and do one-arm dumbbell rows, standing, with my free hand resting on the dumbbell rack and the other hand pulling in a full-range motion up into my hip area. With each draw I can alter it somewhat — maybe five reps into my hip and five a little higher into my shoulder to get the rear deltoid and upper back.

These are followed by semi-stiff-legged deadlifts, an exercise fundamental in the overall strengthening and muscularizing of the body. In my training, it's a practical, everyday way to make the body more powerful realistically than to merely make it appear stronger.

For these stiff-legged deadlifts, I'm standing on a block to get a good stretch in my hamstrings. My knees are slightly bent. This targets everything; back, traps, hamstrings, quads and forearms.

Next are standing one-arm cable crossovers supersetted with one-arm cable pulls. For cable pulls, I'll go down to my knees and position myself relative to the cable where I can get a good stretch in my lat, pulling the cable into my hip so I'm now getting a pump on the same side from both of these movements before switching to the other side. As I slowly pull the cable back, I tug it into my hip, turning my body at the same time to bring into play plenty of lat action. With these two movements you get the chest and lat together, all without releasing the handle.

The final combination for these bodyparts is wide-grip chins supersetted with dips; four sets each, with eight to ten reps for chins and twelve to fifteen for the dips. Chins are either behind the neck or in front; dips are either weighted or with bodyweight. Dips work the chest, triceps and some serratus, but I can really feel them in the rhomboids if I situate myself in the correct hanging position.

Shoulders and arms day begins with forearms, gripping the Olympic bar on my knees with my thumbs under the first fifteen reps, then releasing to let my fingers extend with the bar for another six to eight. I have to be careful to not overtrain or tear an insertion with this one.

These are followed immediately by Zottman curls — palms forward, curling up and in — for six to eight reps. These get the belly of the biceps and the brachia, and strengthen the wrist and cap muscles. Then I may throw the dumbbell overhead and superset triceps extensions for five reps, followed by a dumbbell pressing movement for five reps. This constitutes a long giant set, beginning with the forearms and ending with pressing, but it enhances durability and vascularity.

Next are reverse-grip cambered bar curls for eight reps, then I put the bar down and grab an underhand grip and do another six reps. These are followed by lying triceps extensions with first a regular grip, then a reverse grip to complete the superset.

The next superset is a tri-set of regular dumbbell curls followed by overhead triceps extensions with a dumbbell, seated with my back supported, followed by overhead pulley extensions.

For shoulders, I might choose the press-behind-neck supersetted with a standing upright hammer raise in which I bring the dumbbell from a hanging position to straight before me, to overhead, working lots of front delt, chest, biceps and forearm. It's a heavy movement with good thrust in it, somewhat of a clean with one dumbbell but keeping my arm as stiff and straight as possible.

The next superset is bent-over laterals, bringing a lot of back into play, followed with a lying side-arm lateral raise.

For legs, on the odd day I might do extensions for eighteen to twenty reps supersetted with leg curls for twelve to fifteen reps, four or five sets each. These are followed by squats for twelve to fifteen reps, staying with one weight, supersetted with leg presses for twenty to twenty-five reps with a variety of foot positions.

While this is a superset base from which I might work, I experiment constantly with different combinations, changing even from one workout to the next, training instinctively and trying whatever I think might work best for that day. Sometimes they might be giant sets with four or five different exercises.

Whenever it gets old, I just go to the gym and get something moving and start any combination of things. I give myself a wide margin for hybrid movements, and it inevitably falls into place.

For the past few years, this approach has been popular with me, but I always look back and try to come up with others that were effective, more productive and more condensed. Nothing achieves that total blood-gorged feeling like supersetting. The technique seems to offer a richness of benefits that no other approach can equal: namely, size, muscularity, practical strength and freedom from injuries. The proof for supersetting's validity is there.

SLUMPBUSTERS

Our training will not always be a barrel of laughs. We expect a steady upward curve in our progress and when that appears to stop or decline, we become disappointed, disillusioned and discouraged. Our attitude, which should buoy us up and lead us on, becomes weary, laden with doubt and boredom — down we go like a lead balloon.

As these sticking points plague all of us frequently, we are wise to press on with our prescribed workout, giving it plenty of time to work. Those who endure these apparent voids — these plateaus — have heart; they carry on to grow in both muscle and character. Simply diminishing the demand on ourselves by lowering the poundage and focusing on pace, form and feel often loosens the knot that binds our progress. We grow in stages, improvements being made well beneath the skin line which, much to our surprise and delight, surface after months of steady, hard work. However, the time comes when change is needed, if only for a day. Changes are a relief; they're fun, revitalizing and instructive. Changes can be found in these down and gritty slumpbusters.

Slumpbusters are any combinations of superset exercises that stray from the norm yet retain integrity. Integrity is found in logic and instinct — qualities we all possess but seldom use. Slumpbusters are designed for short-term use (a day, a week), but can be easily merged into your training schedule regularly if it feels right. Because they're unique, they're fresh to the mind, fresh to the body. With some exceptions, the slumpbusting combinations listed here can be performed using the pyramid system of reps and weight, or an eight to ten rep range using a moderate fixed weight. Four sets of any slumpbuster is a minimum. If you're pumping and having fun, take it to five, six or seven. One combo, if pushed, may be all the doctor ordered; two combos can be mixed according to your needs, desire and energy.

The thoughts above are important and should be read carefully. However, thoughts without deeds are just thoughts. For your pleasure and prosperity, put the following thoughts, or slumpbusters, into action.

BENT-ARM PULLOVER AND PRESS — BARBELL CURL

A powerful and tough combination that hits the whole upper body, from longitudinal abdominal to major bis and tris, from serratus and lat to pec and front delt. Standing barbell curls done with thrust put a substantial demand on the erectors and upper shoulder cage — a lot of pump, a lot of heavy breathing, a lot of circulation.

BARBELL CURL — CLOSE-GRIP BENCH PRESS — PULLDOWN

Pecs and front delts get involved with main focus on biceps and triceps. Pulldowns offers relief from demanding curl and press and continues voluminous blood flow. Works lats effectively.

WIDE BENCH — PULLDOWN — STIFF-ARM DB PULLOVER

A classic superset hitting chest, front delt, lat and upper back in a big way with minor work to triceps and biceps.

WIDE-GRIP BENCH — BARBELL PULLOVER — BARBELL ROW

A heavy load, light load and heavy load series. Chest, front delt, triceps followed by serratus, tri and lat followed by upper back, rear delt and erectors.

SHOULDER PRESS — PULLDOWN —TRICEPS DIP MACHINE

The Hammer shoulder press effectively and safely works the entire shoulder, while stimulating the triceps. The pulldown works the latisimus and if done with a focused flexing, the traps, rhomboid and scapula can be brought into play. The triceps press works pecs, triceps and upper back to round things out. (You can replace the Hammer press with any shoulder press machine.)

SHOULDER PRESS — SEATED LAT ROW — DELT MACHINE

Freehand barbell press puts big demand on entire shoulder girth and upper back while nicely tying into the triceps. Seated lat row, my favorite feeling back movement, works the entire length of the lats with major focus on rhomboid. Full forward starting position activates erectors and biceps, forearm and grip are well stimulated. The rear delt action puts the finishing touch on the upper back, getting hard-to-reach details around the rhomboid and scapula.

E-Z CURL ORBENT BAR CURL — TRICEPS PRESS MACHINE

There's nothing like a full arm pump to pick up your training spirits — joined with the chest, back and shoulder action of the triceps press machine, high pump and burn, low demand on cardio.

DUMBBELL CLEAN AND PRESS — STIFF-ARM DB PULLOVER

The dumbbell clean and press is seldom done 'cuz it's ancient and tough. Nevertheless, it's one of the best single bodybuilding exercises working erectors and shoulders, traps and back for power and muscular density. The stiff-arm pullover done with light to moderate weight for simple, sound reps will give you a chance to re-oxygenize while hitting the lats, serratus and some more minor bi and tri.

HAMMER CHEST PRESS — HAMMER HI LAT

Hammer chest press combined with the Hammer lat row does a lot of good stuff to your upper regions, pec, triceps, scapula, rhomboid, traps and a little biceps.

SQUAT — LEG CURL — CALF MACHINE

The one and only lower body slumpbuster I use is the squat, followed by leg curls and standing calves. These are done with high reps and a lot of breathing, sets of fifteen on the squat, fifteen on the curl and twenty-five to failure on the calf — pumps the entire leg, front, back and side.

LUNGE — STIFF-LEGGED DEADLIFTS — CALF RAISES

Sisters — your attention, please. This peak training combination attacks enemies number 1, 2 & 3 — the glutes, the upper thighs and hips with considerable benefit to the lower back and overall muscularity. Four sets of fifteen to twenty reps, depending on your purpose and weight used, will provide both athletics and balance to your training. Ease into this superset and build up reps, pace and weight slowly, patiently and assuredly. This is the ultimate glute blaster of all times, for all ages.

WRIST CURL — HAMMER CURL — O/H PULLEY EXTENSION

Total arm building with the accents on minor syllables — seldom-worked forearm, grip, lower biceps and triceps. Unique series of exercises adds interest, dimension, valuable muscle mass and power to your bodybuilding storehouse. Barbell wrist curls are best performed with forearms resting snugly on the thighs for four sets of fifteen. Hammer curls are thumbs-up curls, performed alternately, and overhead pulleys are done your style for pump and burn.

UP AND DOWN THE RACK

This bittersweet, pumping and burning dumbbell routine can bring tears of bliss and tears of tortured submission to your eyes — curling, pressing, pulling — it's all the same, a total slam of eight to ten sets in four to five minutes, virtually nonstop. Start light for fifteen reps heading up the rack in two and a half or five pound jumps, each consecutive set done to maximum reps with very reasonable form (minimal cheating overlooked) until a two-rep set is reached, then head back downhill, no coasting allowed, until your courage or blood sugar give out. A partner is helpful to spur you on, though the silent and brave who go the trip alone are to be admired. The great burn and ache lasts for days and informs you that this intense slumpbuster can only be done occasionally.

HIGH REP TARGET TRAINING

Keep this aside for a mindless day where the energy is there but the desire and attention apparently are not. Pick an exercise, any exercise that comes to thought, and with a light weight start repping out toward one hundred. See how far you get and see how fast this gets your attention. Concentrate on form and the rhythm of the reps. This will push back the pain barrier. You'll need to take short breaks to allow new blood to briefly flush out lactic acid. Continue until a hundred reps are reached.

10 SETS OF 10 REPS

Nothing intricate here — just dogged set after set with ensuing momentum. Works well with the basic bench, squat, standing barbell curl, press-behind-neck and lat row, although any exercise you dream up will do. Start with a light weight for a set of ten. As you proceed with thirty-second intervals the workload gets tougher until ten reps are a delirious challenge — forced reps and partner assists are allowed. This method of operation can effectively break growth plateaus by thoughtful implementation over a six-week period.

TO WRAP THIS UP

If this is not enough material covering the infinite variety of training possibilities and exercise combinations, I have one last offering. Skim your library of magazines and books and list the vast selection of exercises on separate bits of colored paper. Fold them neatly and place them in a large, wide-mouth jar. When preparing your next intelligent and convincing workout program, grab that overflowing jar, shake it and blindly pick out six or eight colorful surprises. Randomly piece them together and there you have it; the science of chaos, next month's blast, another way to apply our madness. Train hard and enjoy it.

Linda Lima created this drawing from a photo by George Greenwood for a poster presenting The 1980 Senior National Powerlifting Championships produced by prowrestler Billy Graham Superstar. All the giants of the day were there setting records as the big numbers rose like a fever amongst the blistering competitors. I met Dr. Fred Hatfield that day in Phoenix as he moved 1000+ pounds into a squat record. The drawing became the cover of the book you hold.

5

EXERCISE X-RAYS

Be hard as nails. Choose your routine and take it to the max. Squeeze it till it groans. A theory: Breaking plateaus that generate growth bursts come from those wicked persistent struggles we wisely engage in before changing our routine. Endure. Smile. It's happening.

Let's move on to the exercise descriptions. Let me briefly mention that the descriptions are necessary because many readers are beginners or long-time fitness absentees. Therefore, I'll describe them in appropriate detail throwing in bodybuilding talk as I proceed.

Need I remind you that form is of primary importance? Form is followed by focus, pace and then immediately by the weight used. This does not minimize the importance of poundage; it just accents the foremost position of form.

Abdominal — Midsection Work
Bar Hang
Bench Press
Bent-over Barbell Row
Bent-over Reverse Grip Barbell Row
Cable Crossover
Calf Raise
Chin — Wide-grip
Chin Behind the Neck
Clean and Press
Close-grip Bench Press
Close-grip Pulldown

Crunch (See Abdominal — Midsection)
Curl — Bar, Dumbbell, Ez Bar (Bent Bar), Machine
Curl — Seated Dumbbell Incline
Curl — Standing Dumbbell Incline
Curl — Thumbs-Up/Hammer Curl
Curl — Zottman
Deadlift
Dip — Freehand or Triceps Press Machine
Dumbbell Fly
Dumbbell Press—Chest and Shoulders
Dumbbell Shrug
Front Squat
Hammer Strength Machines
Hanging Leg Raise (See Abdominal — Midsection)
Hyperextension
Lateral Raise — Front, Hammer Plate Raise
Lateral Raise — Bent-over
Lateral Raise — Side Arm
Leg Curl
Leg Extension
Leg Press
Leg Raise (See Abdominal — Midsection)
Lunge
Lying Lateral Raise Front
Lying Lateral Raise Rear
Lying Triceps Extension
Military/Overhead Press — Clean and Press
One-arm Cable Crossover
One-arm Dumbbell Row
One-arm Cable Lat Pull
One-arm Overhead Cable Pull
Preacher Curl/Scott Curl
Press-Behind-Neck (PBN)
Pulley Pushdown
Pullover — Stiff-arm or Straight-arm
Roman Chair Situp (See Abdominal — Midsection)
Rope Tuck (See Abdominal — Midsection)
Row Machine
Rubber Tubing — Rotator Cuff Work
Seated Lat Row/Low Pull

Smith Press Behind Neck
Squat
Stiff-legged Deadlift
Sumo Deadlift
Sumo Squat
Wide-grip Pulldown
Wrist Curl — Reverse Wrist Curl

ABDOMINAL AREA — MIDSECTION — TORSO

Not the most popular region of the body to exercise, often because it's one of the first areas to store excess bodyfat and generally reminds us that we're out of shape, in poor physical condition, negligent and vulnerable and ordinary. Attention on a midsection that's becoming more substantial and less muscled day-by-day can be depressing and overwhelming. We eat wrong, eat too much and don't exercise: a formula for devastation that must be undone.

A weak, unmuscled torso presents further problems when we consider the integral part muscle plays in balance, protection and effective functioning in work and play. Obesity and back problems have become mankind's recurring nightmare. (Throw in smoking and it becomes pathetic, the meanness we suffer at our own hands.) The fix is simple; let's get to work.

The exercises below in varying combinations (when coupled with attention on diet) are the most popular and productive in achieving a flat stomach and strong torso. Crunches, leg raises and rope tucks are my favorites.

ABDOMINAL — CRUNCH

Lie face up on your favorite bench or piece of floor, knees bent and feet tightly toward you, shoulder-width apart. Position your arms behind your head and cradle your head in your hands. From this stable starting place, with a minimum of tugging on your head, roll your upper torso forward into a C-like posture, your upper back raising off the floor as the abdominals contract to complete the movement. Think abs. This contraction should be split-second yet super tight — the peak of muscle overload and adaptation. Slowly lower yourself to a full and deliberate starting position and repeat for sets of multiple reps.

A weight plate can be held behind the head or across the chest to add resistance; lower the reps. Right and left obliques and intercostals are recruited as we slightly twist and lead with the right or left elbow as if reaching for the space between the knees. Mix them up, for example twenty to the front, ten left, ten right, ten front totaling one set. Getting warm, oxygenized and movin'— I call this the "super crunch."

Crunches tone and strengthen the entire abdominal area with an apparent emphasis on the upper region. They provide maximum muscle action with minimum expended energy. Mild crunches are a therapeutic exercise and safe on the lower back, a good introductory exercise for the willing and able obese, elderly, injured or beginner. Good stuff.

ABDOMINAL — HANGING LEG RAISE

The ultimate in leg raise effort starts by hanging from an overhead bar with your hands or with the assistance of Brad Harris' Ab-Original Straps. Hang, and with slightly bent legs (or legs bent a lot), raise your legs upward to some point of contraction, lower again to the starting point and repeat.

Easy, until you start swinging out of control and the rest of the gym wants to see you to it again. The hanging leg raise takes a little practice and should be introduced once the trainee is conditioned and confident. The trick is to fast-forward the reps (up.down.up.down without pause) to prevent a pendulum action from developing. I dare ya.

ABDOMINAL — LEG RAISE

The leg raise can be performed on the floor, or off a flat or ten percent inclined bench. They are tougher than crunches, working more of the lower ab, groin area and hip-flexors. They also present antagonism to the hips and lower back if attention to your body mechanics, positioning and form is not acute. According to your readiness, I suggest you extend your arms totally forward and place your hands comfortably under your tailbone. This platform and counter-posing, upper-body muscle action relieves if not entirely eliminates low-back pressure, as will bending the legs slightly at the knees. Now you can rep out with only the abdominals and hip-flexors crying out in muscle-building pain.

The action starts with the greatest intensity from the floor or bench as your extended legs are slowly and laboriously lifted to a near overhead, thigh-perpendicular position. Up and down with a moderate pace governed by the good struggle, you are applying yourself to a classic favorite that's awkwardness diminishes as the workouts go by and you enjoy their benefits. (I sound like I'm selling them by the pound and today is the last day before they go bad.)

Your reps may not exceed ten or twelve as the hip-flexors and muscles of the groin region seldom bear direct resistance. They'll be sore tomorrow; don't freak. Once I thought I had appendicitis, another time a hernia. Turned out to be a rep too many on a muscle too weak.

ABDOMINAL — ROMAN CHAIR SITUP

Simple. Slide in, make yourself comfortable, lean back to a point that is safe, agreeable and effective. Sit back up and repeat. Have fun. See ya later. This is no longer a popular piece of equipment; it's not likely that your gym has a Roman Chair abdominal bench.

ABDOMINAL — ROPE TUCK

This one's my favorite. The rope tuck, while specifically an abdominal exercise, can be manipulated by body positioning and concentrated muscle contraction to work countless details of the upper torso. Start with a pulley system that provides a single overhead cable from which you can attach your favorite rope handle. Choose an appropriate weight through trial and error (approximately thirty percent of bodyweight), grab the rope, kneel down about three feet in front of the system and sit back on your heels. Bend forward toward the weight stack with the rope under tension and close to your lowered forehead. You're ready to practice the movement as you assess the resistance on your abs and throughout the upper body, determine your range of motion and facility to move with muscle-focused efficiency.

The first ten reps are performed with the arms held rigid, rope-grasping fists near the temples, the torso moving up and down by the power of the abs. Important: the entire abdominal muscles are contracted to do the hard work. Don't lunge forward and accomplish the motion with the assistance of your bodyweight. Nice try.

Moving on, continue the action with a slight shift of the body and grip predominance to the right for five longer-motion reps, and, likewise, shift to the left and repeat. These variations add interest and further the involvement of the torso to include the obliques and intercostals. An extended overhead range of motion affected by the cable enables you to bring in serratus and lats while you are continually loading, stimulating and fatiguing the grip and biceps.

We've got the whole family playing, the heart's beating and the sweat's pooling. I don't usually stop there. We're twenty reps into the set and there's five or ten or fifteen left. Five more tucks to the front to complete and balance the abdominal obligation and we can pull ourselves off our knees and in one motion bring the legs around and assume a seated position whereupon we allow the cable to completely extend forward; we're still on our haunches and savoring the relief of extension. The hands are giving way but not until we count five more tugs with the rope to the front of our body, our chest and back arched and contracted. That's set Number One. I love to superset these with light-weight deadlifts for four sets of ten. Perhaps I can forego the aerobics today.

BAR HANG

Nothing to it. Simply hang from an overhead bar with any useful grip (close, wide, supinated, pronated) for extended lengths of time to improve grip strength. Work up to sixty-second hangs. Ouch.

BENCH PRESS

One of the patriarchs of weight training, and one of the three lifts in the sport of powerlifting, a family whose siblings are the squat and the deadlift. This comprehensive movement builds a network of upper torso muscles including primarily the front deltoid, the pecs and the triceps.

Lying on your back, grasp the racked bar with a grip some six inches wider than shoulder width; press overhead with a slight arc to a neutral starting position directly over your shoulders. Once you've momentarily established and briefly held your starting position, lower the bar slowly and deliberately (the eccentric or negative motion) to the bottom of your pectoral muscles. Allow the bar to make full contact with the body before immediately reversing the motion and pressing the weight to its original starting point (the concentric or positive motion). Smoothly repeat until your designated reps are achieved.

Focus on the muscles involved, carefully locating the bar through its range of motion until you discover your groove — the exact track for the bar's movement according to your skeletal-muscular mechanics. Allow one or more seconds to lower the bar and power up steadily after reaching the chest. Practice — there's no failure at this stage, only correcting and re-correcting, trying your best and improving. You'll personalize all your exercises as you grow, perform, learn and understand.

BENT-OVER BARBELL ROW

Bent-over rows are a comprehensive exercise like squats, deadlifts and standing military presses. The thing is, they're the toughest, meanest and most demanding upper body movement. They work large and specific muscles (full back) yet engage the whole system fingers to toes, in their execution. Therefore, systemic growth — whole body growth — is accomplished, along with deep fatigue and an accentuated need for recovery.

Rows are a power exercise and are most effective when performed with heavy weight. The movement is basic, and takes practice and conditioning over months to allow you to perform safely with body thrusts that recruit the muscle mass. The bent torso acts as a lever under the resistance of the bar. The lower back (the spinal vertebrae supported by the erectors) provides the fulcrum and bears an extraordinary load. Be careful.

To protect my lower back, I assume a relatively close standing position, bend over with my ribcage somewhat supported by my thighs; my back's flat and my eyes are focused somewhere ten feet before me to position my head correctly. I grab the bar over-grip some six inches from the collars of an Olympic bar. Settling in, major focus on grip and body position as I breathe deeply three or four times in preparation, I pull the bar tightly to the mid-chest. I lower it deliberately to the starting position, the plates just short of or tapping the floor, up again with muscle power, down again with negative focus.

Pull the bar to the chest at a medium speed; to the high chest works upper back, to mid-chest works mid-back, low pull toward gut works low back. Find your favorite target or vary as needed.

Build your muscle and might over an extended period with minor weight increments and solid, well-formed reps. Small thrusts are okay, but will take their toll on the low back which bears the extreme load of the highly stressed pivot point. Let the lumbar and erectors build in power as you slowly progress.

BENT-OVER REVERSE GRIP BARBELL ROW

Lower lat sweep is accomplished with this unique and compact movement. Performed close-grip with a bent bar, pull the bar tight to the waist, arching the back to engage your full low back, low lat muscle mechanics. Moderate weight allows the safest and surest articulation of this form-demanding movement. Sets of six to eight match the demand.

CABLE CROSSOVER

Cable crossovers are not a power movement but they are significant in shaping and defining the entire pectoral region. Stand in the center of the apparatus with cables in hand. Take a giant step forward and, with stiff arms, draw the handles high and straight forward, leaning as you do to counterbalance the resistance. Continue with a full range of motion, extending and contracting evenly and deliberately. Focus on upper pec contraction for six reps until the burn is considerable, then shift the handle movement to a forty-five degree angle toward the floor. This engages more pec mass allowing you to force out another four to six reps. Vary the angle of movement according to fatigue and to target different ranges of the muscle. Seek rhythm, slow flow and tight contractions.

Cables drawn high across the pec recruit upper chest muscles near the clavicle tying them into the front deltoid; the lower the action the lower the pec musculature recruited. I prefer single-cable crossovers to further the range of motion and direct the resistance more accurately and with greater muscle-building contraction.

CALF RAISE

You can stand, sit or have someone sit on your back while you do the calf raise. Standing, toes and forefoot on an appropriate block, simply raise and lower your heels to engage the calf muscles. Resistance is achieved by bearing weight across your back with a bar or via a machine or by holding a dumbbell in the appropriate hand as you stand on a block applying one leg at a time to the task. Alternatively, the donkey calf raises are performed by leaning forward on a supportive object and having a partner sit across your back as you raise and lower off the by-now-popular block. There are machines that allow you to sit while resistance is applied to the calves in a bent leg position, thereby shortening the calf muscles and directing the effort to the soleus. Mix them as you devise your routine, supersetting seated with standing, for example. The predominantly slow twitch fibers enjoy high reps and frequent training. Donkeys are the best.

CHIN — WIDE-GRIP

Starting from a fully extended hanging position, pull your body up to the bar so the underside of the chin is near contact, deliberately arching and leaning thereby contracting the lats throughout. Lower yourself slowly, extend and continue. Form is everything, pure and controlled. Lat contraction is your purpose, not going up and down roughly any way you can. Here we have the lats totally engaged, outer and lower. Pulldowns work well, but chins are merciless; there's no possibility of cheating without silly body contortions. After a warm-up set, hang an appropriate weight from your waist using a strap or belt to give you a 12, 10, 8, 6 rep sequence. Not everyone is remarkable in chinning. Give it your committed best and you may develop remarkable lats. Added attractions are biceps peak, grip strength, linear abs and minor pec action.

CHIN — BEHIND THE NECK

This modification shifts the resistance from the lats primarily to the inter-muscular activity of the upper back and deltoids. Not my preferred target, but a mean, full back muscle intensifier. Don't project your head forward and endanger the cervical complex.

CHIN — OTHER VARIATIONS

Chins come in all shapes and sizes. There are the wide-grips already discussed with their prevalent over-grip or "supinated grip." And there are the close-grips with both the supinated grip and its counterpart, the pronated grip. I advocate the fully extended starting position once the body is in condition to chin at all; for some, it's the challenge of a lifetime. Pull with all your might from the bottom to the top, a tight contraction to the chin or further, should structure allow, and down slowly to extension. Arch the back in either grip to emphasize the back's exertion. Pronated grip maximizes the biceps engagement while working the lats (adds to the long lat sweep that stretches low), serratus and back. Overgrip does more for the upper back and spinatus region. All chins build grip, wrist and forearm strength.

Full extension too soon, before insertions are thickened and readied, can cause a lot of pain if not separation or a tear in the complex of shoulder, pectoral, latisimus and biceps.

CLOSE OR NARROW-GRIP BENCH PRESS

Not much difference in approach and performance from the Big Guy, the flat bench press, except that the grip is close, eight to twelve inches apart, and the target is primarily the triceps. The tight position of the arms requires that they fold close to the body, elbows forward with the major load on the triceps and, in diminishing proportions, the front delts and chest. The groove is self-defined and logical but can be modified to accentuate the range of muscle contraction. Beware: Too close a grip abuses elbows and wrists.

CLOSE-GRIP PULLDOWN

This pulley movement has a great appeal and serves well as an off-day antagonistic superset movement, i.e. dumbbell inclines with close-grip pulldowns. Perform these with a full range of motion from extension to contraction. As you lean back to allow a tight clearance, pull the bar to a high chest position, contract and continue at your prescribed cadence or tempo. Upper-lat and mid-back respond well to this good feeling movement, an alternative worth its weight in pig iron.

CURL — BAR, DUMBBELL, BENT BAR, MACHINE

A curl is a curl is a curl. Not exactly.

I do all of these movements regularly (doesn't everybody?) and enjoy them equally. The straight Olympic bar rules until my wrists begin to complain; I then switch to a thick-handled bent bar. Stand erect with your feet shoulder-width apart and the bar hanging fully extended before you. Pull the bar somewhat in front of you and up at the same time to a point even with the shoulders. Pause only long enough to reverse the action and lower the bar slowly to the starting position.

Your reps in all exercises will vary according to the muscle, its mass and fiber, your goals and scheme. I work reliably in the six to ten rep range, matching my mood, endurance and level of repair. As I fatigue, and this is evident in all my training, I draw upon a calculated body thrust to enable the completion of the final tough repetitions without losing workload integrity. (Some people might call this cheating; can't fool everybody.) These deep, hard reps call the rest of the body to action. As long as they are defined and directed, they'll work for you. They bite.

These are big, full biceps builders if that's your target. None better. The heavy curls with built-in thrusts put a welcome demand on the system, shifting them from single-joint isolation movements to broad-range muscle recruiters. Dig in.

CURL — MACHINE

Machine curls are like cars; they're designed to get you from one place to another. Drive one, you can drive them all, just that some are a better ride. Hop in, wiggle till you're comfortable and pull. Now you've got it. I'll be over here doing dumbbell alternates with Leroy. Don't fall off.

CURL — PREACHER OR SCOTT CURL

You know the drill. You approach the bench when it least expects it, sit down like you were going to take a breather and then suddenly and fiercely wrap your legs around the thing, grab the suspiciously close bent bar and start curling in hungry reps over its padded and perfectly angled post. Some people claim tendinitis from the outward slant and prefer to curl from the pad which allows the arms to drop straight down; no hyperextension, no elbow aggravation, no over-curling to stress the brachialis. Instead, lots of screamingly intense, isolated biceps pulling and slow, vascular, mind-altering descents. Let someone else count if anyone's keeping score.

CURL — SEATED DUMBBELL INCLINE

Choose your favorite incline to give your biceps the extension and mechanical advantage you desire. Stay tight, let the dumbbells hang and pull them, palms forward, toward the shoulders; contract and slowly lower. Same ole' curl yet different enough when you fight the metal going down to the count of three or four, rep after rep, or curl them outwardly from a super-extended palms-out position, up and down like fire and ice.

CURL — STANDING DUMBBELL INCLINE

Injuries cause you to try different exercise positions. Not long ago, a bruised shoulder prevented me from effectively doing seated dumbbell incline curls. Seeking an option, I stumbled across a mighty, somewhat isolated biceps builder, a stray from the norm. At a seventy-five degree incline, I stand with my back against the pad of an adjustable bench. I bend at the knees slightly to gain a position of sturdiness and let the dumbbells fully hang at my side. I engage the weights one arm at a time and proceed to do four sets of alternate curls. Dig in and pull to the shoulder and since we're on the subject, I like six to eight reps. Fully extended, dig in and pull. Put total attention on each arm, separate and alone, concentrate, back and forth. You've got it!

CURL — STANDING OR SEATED DUMBBELL

Let's see. How does it go again? Assume either the standing or seated position with the dumbbells hanging by your side, fully extended and palms forward. Just as you would in the barbell curl, pull the weights slightly forward and up to shoulder height. Don't do anything fancy as if it would make a difference. Pulling the weight with all you've got and looking for more is sufficient. With each new rep, focus all your attention on the movement of the weights, the path they travel and the team of muscles aching, pumping and burning to finish the rep. Notice the change in demand as the dumbbells are lowered, stretching and taut, to the starting place. Note the relief that comes with the pause, the drawing in of air and the tightening of the body as the glorious process is repeated until it can't be repeated again.

I will remind you every once in awhile: I like supersets. Dumbbell curls go nicely with lying triceps extensions and a dark Zinfandel (non-alcoholic). They work the biceps, completely and throughout. You will hear different stories about high sets and reps (ten or more) and low (six or less), single sets, ultra slow reps, rest periods; "I read it on the Net," "my uncle said." You've got to experiment and mix it up at first, listen to yourself, dig around inside, match your personality. It'll come to you, have fun and don't give up.

CURL — THUMBS-UP/HAMMER CURL

A variation of the curl that I've been doing since an injury fifteen years ago that urged me to stray from the norm, the thumbs-up curl and I have come to know each other quite well. Stand as indicated earlier, only now the bells are held palms facing inward. Here again, drag the weights upward but in a slightly modified groove, one that brings the plates toward the face — the cheekbones, to be precise. This positioning clearly puts a demand on the forearm and across the biceps, a welcome and productive diversion.

Moreover I, who seek water from a rock, find that with a mind on the back muscles, front delts and minor pecs, this movement with explosive yet controlled thrust and emphasized negative hammers nearly the whole upper body. Sets of 12, 10, 8, 6, 4 are common with me, supersetted with wrist curls and pulley pushdowns, just to be sure.

CURL — ZOTTMAN

Biceps, forearms, wrists and hand cap muscles all in one tidy little package. However, open this package and you've got your hands full. Again, stand upright, dumbbells a' hangin'. Zottmans are done alternately. With total attention on one arm, pull the weight upward and toward you; as it approaches the shoulder, rotate the hand into the body and lower it with restraint to the starting position — a tough journey down as power advantage is lost to the reverse grip and altered muscle mechanics. This flexing and flaring of the biceps and forearm produce compound muscular demand and account for pronounced muscle shape and delineation.

Complete extension and flexion accomplished, switch your attention to the other arm and repeat. Look for rhythm and building momentum as you seek your limits in the sets and reps. Yet again a caution: Use a lighter weight to protect the tendons and insertions.

DEADLIFT

Deadlifts are a simple exercise really, made difficult by over-trying and over-thinking. Stand before the weight in a solid, shoulder-width stance (or up to six inches wider), shin to the bar. You are about to bend over and pick up a heavy object and this should be your mental approach.

Bend at the waist and at the knees equally and at the same time. Grasp the bar fully and securely, over-grip or in an alternate under/over grip, about waist width, hands just outside your legs. Looking straight ahead, your spine in a powerful flat position (not stooped over or rounded), focus, regulate your breathing, breathe deeply and steadily pull the bar to a full, standing military position. Keep the bar close to your body and exhale as full force is exerted. Pause for a second of contraction and slowly bend your knees and low back as you return to the starting position and repeat.

Three to four sets of ten reps, twice weekly with a light to moderate weight should be of substantial benefit during your first six weeks to condition the many muscles involved, to discover form through practice and the possibilities of application to your goals and system of training. A safe placement for this exercise is at the end of your leg workout as it complements quadriceps work or at the end of your back work. Seventy-percent output should suffice in the early stages to set the foundations, build muscle and prevent training overload and injury. It takes time to prepare the thigh and hip girdle and erectors for heavy powerlifting.

The day will come for many, if it hasn't already, when the urge to lift a maximum weight from the floor to your waist for a single rep will challenge you. Be ready — wisely done, deadlifts that approach triple, double and single reps after warming up are exciting and productive. Exceedingly heavy workouts done twice every four to five weeks are a valuable addition to your training regimen: systemic muscle growth, increase in overall core muscle, power and bodyweight. Workouts producing personal records (PRs) are truly memorable.

Women who seek to strengthen, shape and tone their buttocks, hip and thigh area will respond well to this formerly all-male power movement. A comprehensive and stabilizing exercise, deadlifts should become a standard practice throughout your years of training. They will produce most agreeable changes in your shape and performance. Throw in squats and you'll delight.

Don't hesitate. With care and daring and proper instruction you can humbly boast of their presence in your scheme. Finally, only practice and experience will teach you.

DEADLIFT — SUMO STYLE

I don't talk about science much in the building of muscle any more than one does in talking about crossing a road to get to the other side. And, I can't say I've logged a lot of hours in the sumo deadlift, either. But, I reckon I've got a lot of years left and this odd, multi-joint exercise is interesting and shows promise in its lumpy architecture.

Maybe it's the grip. Stand with the Olympic bar grasped in a staggered over/under grip twelve to fifteen inches apart, head forward and up. The legs are wide apart (up to thirty-six inches) and feet toed-out to forty-five degrees, the knees and hips a tad short of locked. Here we observe both the starting stance and the stance of the rep's completion, an effort requiring power and practice in itself. We've got a lot of adjusting and adapting to do with the unusual resistance we now experience in a dozen different places; the grip and forearm, angular knee and hip insertions, compromised quad engagement. The overloaded traps and back are pulling and stabilizing through an unorthodox track, deep breathing restricted by the hanging, closely gripped tonnage and thoughts of traction in a lonely hospital outpost.

Down you go in a slow and erect body posture, no giggling. The plates on the bar touch the floor, and, though you're tempted to leave it and run, you pause briefly to mentally mark your placement, slightly relax and explode into your sure, all-consuming ascent.

Practice this baby monster using a friendly weight for reps of eight, sets maybe four. Take your time achieving this working range and develop a scheme of progression, if you think it's really necessary.

I believe six to eight weeks of logical and freely presented overload is one of the main keys on the strength and muscle builder's key ring.

DUMBBELL FLY

Flys are performed to engage the pectoral muscles in their most complete and isolated action, drawing the extended arm across the chest. They are performed on the flat bench or any intelligent degree of incline or decline. Assume a position lying on your back with a pair of lightweight dumbbells overhead. Maintain a semi-straight-arm advantage, palms facing each other, lower the bells outward until they are in line with the body or parallel with the floor, pause and return with willful pectoral contraction. Bone structure, insertions and muscle mass frequently determines the effectiveness or success an exercise has on one person or another. The upper arm wants to take over in the execution of the fly and the movement then does little to shape and define the pecs and lots to shred or tear the biceps. Consider this.

Flys make for a burning and pumping secondary movement in a chest pressing superset, so I've been told.

DUMBBELL PRESS — CHEST AND SHOULDERS

Whether done on a flat bench, decline or incline, this is basically the same mechanical movement. Simply put, as the flat bench press position engages the center chest mass and front deltoid, the incline shifts the resistance to the upper chest mass and demands more shoulder; the decline conversely gets lower pec and minimizes deltoid involvement.

Sit on the edge of the bench with the dumbbells plate down on the lower quads. Draw the dumbbells to your waist as you roll back to a lying position, immediately thrusting the weights up to an overhead starting placement. Palms forward and elbows facing back, lower the weights to the side of your body not quite even with your head and power back up. Practice, seek your groove, focus and you're on your way.

Dumbbell presses are a better and healthier exercise than the barbell bench press in many ways because the hands can rotate to accommodate the needs of the frequently overused and abused rotator cuff or shoulder device. The barbell bench press is rigid and unforgiving. Also, with three hundred and sixty degrees of direction in each hand there's a need for a lot of muscle stabilizing and coordination, meaning more demand for muscular health and growth.

Dumbbell inclines are the favorite big deltoid builders of pro body-builders over the years. A forty-five degree incline up to seventy-five degrees is a nice range of variation for the years to come. Muscling your dumbbells into place is also a structure and skill-building process. Don't drop them, don't clang or crack them at the top. Control them. Be nice.

DUMBBELL SHRUG

The dumbbell shrug is for muscle weaving and posture restoration. Shrugs primarily work the powerful pulling muscles of the back — the trapezius — which stand out amongst lifters as predominant mounds below the ears and across the shoulders.

Stand erect with dumbbells of an appealing, moderate weight, with shoulders back, head high, lats flexed, gut in. Smile. Slightly bend the knees, stoop imperceptibly forward allowing the dumbbells to drop some four inches as you release your traps and softly round the back — the starting point. Pull the dumbbells up high with all your might, shoulders to ears and roll them to the fully erect starting position. Confidently flex the entire system as if ready to salute. Repeat with flourish until you complete the set. This can get serious at some point and the weights can get heavy. Superior grip work is a great simultaneous accomplishment; those bis and forearms don't just hang around shootin' the breeze.

FRONT SQUAT

For ultimate thigh development, front squats are a superior leg exercise and deserve to be ranked alongside the honored full squat. Step up to the racked bar and settle it high across the front deltoids; raising the upper arms, bring the hands to the bar for support. The exact hand-arm arrangement is to be worked out individually by trial and logic.

Stand fully upright and prepare to squat. Complete quadriceps action is achieved as you squat directly up and down precisely as in the standard squat. The resistance in the front squat is located forward of the torso in deference to the standard squat in which the resistance is behind the body's center. This alteration in resistance is significant and accounts for a modification of the intensity of quad muscle recruitment as well as demands made on the torso musculature.

The bar across the shoulders is precarious and can be painfully abusive to the upper shoulder cage should you choose to go heavier and heavier. Select a modest weight and practice this winner, allowing the entire body to adapt and strengthen together in time. Wisely settle on a lighter load and more reps to gain the benefits of the front squat demands.

HAMMER STRENGTH MACHINES

Hammer came on the gym equipment scene in the early 1990s. Pictures of the preposterous-looking stuff filled the pages of the muscle mags and I thought, "What a joke. These things will behead a person before they build his or her muscles."

It was two years before assorted pieces for various muscle groups popped up in gyms across the country. Today, Hammer has a rugged plate-loading machine for every sinew in the body and they work — big time. More or less, you sit down and either push or pull as indicated. I mention this here because I often note them in my routines and on occasion get queries from the confused, asking "What's he talking about now?" Easy to use, sure to do the job.

HYPEREXTENSION

An important movement for lower back development and stability, the hyperextension is performed on a specific piece of equipment. Hyperextension benches are all a little different. You eventually find yourself lying face down across an apparatus, the back of your lower legs held rigid to support your upper body, which is precariously extended from the hips. Slowly raise your torso upward and approach a horizontal position, hold the contraction for a split second and lower in a two- to three-second count. Short trial movements will prepare you for and familiarize you with this unlikely exercise. Your ascent is slow and thoughtful, cautious not to come up too quickly or too far and distress your low back. Hypers are more agreeable than they sound and their benefits are sterling. Twice a week on a compatible day of your choice.

LATERAL RAISE — BENT-OVER

Stand before a pair of iron knuckle-busters. Greedily pull in some oxygen, with the back of your hand wipe the sweat from your brow, bend over and firmly grasp the dumbbells. Bend your knees and rest your ribcage as best you can on your quads to protect fatiguing erectors from overload. Allow the dumbbells to hang, palms facing each other. Pull the dumbbells high and outward to a position even with or above your flattened back. Contract the rear delts, concentrate on the negative return and repeat. Go two reps per breath. Done.

LATERAL RAISE — FRONT, HAMMER PLATE RAISE

This is my version of the front lateral raise. Most of what I do is tainted by time and injury, not that I'm a hundred years old or falling apart. Just a few almost pleasant limitations encourage me to modify and sometimes eliminate a few of the movements of my trade. This solid counter-pose plate grip "fixes" my shoulder and enables front delt action I would otherwise be unable to enjoy. Sitting on the edge of a bench, feet planted but with legs extended and spread out for stability, grasp a flat plate with both hands and allow it to hang, ready for the first rep. Easy.

Raise the plate with rigid arms directing the resistance through the hands and onto the front deltoids. Peak resistance is reached at a point some forty-five degrees above horizontal and rotation beyond this range becomes a risk. Lower to the starting position using the eccentric properties of the exercise to load the delts. Feel the compressing action of the grip in the pecs, the upright thrust within the traps, the peculiar demand on the straining biceps, the muscular stabilizing throughout the back and torso as they fight for balance. A light weight serves to warm up the rotator cuff; heavier weights with a clean-like motion can be serious. Don't underestimate the dinky stuff.

LATERAL RAISE — SIDE ARM

This ever-popular, single-joint dumbbell movement isolates the outer head of the deltoid; it shapes and completes that which presses begin. You won't see a lot of powerlifters practicing the lateral raise, but it's not because it doesn't add muscle. The best way to learn the exercise is to start very light with a pair of chrome dumbbells (or those little blue ones work well) hanging by your side, slightly to the rear of your body, palms facing inward. With arms rigid, raise them outwardly to a position slightly above parallel or just above your shoulders, palms remaining down. Repeat the movement for a set of ten repetitions and notice how cleverly we modify the action to reach our goal as we fatigue, a teeny lean forward, an imperceptible bending and shortening of the arms, a mini-thrust and a crossing of the eyes. Fact is, you're on your way to the perfect side arm lateral raise to give your delts the cannonball look of your dreams.

Don't stop now. Work up the rack, eventually, and improve your form and thrust with tight contractions at the top and negatives that rake striations across the shoulders and traps. Who said these isolated, simple movements are simple and isolated? Get rolling on these creature-makers and you have grip work, lower, middle and upper back jamming in concert, heavy breathing, and some random parts of the outer biceps burning. Here's a novel idea: superset side arms with seated press-behind-neck. Original.

LEG CURL

The leg curl is a machine exercise that works the muscles on the back of the thighs, the hamstrings, also know as the thigh biceps. Typically an under-worked muscle, it is important to bring the thigh biceps into balance with the quads to provide overall strength, protect the leg complex from injury and add appealing symmetry to the body. Position yourself according to the mechanics of the apparatus, adjust carefully and perform the reps as indicated. Four or five sets of six to twelve reps twice a week work well. I practice one-and-a-half-second eccentric, with a half-second pause and a two second concentric tempo. I seek tight contraction and commonly do curls as the second part of a leg extension-leg curl superset, doing single-leg calf block stretching during the pause between supersets.

LEG EXTENSION

Performed with the assistance of a machine, the leg extension works the powerful four-part muscle structure of the front thigh, the quadriceps. It has its place in the training of the thighs, though I reserve it for the first part of my leg extension/curl/calf raise tri-set. This demanding union placed before my squat workout serves as a significant warm-up and heavy-load preparation. It strengthens and shapes the quads, yet I am reluctant to apply more than a guessed eighty-percent last rep overload as a caution against knee risk. Remembering adjustments for personal needs, I do 5x12-15 slow and steady reps, moderate weight, no momentum, brief mid-rep contraction. Lactic acid exudes, fire everywhere.

LEG PRESS

We're stuck on machine work here, aren't we? Though quality, efficiency, comfort and load bearing roam a wide range, all leg presses are basically the same. Sit down, secure your feet on the platform, make yourself comfortable, unlock and press. Secret: a good leg press works a lot better than a bad leg press.

Foot placement makes a big difference in targeting development or engendering an injury. Feet too close or too low on a platform often result in knee abuse. Legs angled too far out or placed too wide (uselessly hoping to recruit adductors and trim loose flesh from the inner thigh) cause pain and damage as the natural knee tracking has been severely compromised under stress. A common sense shoulder-width, toed-out footing that is thoughtfully high on the rack will provide the safest and most productive arrangement to power through your muscle-building reps. Pushing through your heel and traveling slowly through your reps and sets will maximize their effect. Don't go too deep at the bottom of the action or you'll eventually cause a muscle tear or hip, low-back, knee or ankle stress. Makes ya grouchy.

LYING LATERAL RAISE FRONT — L-FLY

These prone raises isolate the deltoid caps as they draw upon the surrounding attached muscle groups to spread its good work through the entire upper body. Lie sideways on a bench with one shoulder to the vinyl and the opposing shoulder upright. Allow the arm closest to the bench to extend comfortably forward and out of the line of action, while your leg likewise seeks its own comfort. The upper leg is extended forty-five degrees forward and can reach toward the floor to act as the stabilizer. (Alternatively, you might put your non-working hand on the floor to your side.)

A dumbbell of light weight (five to fifteen pounds) is extended above your body to a neutral starting position. Slowly, with the working arm rigid, lower the weight forward of the chest to an agreeable extension, almost as if reaching for the floor. With power and control, return it to the starting position, elbow tucked tightly against your ribcage during the entire procedure. Repeat for a set of eight to ten reps and conclude by putting the dumbbell to the floor and rolling it under the bench to the other side. Flip your body position and repeat. Three or four sets of 10, 8, 6 reps at the end of your delt routine is a treat.

Awkward at first, this body mover as it is practiced and perfected targets the front and side delts. Yet full range of motion, focus and elaboration will bring in a long lat sweep, mucho back stuff and rear deltoid contraction. A persuasive body thrust with heavier weight involves and exhausts the larger system of integrated muscles. It can get mean.

LYING LATERAL RAISE — REAR

The lying lateral to behind the torso requires similar body-limb stabilizing as the front lying lateral (L-Fly) above and follows the logical track behind the back with similar cadence and power-thrust. The shift of muscle action continues to bash the delts — these moves require a bit of unhurried investigative trial and error, a willing mind familiar with the learning process and the characteristics of finesse. They'll work for you if you work with them. Toughen, pack and etch. Sets of these crazy spider lateral raises are done alternately, nonstop.

LYING TRICEPS EXTENSION

Lying on a bench with your arms extended overhead in a narrow (six-inch) grip, start the triceps extension by lowering the bar to your forehead or beyond. The upper arms are to remain elbow-tight and upright to emphasize the load on the triceps and guarantee maximum development. The triceps extension is a major mass and power builder. High reps pyramided with low reps work well to saturate the three-headed muscle.

The overhead triceps extension performed similarly from a seated upright position (wisely using a back-support utility bench) with the elbows straight overhead is another aggressive triceps builder. The employment of the bent bar is a popular alternate. Remember, tendinitis prowls. Warm up, don't overload excessively, rest properly.

LUNGE

I prescribe lunges for a stretchy, pumpy movement between sets. That's all. Then again, Laree likes 'em a lot more. She does them off a raised platform, protecting the knees while offering a more complete and targeted range of motion. Sisters of Steel may want to experiment making the prime target the glute and hamstrings tie-in.

MILITARY/OVERHEAD PRESS — CLEAN AND PRESS

Standing or seated, this is tough. Grasp the bar just outside shoulder width and position it across the front of the shoulders, just under the chin. It will require some practice, trial and error to pull the bar from the floor in one swift and directed motion to the target starting position.

Hint: Partially bend over and partially squat down to grasp the bar and then, with focused might, pull the bar up to the shoulders and allow the weight to cradle on upturned palms and front shoulders. The power comes from the concerted effort of the thighs and back. This is an amazing exercise all by itself, called the power clean, part of an Olympic lifter's clean and press exercise. It's a very comprehensive movement for dynamic overall structure development and explosive power: lots of trap, low back, hamstring and quad. A favorite of serious football players for the kind of explosive power needed to crush the opponent. Fun stuff.

Once in place, press the bar continually to a locked-out overhead position, briefly hold and slowly lower to your shoulders and repeat. This is to be done with a minimum of back lean or leg thrust. I highly recommend you use a tough leather lifting belt to girdle the midsection and protect the lower back.

This is not a low-level or medium-level movement. It is a high-level movement, comprehensive and systemic, meaning in simple terms a full-body, major-muscle, multi-joint exercise, responsible for sending messages throughout the entire body to grow — to adapt — and meet the demand. This includes enzymes, neural pathways and hormones. Cleans and presses growl. They bad.

ONE-ARM CABLE CROSSOVER

The one-arm cable crossover beats the dual-arm in that you can give superior focus to all ranges of pectoral activity, achieve a greater range of extension and contraction, work one pec at a time with maximum output and modify the action to incorporate surrounding, hungry muscle groups: serratus, lats, bis.

Position yourself alongside your favorite cable apparatus as if you were about to perform a typical two-hand cable crossover. Crouch slightly in a position of readiness and with shoulders remaining in a straight line with the cable system, draw the single handle with a rigid arm high across the pecs. Back and forth, contract, extend, contract — Look for rhythm, continuity, flow and burn. As high-pec muscles fatigue after four reps, drop to a stronger mid-pec hand-and-cable groove forty-five degrees toward the floor before you. Another four reps and finish with a shift in body to bring the cable directly down toward the floor as you locate low pec recruitment.

Have fun with this rangy exercise: improvise, feel, isolate, customize. Make it yours. Back and forth.

No supersetting here; apply this combination to the end of your pec routine, three to four sets of twelve reps, one side followed immediately by the other. Form, muscle-location, isolation and burn is everything.

ONE-ARM CABLE LAT ROW

Stand sideways, three feet (more or less) from the base of a low pulley system, handle in the hand farthest from the cable apparatus. Assume a wide stance, bend at the knees and hips and let the weight stack extend to near-touching. Your working lat and arm should be in full extension, an appropriate starting position. Settle in, shift footing for movement efficiency, hand on knee for support: Ready, steadily pull the handle to the mid-torso, contract, slowly return, stretch low-lat insertions and repeat.

How you pull, to where you pull, the arch and contraction of your upper torso, the position of your body in relation to the cable system all determine what part of your musculature you will affect. You put the paint on the canvas; you're the artist. You paint the wall, it's your building.

Back and forth, nonstop. No supersetting here; apply this series to the end of your back routine, three to five sets, 12, 10, 8, 6 reps. Focus, trust yourself. It's worth it.

ONE-ARM DUMBBELL ROW

This potent exercise stands alongside barbell rows in mass and power-building seriousness. Executed with the same intensity, they are wisely done as alternatives to the barbell. Stabilized in a powerful tripod stance — none of this knee-on-bench stuff — one-arm dumbbell rows remove the load from the lower back, enabling you to tough your way through lumbar overload. Relief in this overworked area is priceless.

I stagger my legs, bend at the waist and lean on the dumbbell rack before me, extend my free arm to grasp the dumbbell, position myself for desired muscle recruitment and pull the weight to the body in a muscle-intense movement with an ample twist of the torso at the top to accentuate contraction. Too much thrust early on and the effect is lost to momentum. The target of the tug is important: high on the torso (toward shoulder), more upper back; low on the torso (toward the obliques), more lower lat.

In all your exercises focus, form, and practice yield perfection of some variety.

ONE-ARM OVERHEAD CABLE PULL

The one-arm overhead cable pull is odd and rarely practiced, yet has a sharpening effect on the linear lat — from insertion A to Z (so much for physiology — ve must 'av imagination). Tough explanation: Grasp the single handle of the overhead cable crossover in your right hand. Position yourself in a wide-footed stance, right side away from the machine. Extend your arm over your head and pull to the right as you stabilize yourself against the resistance. The resistance will travel through your hand and arm and into the entire length of the lat as you tug. Lean and tug, return, lean and tug. This is one of those improvising, adapting, shifting and locating movements that challenge our training talents and create sweet touches to the muscular system. Practice and stick it out. Onlookers will be impressed or think you're strange. It's all a matter of expression and the way you chew your gum.

PRESS-BEHIND-NECK (PBN)

PBN is similar to the military press except the starting position is from the shoulders, bar behind the neck. A suggestion here is to sit before the bar in its racked position. (You do have racks, don't you?) Grasp the bar with reasonable shoulder allowance, duck your head under the bar, shift forward settling bar on your shoulders and sit upright. Now proceed to press the bar straight overhead and lower to a point somewhere even with your ears and repeat. Keep your head in its natural posture, not compromising the neck to perform the movement. That is, don't project your head forward with your neck under resistance; the bar needs to track further back. This may be a chiropractor's nightmare, but it sure is popular. Same with chins and pulldowns behind the neck. 911.

PBNs work that network of muscle throughout the upper back and shoulder carriage. Contract with fierceness — posterior and lateral deltoid, the spinatus, triceps tie-in.

PULLEY PUSHDOWN

Not a power or mass exercise, the pushdown effectively forms the triceps and adds to their health. Grip your favorite handle and stand approximately one foot away from the overhead pulley. Bend your arms at the elbows and locate them close to your torso, directing them slightly forward. Extend the handle downward to a straight-arm position, contracting the triceps tightly. Slowly return to the starting point with an accent on the negative for maximum advantage. I regard the pushdown with affection and apply ample body thrust to load the triceps totally while properly engaging an army of associated upper body muscles (erectors and torso stabilizers, serratus, minor pec, and upper back). This vigorous performance transforms the minor isolated action into a more substantial movement packed with energy and spirit. Ideal for supersetting with sets of twelve to fifteen reps.

PULLOVER — STIFF-ARM OR STRAIGHT-ARM

Performed with a barbell or a dumbbell, it's a feel-good power stretch that engages the lats, the underside of the bis and tris and minor pec as it puts the rotator cuff through its ranges. Longitudinal abdominal muscles come into play to stabilize the torso. Did I mention they build the serratus like the mason builds walls of stone?

If you like supersetting, a stiff-arm pullover between sets is gratifying and productive. A moderate-plus weight allows you to stretch, revives the muscle cells and adds immensely to upper latisimus building. Keep the secondary pullovers at eight to ten reps.

Lie on your back, head on one end of the bench, feet on the other end and a dumbbell or barbell grasped in your hands straight overhead — your starting position. Take a deep breath as you slowly lower the weight behind your head with stiff arms (elbows near locked). When your arms are in line with your torso — parallel to the floor — reverse the motion and return to the starting position, exhaling as you do. Pause momentarily and repeat. It's a great stretch, great lat pump, great relief movement that promotes posture awareness. Lots of blood circulating oxygen and nutrients to wake up, stimulate, revive and refresh.

ROW MACHINE

Adjust the weight, grab the handles, place your feet securely on the footrest before you and sit with your arms extended and under the resistance of the cable. The starting position has you in an erect, slightly arched upright posture as if elegantly seated in a straight-back chair. Lean forward slightly as the chest pad allows, pause and begin your motion by pulling back while simultaneously drawing in your arms. As you approach the ending position begin to arch your back recruiting your mid-back muscles, further drawing in your arms to your midsection (just below rib cage) to complete the movement.

There you are: seated upright, back arched and flexed, arms drawn in and flexed. Grand. Continue this terrific action that simulates the rowing of a boat for twelve to fifteen reps. Practice and you'll find this will become an all-time favorite — most productive for practical strength and wonderful for muscular growth.

RUBBER TUBING — ROTATOR CUFF WORK

You know the drill; stand rigidly with your arm by your side, bent at the elbow. Resistance properly directed, rotate your hand inward, thereby achieving the therapeutic propine action. Redirect the tube resistance and rotate your hand away from the body to complete the supine action. Complete four sets of twenty-five smooth, high-pace reps of each action for both left and right sides as an upper body warm-up.

Five years ago this exercise combination was seldom witnessed at our gym and was considered for saps only. Today we have a dozen multicolored tubes of various tensions being pumped in every corner of the gym giving it the appearance of an amusement park. This movement is serious, deserves focus and one-hundred-percent effort. It does wonders to develop the minor rotator cuff muscles and tendons that stabilize the shoulder and provide resistance and muscle fullness. The usual presses and laterals don't effect the shoulder straps and require their loyal and tenacious support to help you blast away. Delts need to be warmed up and treated kindly. Perform these cuff rotations regularly to maintain health and achieve full deltoid potential. I dare ya.

SEATED LAT ROW — LOW PULL

The knees are out of the way and your favorite close-grip handle is extended as you reach forward. Pull the handle tightly toward the waist as you arch your back to contract the rhomboids, ending in a upright seated position with a very slight, five to ten percent lean to the rear. Very nice; have fun with the purposeful negative. No thrusting, no momentum — strictly muscle, power and form. This can be supersetted with your stiff-arm or bent-arm pullovers if you like to keep your hands full.

These low pulls are a loveable exercise even when they're nasty. Nice positioning, energizing, catlike stretching and extending, followed by might in the controlled contraction. The reliable 12, 10, 8, 6 sequence with intense muscle work, fifty-five mile-per-hour pace, tightly arched contraction, no pointless leaning back or dangerous excessive forward lean. Mid-back and low-lat sweep are the direct targets of this all-time standard. Good for moms, their spouses and kids. My dog likes this one.

SMITH PRESS-BEHIND-NECK

This is best performed wearing a leather lifting belt with your back against the seat back of a utility bench. Position yourself so the bar of a Smith Press grazes the back of your head without projecting your head forward. Starting at the top of the movement is logical and gives advantage to complete the set-rep execution. Full range of motion is good at the top, but limiting the depth of descent is wise to protect the rotator cuff. Face it: it doesn't need any more abuse.

The reps may be performed with a sure pace and abbreviated range of motion. This rep execution saturates the upper back ridges, full deltoid area and the outer triceps, giving you the sense of one continual breathless rep. High-level pump and burn result. Low volume, throaty growls are fitting for both men and women.

SQUAT

Another big daddy, a comprehensive, systemic, full-body growth builder. Add power and mass with the squat and improve your athletic ability and durability. The accent is on the glutes (butt muscles) and quadriceps (thigh muscles). Unless you have racks from which you can retrieve the bar, you'll clean (Remember? Hoisting it up from the floor?) the bar to locate it across your shoulders. This is no easy task and will result in your using a light weight for high repetitions. Fine. Gives you the opportunity to practice your clean and press (a mighty movement requiring technical skill and practice) and get your lower back, knees and thighs well-prepared for your future of heavy squats — a must if you can and will. S'cuz The Bomber trivia.

Bar in place across the traps and shoulders, padded if you choose with a folded towel or Manta Ray, slowly lower yourself as if you were about to sit down on a chair. The butt goes out and down; your lower back, hips and knees bend in concert. Down you go, keeping your eyes straight ahead, bar steady and over your knees, with feet flat, until your thighs are near parallel to the ground. Up you go, pushing off with your heels. Be careful not to tip forward allowing the back and bar ascent to lag behind the leg thrust. Upright, take a deep breath and hold it going down keeping the torso muscles tight; reach parallel, push up and exhale as you ascend. Repeat till the reps are achieved — one and a half to two

174 Brother Iron, Sister Steel

seconds down, one and a half to two seconds up. You got it? You got it. Don't try to walk up or down stairs for a day or two. It'll be ugly.

You've arrived.

SQUAT — SUMO STYLE

This is an ultra-wide stance squat. Not popular in my neck of the woods, but effective nonetheless.

STIFF-LEGGED DEADLIFT

A lighter variation of the bent-leg deadlift or powerlifter's deadlift, stiff-legged deads are practiced using relatively milder weight with the aim on deeper repetitions for hamstring stretch and flexibility and the resulting health, strength and performance enhancement. Standing upright with the bar in hands, palms toward the body, lower the weight to the floor as previously described; yet the action is performed with only a slight bend in the knees. Look straight ahead as you focus on the descent, keeping the resistance safely close to the body along the shins to a near-ankle pause and steadily pull up, shoulders back, arms extended and in control.

In the case of both bent and stiff-legged deads, at the moment of descent the glutes jut backward as the lowering weight is kept close to the body (the center of gravity) in obedience to the laws of physics. Expect this logical compensation and you'll find the movement more appealing and achievable.

Repeat for eight to ten or fifteen reps for the number of sets defined by your purpose and drive. These bombers — like pieces to a puzzle — fit where they belong.

WIDE-GRIP FREEHAND AND MACHINE DIP

Wing-whackers, these wide-grip dips. Lean forward, round the back and direct the effort toward your mid-back via partial reps. The more you lean forward and the deeper you go, the more the pec activity. The narrower the grips and the more totally you lock out your elbows, the greater the triceps effect. Bar dips are, of course, more demanding and potentially more mass-producing than regulated machine dips. When your rep ability exceeds twelve, you can always hang some weight from a harness around your waist.

Machine dips allow resistance control, muscle targeting and partial range of motion when limited by injury. When I first learned how to walk, I walked over to the dipping bars and began to dip. My mom had to count out the reps; math was tough.

WIDE-GRIP PULLDOWN — FRONT AND BACK

To the front: Positioned directly below the overhead pulley, legs held steady by the kneepad, arms fully extended, pull the bar to just below your chin as you look upward. Your back should be arched, your chest straining toward the bar with your elbows back, not forward, all positioned to fully recruit the entire lat complex — width and length.

Allow a sufficient lean and tug to accomplish your well-formed reps, but no excessive thrusts. Don't cheat — no momentum — you lose. Feel, locate, pump, burn and grow.

If chins are your challenge these days and dern near impossible, by all means do the appropriate pulldowns to enable you to aspire.

To the back: Use a medium grip and situate yourself slightly forward of the overhead pulley. From the fully extended starting position, pull the bar deliberately down directing the resistance to the upper back muscles, rear delt, biceps and lat. This is best achieved by concentrated isolation of this region by pretending you are onstage, before the judges and instructed to hit a back pose. Contract up and down smoothly, tightly, rhythmically.

Here's a long time combo-strategy I use to bomb everything in sight: Tightly contract the upper back muscles as you pull the bar to the base of the skull for six reps. Use the negative return for full muscle recruitment — lats, scapula, etc. Position yourself so there will be no need to dangerously thrust your head forward to allow the passage of the bar. Continue the final six reps to the chin as described previously with sufficient tug to overload the back. You're flying.

WRIST CURL — REVERSE WRIST CURL

Choose an Olympic bar for balance and smooth plate rotation; straddle a bench, grasp the bar with a complete finger and thumb under-grip and rest your forearms on your thighs for cushion and stability. The bar in hand extends just beyond the knees and is slowly lowered to a full and safe range and curled back up to a tight, contracted position. This is done with slow, concentrated might to ensure maximum muscle growth and avoid wrist injury. After twelve to fifteen reps release the thumb and allow the bar to roll down the length of the fingers and partially curl again for a pumping and burning four to six reps. This mean tag engages the complete hand, wrist and forearm mechanics. You're cryin'.

To superset this with a reverse wrist curl, grab the bar with a hands-over grip, similarly place the forearms on the thighs for stability and logically perform the isolated, reverse wrist curl. This is an awkward movement with little muscle mass to recruit. A light weight with focus will efficiently add to your wrist's balance and might.

EXERCISES BY THE TRUCKLOAD

We could go on and on. There are as many exercises as there are pounds in gravity. We covered the good ones and I expect you'll invent some of your own. Every exercise has a dozen or more hidden inside it, which you discover as you lean this way or that, modify your grip or alter your footing, stand or sit, arch, bend or extend your torso, straighten your arms a little or a lot. There's an angle and twist and range of motion for every need. Be curious; discover and uncover them, make them yours.

8

NUTRITION RULES

Good nutrition, like good training, is simple — learn the basics and practice them consistently. A little knowledge and a lot of discipline is the secret. Apply yourself diligently; look ahead, don't look back and don't look for shortcuts. There simply aren't any.

Health and fitness has climbed to the top of our popularity list and has become big business. As you've noticed, there's a gym on every corner and a glut of diet and bodybuilding formulas to pack on muscle and burn off fat.

Competition is fierce, the promises are bizarre and we're all confused, suspicious and eventually numb. We have on our hands a zillion ways to diet, feed ourselves and live our lives for fitness. Let's summarize the fundamental nutritional facts, manipulate them and determine an eating plan that is sensible, agreeable and appropriate for you. We'll do it together. Not a high-wire act under which there is no net, but an on-going, rewarding and healthy lunge forward.

First, let's clear the air and put a few things in order.

THE TWELVE RULES

RULE # 1 — Be tough. Stay away from nasty fats, excessive salt and simple sugars. This eliminates ninety-nine percent of the fast foods, munchies and soft drinks. Who needs them? In a few short weeks, you won't want them, wonder why you ate them and feel sick if you do! I don't mean to be rude, but ... junk is for jerks.

RULE # 2 — Eat a basic breakfast of complex carbohydrates, protein and fat to establish your metabolism for the day and provide fuel and muscle-sustaining ingredients. In a nutshell (and setting aside for now the hormonal and enzyme chemistry taking place at all times), protein builds muscle and carbohydrates and fat supply fuel for energy. Breakfast can be an easy-to-prepare meal from a quality protein shake to a bowl of oatmeal, scoop of cottage cheese and fruit. A gulp of flaxseed oil (or a couple of tablespoons in your protein drink) works extremely well to set up your day's efforts. If you don't feed yourself a wholesome meal in the morning, your body will draw on your muscle stores as a source of energy, putting you in a slump and muscle deficit. Major insurance policy: Add a good vitamin and mineral formula and a gulp of flaxseed oil each morning to put order and efficiency in your body chemistry.

RULE # 3 — This one can be the rascal — with whatever effort it takes, feed yourself every three to four hours throughout the day; again, each meal consisting of protein, fat and carbohydrate. Any combination of the following is perfect: tuna and brown rice, hamburger patty and red potato, cottage cheese and fruit, chicken and salad, etc. You'll notice that sandwiches are not in my top-five list. Discover TupperWare™ and packet-size meal replacement powders.

RULE # 4 — Newsflash: To gain weight, eat more. Assuming you're hitting the weights, be prepared for solid bulk weight; lean muscle mass exclusively is a daydream. To lose weight, eat less, still as often. Don't starve the muscle.

RULE # 5 — I have always instinctively leaned toward a higher intake of protein over carbohydrate to build a lean body. Emphasize protein. Vegetarians, take particular care in order to get plenty of protein in your diet.

RULE # 6 — Between-meal snacking for the trainee looking to gain weight is okay if the snack is truly nutritious — no junk. Don't let snacks be a substitute for a complete meal or become a weak habit. You who are seeking weight loss, consider snacking counter-productive.

Good snacks are fruits or vegetables, jerky, protein energy bars, yogurt, cottage cheese and light protein drinks.

RULE # 7 — Simple carbohydrates (sugar, honey, soft drinks, candy and cakes) provide us with a quick pick-up but let us down just as quickly. Excessive sugar plays havoc with our insulin metabolism and leads to fatigue, poor performance and fat storage. Not good.

RULE # 8 — Fuel up before your workout. Eat a small, easily digested meal about an hour before you train (also a good time to stock your creatine stores). With protein and complex carbohydrates in your system, you'll train harder, longer and with more enthusiasm. You won't experience low blood sugar jitters or dizziness; you'll get a great pump and probably hit that last rep.

RULE # 9 — Similarly, you need to eat a hearty protein meal with plenty of carbs within forty-five minutes of completion of your workout. This is necessary to provide the muscle-building materials to repair depleted tissue and begin the process of building new muscle. Big Tip — whey protein drinks work great here, as well as for pre-workout fuel. Again, restore creatine levels.

RULE #10 — The most important ingredient in your body is plain water. The quality of your tissues, their performance and their resistance to failure is absolutely dependent on the quality and quantity of the water you drink. Flood yourself throughout the day, especially during the workout.

RULE #11 — Sleep, rest and relaxation are of prime importance. It's during periods of sound sleep that our bodies recuperate and build muscle tissue.

RULE #12 — Regard the twelve rules listed and the underlying premise of the chapter (to build muscle and lose fat) as a regular life-long, life-rewarding priority, one that hones discipline and is honed by that same discipline. I dare to say that only a fool regards them as less. Delight in the journey, day by day, for good.

Logical, easy to understand and time-tested, these basic precepts and their observation are not a disciplinary nightmare and do not lead to depression and withdrawal. Pause for a moment: Think clearly. You have not taken on a project like cleaning out the garage or improving your golf swing. You have undertaken the life-long process of fitness, building and maintaining vital muscle, losing burdensome fat. Does this overwhelm and dishearten you? I understand. What disheartens me is the dismal alternative.

The task is easy, a daily practice without beating yourself, expecting perfection or scrutinizing the subject. Discounting laziness, lack of ambition, irresponsibility and other similar disabilities, only one enemy stands in your way: doubt, the devil's deception, also knows as negativity, misperception and poor attitude. Persistent, positive performance, confrontation and contempt the enemy cannot withstand. He will fall and fall hard. You might have heard me say this before: The fight is good, the fight is yours — fight the good fight.

The matter before us is neither a scientific dissertation for a research journal, nor is it five pounds of clay to be artistically molded into a decorative vase. Nutrition and food balancing is best understood when discussed in terms of a few facts and figures. Let's make a short list and go from there.

Whole foods provide the ingredients we need to sustain a healthy life. Very generally, they are categorized according to their structure to be proteins, carbohydrates and fats. Further, proteins, composed of smaller units called amino acids, intricately build the body. Carbohydrates provide most of the initial fuel for its activity and fats fuel the body and reside within the body's structure to complement its well-being. Unfortunately, sixty percent of the people of affluent nations store fat in great excess and suffer the diseases attributed to being overweight.

These macronutrients, marvelously complex and interdependent, are joined by micronutrients (vitamins, minerals, trace minerals, antioxidants) to facilitate the chemistry of the body.

All macronutrients have additional value determined according to their ability to supply fuel to the body as if it were a furnace. This is called its caloric value or food value, something like log-size to a fire. A calorie is a unit of heat energy (you know, the log).

Here are a few gems of reference to guide us:

1 gram of carbohydrate = 4 k-calories (a.k.a. calories)
1 gram of protein=4 calories
1 gram of fat=9 calories

One pound of fat contains 3,500 calories. Drop 500 calories a day from your minimum daily requirement over a one-week period and you lose one pound of fat … maybe.

One pound of muscle equals 600 calories but takes as much as four times that in energy to synthesize the tissue.

Metabolism is the ability of the body to convert ingested food into macronutrients and micronutrients — the chemical and physical process the builds, maintains and energizes our bodies. Factors of metabolism are complex and highly individualized. None of us are the same; we each require different diets just as we require different exercise.

Metabolic rate refers to the number of calories we need or burn each day to sustain our bodies. Basal metabolic rate (BMR) is a calculation of calories needed just to maintain the body at rest, an idling engine — our resting energy expenditure.

Our metabolic rate climbs as we increase activity — by, say, thirty percent if we engage in light work and chores, doubling if we blast and bomb away. Busy people have higher metabolism. Sedentary people have lower metabolism. Brilliant.

It's been observed that the body requires more calories to support muscle tissue than fat tissue. The more muscle mass you have the more calories you burn to maintain it. Good for the big eater tending toward a lean, muscular build. Conversely, the less muscle you have, less of the calories you consume are burned to support the body and more are stored as fat. I have some muscular and fit friends for whom required eating is hard work just to sustain mass. Go figure. Perhaps the latter need more fat calories from essential fatty acids (EFAs) to provide more fire for the furnace.

Aha — Essential Fatty Acids. Some of the most important ingredients for our health, which we almost refuse to recognize because they are fats, had slipped my view until only recently. Did you know that EFAs cannot be manufactured by the body and therefore must be gained through our diet? Failure to ingest enough EFAs contributes to hardening of the arteries, abnormal blood clot formation, coronary heart disease, high cholesterol and high blood pressure. EFAs are poly and super-poly unsaturated fats and are utilized in rebuilding cells and producing new cell membranes. Almost incidentally, they can improve skin and hair health and appearance.

Two basic categories of EFAs are Omega-3 and Omega-6. Omega-3s are found in deep-water fish, fish oil and certain vegetable oils (like canola and flaxseed). These oils must be consumed in pure liquid or supplement form. Omega-6 oils are found in raw nuts, seeds, legumes, sesame and soybean oil. Extra care must be taken in their handling and storage, as even low heat will destroy the essential fatty acids.

What this means to you is that if you don't regularly eat saltwater fish and nuts and seeds, you'll do better physically by supplementing with these oils. The flaxseed oils need to be refrigerated; regular grocery stores or inferior health food stores either won't carry them, or, perhaps, won't handle them properly.

I supplement with three to four tablespoons of mixed Omega oils a day and I'm able to maintain my bodyweight and energy with less carbohydrate overload. My joints feel better and my cardiovascular system has improved over recent years, as has the health of my digestive system.

Getting to the point of it all, these are the most common loose ends of facts and terms we need to know, along with some common sense, to arrange our initial, most ordinary menu. The fact remains, to gain weight (muscle, if you please — thanks) we need to increase the intake of our most important calories; we must eat more calories than we burn. To lose weight (goodbye, fat) we need to decrease the intake of our least important calories; we must eat less calories than we burn. Cutting edge stuff.

Okay, you're with me, I see. It's been intelligently estimated by Lyle McDonald (author of the fascinating book The Ketogenic Diet listed in the resource appendix) that the average person burns somewhere in the vicinity of fifteen calories per pound each day. This, of course, varies depending upon body composition, gender, activity, environment, stress and more, but we need a starting place.

Formula Example: I weigh two hundred and twenty-five pounds. 225 multiplied by 15 calories equals 3,375 calories required each day to maintain my bodyweight and activity. Providing my activity remains the same, I must eat an intelligent proportion of either more or less calories per day to achieve a safe and efficient weight gain or weight loss.

Question: What should these calories consist of and where should they come from?

Here's where the manipulating comes in. Here's where the differences of chemistry, workload, goals, life-style and personal preferences come into play. You new at this? Apply the balance of macronutrients put forth below, a good place to begin your disciplines and applications with confidence and pleasure. The percentages are simple and direct you to include more protein, I'm guessing, than you're accustomed to ingesting. It's about time. Help is on the way. The process of tweaking these combinations to suit your system and program becomes clearer day by day.

Protein=40% of daily intake
Carbohydrate=30% of daily intake
Fat=30% of daily intake

Note: a smart practice is to weigh yourself in the morning before breakfast, unclothed and after elimination to establish an accurate bodyweight reference. Use the same scale always and don't become a slave to the gadget; you are flesh and blood, after all, not a number. Twice a week when you get the urge is sufficient for this event.

Hello. You're ready for steps one, two and three in your quest to gain muscle and lose fat.

Step 1: Preparation. The difficult, often procrastinated step of commitment has already been taken. Take time to fix your decision in place as you astutely and diligently apply The Twelve Rules. Be generous with yourself and allow time to learn and re-learn, practice and adjust. Put your arm around your shoulders and be a good companion. You need all the help you can get and there's no better place to start than home. Get comfortable.

Let no part of the endeavor to gain muscle and lose fat threaten or overwhelm you. Need I remind you it's a step-by-step, one day at a time process where every step forward should be appreciated and recognized as successful? Together the steps, many of which appear to be backwards, define the distance between you and the ordinary. Self-assessment is inevitable and mistakes will happen. Be intelligent and beware. Don't fall victim to guilt. Like the grim reaper it will stop you in your tracks. Be happy.

Step 2: The Calculation. Apply the caloric formula outlined to determine your approximate daily calorie consumption.

Weight x 15 calories of average expenditure
per pound of bodyweight equals:
Total calories per day

Calculate your protein, carb and fat proportions according to the basic guide above. Chose the foods you want to eat according to their caloric and macronutrient values, an easy trick with which you may have years of practice. A simple calorie-converter found at any market checkout counter is invaluable in these calculations.

Step 3: Application. Once familiar with the ground upon which you stand, lock your plan in place. Add five-hundred calories per day to gain a sensible pound of mass a week. Subtract five-hundred calories per day to lose a pound a week. Note the simple calculations on a notepad or, better yet, in a logbook.

You're looking at nutrient percentages commonly known as 40/30/30, or fifty grams of protein, thirty-seven grams of carbohydrate and seventeen grams of fat, more or less food per day to make up this relatively easy five-hundred calories.

The subsequent steps to take consist of the ongoing practice and continued training that provides fulfillment and leads you to your ultimate goal. This is old information to many of you and its application has recorded triumph. Time and trial, scrutiny and curiosity guide us to variations in our initial percentages. Our individuality requires that we alter our carbs, protein and fat intake to meet our different needs. Still, as in exercise, some will insist their way is "the" way. The arguments, the charlatans and cults are preposterous and boring. Listen to yourself, ultimately. Trust yourself in both exercise and nutrition, as soon as possible. You the man. You the woman.

Where does failure originate? What is the chief cause of frustration due to a stall in progress? Straying from the course you set out to follow. Simple as that, partner. You mistakenly, carelessly or weakly widened your margins. You missed your workouts or neglected your meal plan. Re-focus. It's okay. Get back on track. You learn and improve. Keep going. Don't look back. The dust has already settled. Move on with renewed vigor, Godly creature.

ZigZag in both training and menu is a popular practice, once you are invested and stable in each area. Briefly, as applied to training it is the method of training systematically to extreme overload in sets, reps and weight for three weeks and pulling back for an equal number of weeks to a moderate training level where form and pace rule and restoration is nurtured. The variation between blasting and cultivating is well received mentally and physically. Freedom reigns in the spirit of the bodybuilder. The same approach can be practiced in your diet plan as a bodybuilder looking for muscle mass and no fat. Closely follow your maintenance food intake for five or six days (estimate by trial) and power-up on the sixth and seventh days to pump the restoration process and provide energy for some mighty and loaded workouts. Follow the zigzag regularly and record the procedure and the results. This is not a scheme to allow for a cheat day as if you needed one. Fact is, cheating is for weaklings and "weak" is a characteristic we aim to eliminate. You with me?

Me? I slam down the animal protein and in doing so am not short on fat consumption. My carbohydrate intake is considered low. I eat no processed sugar, few processed carbs (the occasional pasta side dish), little starch (small microwaved red potatoes), lots of salad and green vegetables. Protein drinks of milk, whey, banana and eggs fuel my system before and after workouts and throughout my heavy daily demands.

The other factor to consider carefully when losing or gaining weight is your training output and the style and combinations you apply; that is, aerobics (what and how hard, how often and how long) and weight training (style, frequency and intensity).

THE DRAPER MENU

I have a life, thank you. Listed below is an outline of my daily menu. It is designed to service my needs: aggressive weight training to maintain or gain muscle mass through my perception of the off-season (October-April). I'll repeat here for calculation purposes: I'm a fifty-eight-year-old male, six feet tall, two hundred and twenty-five pounds, bodyfat under ten percent, weightlifting five days a week consisting of about two hours per workout.

Meal proportions may vary to control target accuracy. Sources of protein, fats and carbs vary only slightly. I am well fed and denied of nothing. Cheat days — ha! — are defined by my eating a bran muffin or a meal replacement bar. Fact is, I enjoy the order and rigidity of my diet — It brings me peace. No regimen, I feel sloppy and careless, guessing and out of control.

Discipline to me is as flight to an eagle; a prize to the champion before the race has begun, a dark-toned and heavily-textured straight line through the wilds and across the peaks and dunes. Discipline — It's yours if you want it or need it. Help yourself.

BOMBER DAILY MENU

Morning supplements:
Super Spectrim vitamin/minerals, vitamin C, creatine, MSM, glucosamine, EFA oil

Meal 1

Pre-workout — Whey protein drink (2 scoops Bomber Blend, 16 ounces low-fat milk, 2 eggs, small banana, tablespoon peanut butter)
1,191 calories (131 g protein, 79 g carbs, 38 g fat)

1 piece of toast (whole wheat)
70 calories (2 g protein, 13 g carbs, 1 g fat)

Meal 1 total:
1,261 calories (133 g protein, 92 g carbs, 39 g fat)

Pre-workout Ripped Force drink
90 calories (0 g protein, 23 g carbs, 0 fat)

Meal 2

Protein drink (2 scoops Bomber Blend, 16 ounces low-fat milk, 2 eggs, small banana, tablespoon peanut butter)
1,191 calories (131 g protein, 79 g carbs, 39 g fat)

Meal 2 total:
1,191 calories (131 g protein, 79 g carbs, 39 g fat)

Meal 3

Post workout — Large hamburger patty,
579 calories (66 g protein, 0 g carbs, 35 g fat)

2 micro-waved red potatoes
290 calories (6 g protein, 68 g carbs, 0 g fat)

Meal 3 total:
869 calories (72 g protein, 68 g carbs, 35 g fat)

Meal 4

Post workout — Large hamburger patty
579 calories (66 g protein, 0 g carbs, 35 g fat)

2 micro-waved red potatoes
290 calories (6 g protein, 68 g carbs, 0 g fat)

Meal 4 total:
869 calories (72g protein, 68 g carbs, 35 g fat)

Late-afternoon snack

2 pieces beef jerky
162 calories (13 g protein, 4 g carbs, 10 g fat)

Late-afternoon snack total:
162 calories (13 g protein, 4 g carbs, 10 g fat)

Meal 5

Low-fat milk
137 calories (10 g protein, 14 g carbs, 5 g fat)

Turkey breast meat
188 calories (38 g protein, 0 g carbs, 2 g fat)

Pasta, 6 ounces
222 calories (9 g protein, 39 g carbs, 3 g fat)

Vegetable
20 calories (1 g protein 3 g carbs, 0 g fat)

Cut vegetable salad
50 calories (3 g protein, 14 g carbs, 0 g fat)

Meal 5 total:
617 calories (61 g protein, 70 g carbs, 10 g fat)

Meal 6
Can of tuna
100 calories (22 g protein, 0 g carbs, 1 g fat)

Cottage cheese
50 calories (8 g protein, 2 g carbs, 1 g fat)

Meal 6 total:
150 calories (30 g protein, 2 g carbs, 2 g fat)

Evening supplements:
Super Spectrim aminos and vitamin/minerals, C, creatine, MSM, glucosamine, tablespoon Metamucil™ fiber

Meal 7
Can of tuna
100 calories (22 g protein, 0 g carbs, 1 g fat)

Cottage cheese
50 calories (8 g protein, 2 g carbs, 1 g fat)

Meal 7 total:
150 calories (30 g protein, 2 g carbs, 2 g fat)

Total consumption for an average day:
5,356 calories (542 g protein, 480 g carbs, 137 g fat)

Approximate average daily nutrient percentages:
40% protein, 35% carbs, 25% fat

A review of this menu may cause you to gag or give you the shivers. Or you may ask, "Where's the pork?" Good question. I get to it eventually: lamb and buffalo, as well. It's interesting to note that this same outline could have been written thirty years ago, or in 1980 or 1990. Not much has changed. Me? I'm just older and leaner and bear a few more dings. Of course, for all of this I thank God.

IT'S TUNA AND WATER TIME

Think hard. I have three big questions for you:

You want to lose some bodyfat and keep the muscle, maybe gain some while you're at it? How's your resolve? Are you fed up?

The following technique is one I've strongly wanted to suggest in the past but hesitated because it's hardcore and doesn't follow the rules. Athletes — bodybuilders in particular — practice this protein exclusive principle to muscularize before competition. You are going to eat tuna and water for three days. Only the strong shall survive.

Psyche up. Starting Monday you will be consuming water by the jugs — sixty to a hundred or more ounces a day — and one to one and a half grams of protein per pound of bodyweight in six equal servings throughout the day. Back this with your vitamins and minerals two times a day, branch chain amino acids before and after your workouts and a nightly portion of Metamucil™ for fiber.

Forget what you want, what you feel like, what you read. You are in the trenches on the front lines where you will make the difference. Your energy may dip before it rises but your body chemistry will soon adapt. Be strong.

Amazing. We fret and agonize over our excessive bodyweight. We have for months or, more realistically, years. We gobble down all the colorful diets printed in bold captions on the magazines at the checkout counter. Asked to do The Big One and we fold. Almost. As needed, grumble to yourself but master your attitude. This harsh jumpstart never fails to kick in the metabolism and set the weight tumbling.

Later in the week bring in chicken, low-fat cottage cheese and salad or your favorite steamed vegetable to fortify your menu without expanding it significantly. You're feeding the muscle. Here's a delightful bedtime snack ... tuna outta the can, scoop of cottage cheese and cool, clear water ... Combine this with some nocturnally released growth hormone and ... presto.

Exercise with moderate weights for clean reps to accommodate a temporary low-calorie strength loss. Press on as the body adapts and you become familiar and confident. This is a stiff practice to test your resolve, investigate your chemistry, break some troublesome habits and narrow ever-widening margins. It will bring you to the doorstep of the ketogenic diet where protein intake, exclusive of carbs, creates a ketone burning system for energy. Remember, certain amino acids combine to form glucose for energy as well.

FOOD SUPPLEMENTATION

Here many of us come to a crossroads. The gathering signposts of information point in both directions. Yes, supplements work — No, they don't. Put the burdensome information aside and listen to your logic and instincts. Foods are highly processed, soils are depleted, hybrids propose new dangers, chemicals associated with growing, storing, coloring, cleaning damage produce purity, toxins in the environment demand greater body resistance than we can provide by natural micronutrient ingestion and we may very well need bushels of this vegetable and baskets of that fruit to supply our real daily vitamin and mineral micronutrient needs.

How can the body do well without them? At least take a good vitamin and mineral and a whey protein powder, forever and with confidence. They work hard for you and should be regarded as an essential part of your food budget. Here's what you can expect: increased muscle growth and strength, decreased bodyfat, extended endurance, more energy, improved muscular recovery, resistance to injury and illness, and enhanced metabolism.

I've done a lot of examining, experimenting and comparing with my peers over the years both in training and nutrition. You learn to glean through the heap and separate the trash from the good stuff.

A top-quality vitamin/mineral will dial in your body chemistry and aid in muscle growth, recuperation and resistance. Your protein drinks serve the protein and nutrients you need during your busy, hard-pressed days; they are inexpensive meals if prudently mixed with low-fat milk, a banana and ice. (Eggs are optional. I use raw eggs and have for thirty years — Laree made me take 'em off my recommendation as they may carry salmonella bacteria and we don't want you to get sick following my advice after all.) Again, protein drinks are quick, convenient fortifiers that lift you up, take you forward or, at the very least, keep you from sliding back. I count these as part of my food intake and don't shortchange myself by viewing them as costly supplements for the rich and famous.

WHEY PROTEIN

Like proud and impetuous peacocks the mating fields of marketing are dense with colorful protein powders and exotic meal-replacement formulas; each, of course, struts and fans his feathers in an embarrassing display. Whey protein from milk has been underlined as the best and casein has been relegated to a less important position on the scale.

Marketing and product sales — the buck — have brought about this exaggerated commentary. Truth is, both whey and casein are excellent and provide complementary biological value. Because of molecular structure, whey protein is more rapidly absorbed (catabolic), yet is often lost to energy provision. Casein on the other hand is more slowly absorbed and offers a long-term amino synthesis (anti-catabolic).

A recent statement by Bryan Haycock writing for ThinkMuscle.com on protein supplements and sources sums it up. "Both whey protein and casein provide beneficial effects. They're absorbed at different rates and elicit different metabolic responses. In reality they complement each other and should be consumed together for maximum benefit." He goes on to say in response to extensive legitimate research that "soy protein offers little benefits for bodybuilders. Also, the amino acid pattern in soy is inferior to that of milk proteins and not as favorable for promoting growth." Echoes of the primitive bylaws called forth in the sunshine of Muscle Beach.

Ah, the sweetness of truth. Significant research by, er, unbiased government science clearly points to whey as the most efficacious source of protein. If properly treated, it has what we want: all the essential and non-essential amino acids, it's highest in the branch chain amino acids (BCAAs) plus glutamine found in nature and necessarily low in sodium for maximum protein uptake.

Another recent study by a medical force devoted to catabolic trauma patients requiring fast protein absorption proves that failing immune systems are significantly boosted by low molecular-weight whey peptides. AIDS patients, burn victims and bodybuilders like us whose immune systems are compromised by physical overload will benefit from the whey proteins now being produced by the seventh-generation high-tech treatment.

Whey protein when consumed appropriately releases CCK, an appetite-suppressing hormone — great for the overeater.

Whey protein has a low glycemic index, which optimizes insulin production thus minimizing glucogon production. More simply put, it helps us to burn fat while it lowers cholesterol.

Whey contains quadra-peptides, opioids, which produce natural pain-killing activity. Sounds good to me!

Finally, whey protein is handy. Protein drinks make up two of my daily meals both for whey protein value and for convenience.

CREATINE

I've used creatine regularly for several years since it first came on the market as an athletic supplement. Having observed no adverse side effects, I simply enjoy the benefits — maximum muscle contraction, the strength boost translating into hard, efficient workouts, and the resulting vitality and muscle pump throughout the workout.

Creatine monohydrate is an amino acid derivative responsible in the production of adenosine triphosate (ATP) in the body's energy cycle. ATP is the spark plug of cellular energy that enables us to contract our muscles for the initial ten to twelve seconds of intense muscular performance. The efficiency of this energy is observed in short-term explosive movements: sprinting, weightlifting, martial arts.

We bodybuilders engaging in sets of eight to twelve reps benefit greatly by increasing our ever-diminishing stores of creatine by quality supplementation. Red meat is the primary source of this ingredient and unless you are a large consumer, chances are your reservoirs are low.

Creatine's enhanced short-term energy is reflected in increased and enduring strength, maximum pump, the resultant heightened training spirit and performance, and ultimately muscular growth. Bingo.

Research supports drinking lots of water when using creatine. Load as suggested (a teaspoon three times a day for four or five days is a simple loading dock). Powder over caps is preferred and to ensure its full benefit mix creatine in a glass of warm water. Avoid drinking caffeine directly with the creatine as it causes the body to surrender water. The efficiency of creatine depends on the high content of water and cell volumizing — that tight and firm feeling. Many suggest grape juice with its high sugar content to transport the creatine into the tissues more quickly — Give it a shot to see what you think. It's legit.

HORMONES: PRO AND CON

I don't presume to know anything comprehensive about hormones, a subject which can be compared to the cosmos in its complexity and dimension. Hormones are chemicals responsible for mankind's unique and defining male and female characteristics at the cellular level. Their effects are evident in our emotional and physiological structure as well. They are numerous and inter-related, traveling throughout our bodies at the command of our endocrine and pituitary glands; they are stimulated by workload and rest, supported by the intake of naturally occurring and artificially made ingredients, and diminish and alter with age and debilitating disease.

Prohormones are hormone precursors that show evidence of improving testosterone output in both aging male and female users. These substances invaded the muscle and strength building market at the end of the '90s and have caused an annoying stir amongst the steroid fringe of bodybuilders and the pirates. Alas, bucks and butts are big when it comes to building muscle. Hopeful scientific bodybuilders are stacking DHEA, androstene, androstenediols with norandrostenediones in their gorilla concoctions and attacking the gyms with new fury. Partly for this reason, many expect the commercial prohormones to become unavailable to legal purchasers in the not-too-distant future.

I've observed intelligent discussion amongst scientific experts, medical doctors prescribing the substances and legitimate users with credentials. The exchanges at best become an egg-tossing contest in which one may better serve his muscular growth by eating the eggs than assimilating the arguments. A doctor with whom I trust my life proclaimed prohormones as valid substances, which he prescribes with careful follow-up. They are as complex as your hormonal system and can cause it to shut down completely if administered carelessly. His admonishment: Proceed with caution.

We're getting older and smarter. One would only hope we are getting better. Science, by popular demand, is engaged in the pursuit of a longer and improved life for mankind. This has us poking around in the hormone warehouse with particular interest in testosterone, human growth hormone, DHEA and cellular synthesis. Female, and more recently, male hormone replacement therapy (HRT) has become en vogue in this brand new century as pharmaceutical companies are unveiling their topical testosterone preparations in the form of pills, patches and gels. Are you on the slippery slope and observing some loss of footing? You may find help from your family physician.

The field is young, fertile, budding (I'm an old farmhand) and promises good fruit. Every change in the natural course of events has a trade-off, however, and we need to be vigilant and prepared. A friend of mine suggested that the best way to stimulate human growth hormone (HGH) and testosterone is to do three extra sets of heavy squats, deadlifts and presses each week. I'm all for that. Some folks would rather change their oil.

GETTING A BITE ON NUTRITION

Where do you stand? Big pounds? Big changes? Are you dumbfounded? Will moderate alterations suffice? Are you right on, or freaked out?

Whatever you do, I suggest two steps immediately: one, start today, and two, don't hesitate.

Another viable step is to jot down everything you eat during an average day and evaluate it according to the information recorded here. Plan a little trimming and some minor exchanges, logical and non-threatening. When the mood is right in the next forty-five minutes, review yourself with an affectionate eye and determine a general direction — like left or right, up or down, this way, or that ... some direction. Write it down in twenty-five words or less. Go back to steps one and two. You're doing fine.

I swear by nothing. I guarantee nothing; yet, the tuna and water diet is not as fishy as it sounds. Go back a few pages if you haven't already ripped them out. Reconsider the uncomplicated and simple approach to attending a shapeless and uncontrolled menu. Begin at the beginning. It's a wholesome step above an all-out fast that will put you on track, clean the slate, start from scratch and put the past behind you. Clean out the fridge and closets if "they'll" let you; it's for them, too.

Can you do this? Can you whistle? Start whistling. This tuna and water thing works.

Wearing my Super Spectrim tank top as Laree clicked away one hard-working Sunday afternoon in the late1980s. Dr. Carlon Venus and Dr. Anthony Pescetti prepared a fine time-release formula in 1978 and I've been taking it ever since.

9

OVERCOMING

My fingers don't float over the laptop with the greatest of ease. Eventually, they find the keys as if they were lost and manage to depress two or three at once. I mutter and tap, delete, backspace and tap, mutter, tap. We're moving right along.

Thus far, if you started at the beginning, you've read of the early days, Muscle Beach, my emergence as a bodybuilder, the training styles I embrace and the exercises I do: how, why and when. Nutrition and its role were outlined and hopefully caused you to consider how, when, what, why and how much to eat. A variety of obscure peeves were addressed and lesser-recognized attributes applauded. What's left?

How about the daily obstacles that detract from the joy of lifting? Let's scrape together a heap of the most unpopular and revolting stumbling blocks we can recall and give them a toss. The pungent pile should sufficiently beat us up and make us stronger.

Overtraining
Plateaus and Sticking Points
Genetics
Discouragement and Lack of Motivation
Negative Conditions
Nausea After a Workout
Packed City

Abandoned Workout Routines

I Ain't Got No Time and I Ain't Got Nobody

Changes

Pain and Injury

Rotator Cuff — The Most Common Injury

Injury Rehabilitation

Steroids

Aging

Smoking

Slumps and Seasons

Training Partners and My Dog, Spot

Training On and On

OVERTRAINING

As we move along in our training and vigorously apply the six basic keys (if you forgot 'em, see page 33), we need to be aware of the various bodybuilding snags and pitfalls. At any and every level of training our deadliest and most subtle enemy is overtraining. After an initial surge, muscular gains come slowly at best and only from a lot of hard work. We therefore conclude that the harder we work, the greater our growth. This faulty "more is better" logic will surely lead us to a discouraging deadend. In our eagerness to build muscle, we exceed our beginning training limitations and tear down more muscle tissue that the body is able to repair.

The major symptoms of overtraining are chronic fatigue, insomnia, loss of appetite, proneness to injury and illness and the inability to achieve a pump. You may think you have the flu as muscles ache, bodyweight and strength drop and you have a nagging loss of interest in your training.

If any of these symptoms of overtraining heap up on you, ease off your training immediately and take time out to re-evaluate yourself and your workouts. Recovery from overtraining is often brought about by decreasing your training levels, either the number of workouts, number of exercises or number of sets.

This may be a good time to be creative. Try something new or alter your training to reactivate your interest. Check out your diet. Make sure you're getting plenty of muscle-building protein and carbohydrate before and after your workouts. The body feeds off its own tissue as an energy source if not adequately supplied by food intake. It's vital to keep your attitude up and seek encouragement from partners and friends. This healthy sharing and introspection furthers your learning experience and overall awareness.

You may wisely choose to take a layoff entirely, giving the body a chance to recuperate and your mind the needed time away from the gym. You'll come back after the rest days mentally and physically refreshed and with renewed enthusiasm.

The information and advice given above is standard: concise, clean and safe. I feel like Percival the Nobleman. You may all go about your busy business and build concise, clean and safe muscles. I must admit that I have generally overtrained in adherence to my obstinate theory that hypertrophy must be an insistent process. Slam the workouts, eat big and in smart balance, rest as you must equals The Draper Formula (a.k.a. The Bomber Formula).

Slam means slam: sets and reps and numerous movements in volume with heavy doubles and triples on the systemic movements two or three times a month. No misses, no layoffs, the head and body hard at work. I'm not saying it works. I'm not telling you to try it. It's what I do.

There's a term, "periodization," we talked about earlier attached to a method of training that I've always practiced, undoubtedly one of the most common training methods employed by bodybuilders and attributable to their common sense. Simply (minus all the technical garbage), periodization means training for a given goal over an extended period of time with appropriate changes in sets, reps, exercises and phases. Such an approach intelligently and comprehensively works the different muscles in differing ways to satisfy their respective and varying growth components without overtraining or overloading: maximum efficiency accomplished. I believe I apply the principles of ... ahem ... periodization to the max, accidentally.

PLATEAUS & STICKING POINTS

Closely tied to overtraining is the puzzle of sticking points or plateaus. Gains come fast at first. The sport is new, hopes are high and there's victory in achieving your goals. Increase in muscle size, strength and tone are evident. Now we come to the hard part: As growth begins to normalize, progress slows down to what seems like a screeching halt. Here time groans by and the less serious lifters are taken to the mat.

Be confident that providing you're vigorously applying the basics, improvement is always taking place. It's here where the qualities of discipline, perseverance, determination and patience are developed and are called upon. And here is where real growth takes place in your soul and in your physical self.

Chances are you've become anxious, too close to yourself and far too critical. Changes in muscle density and skin tone are very subtle and often appear only after you become weary of examining yourself. Have faith and press on. Don't submit to a child's disappointment and don't give up the front line trenches.

Bodybuilding curiously parallels all of life itself. Each one of us faces these periods of struggle and stagnation and it's from them that we learn and grow.

The plateaus, the sticking points: Where do they come from? What causes them? Why do they happen? They are an eventual part of the process of adaptation to muscle resistance. They are overcome by progressive resistance training (overload) achieved by persistent, systematic rep-per-set, weight-per-rep incrementing. That is, over a given period of time one increases the repetitions of a set of an exercise of a given weight by one rep each workout to complete a sensible preplanned, rep-and-set scheme. Explanations get complicated so I'll lay it out for you. It works. It's as old as Muscle Beach, as simple and as original.

Let's use the popular classic bench press for a cycle of eight weeks using the rep-per-set system. Start on Workout One with a weight you can handle comfortably and regularly for four sets of eight repetitions. This can be based on a percentage of your one rep maximum — that is, approximately sixty percent of the maximum with which you can perform the exercise for one rep. You're the boss. This routine can usually be practiced two times per week successfully. Break out your log and prepare to make notes.

> Workout One - 4 sets x 8 repetitions
> Workout Two - 3 x 8 and 1 x 9
> Workout Three - 2 x 8 and 2 x 9
> Workout Four - 1 x 8 and 3 x 9
> Workout Five - 4 x 9

Having fun? Continue this progression until Workout Nine when you complete four sets of ten repetitions. At this point, the battle is on and you're a month into the fight. Go for another month as you pursue (seek, chase after, beg for, worship or decry) 4x12. Another popular option: increase your base weight by the smallest increment possible, two two-and-a-half-pound plates for a total of five pounds, two one-and-a-quarter pound discs for a two-and-a-half-pound increase, or less if you have washer plates or magnets, and continue on your merry way.

This scheme is for the hardcore slammer or for anyone with goals and a will. It'll aggressively attack the plateau, beef up the discipline, expose the weaknesses and afford an experience of learning you will use again and again. The system secures stable and persistent training as we continuously reach for and enjoy the successes. The order we need in ourselves and our training begins to form with the prescribed routine. Our muscles grow to meet the demands and a confidence, a certainty, fills our hollows.

Waving flag: Don't become bogged down with this method or your workouts will falter. They'll become unyielding, pre-packaged and bland, robotic and sterile.

GENETICS

There are ruling differences in all of us determining our body-building potential, based on a long list of variables: need, attitude, knowledge and understanding, discipline, spirit, confidence, support, time, money and application. Add your own variables. These factors woven together are ultimately limited by genetics. DNA maps out bone structure, muscle shape, maximum muscle size, relevant fat proportion and deposition, muscularity and vascularity.

As we apply ourselves to the principles we perceive as best for us, correcting and re-correcting through trial, error and adaptation, we grow and learn. Never too soon, never enough. As we approach our genetic limits, our progress slows down to halves of halves. Plateaus, frustration and doubt bite at our heels. Unless we recognize this as real, eventual and, well, sort of okay, we live in illusion. Don't get beat up in the fight, don't give up, don't turn and run, don't whine. To keep going takes hope, courage and inspiration.

We take our limitations (we all have them in vast supply, as I said, my most recent one being age), we take our structure, chemistry, brain and soul and continue to manipulate them, pushing and pulling, arranging them in their best possible balance. That's what you're doing right now, seeking answers. It's on-going. Digging around for another intelligent routine, dialing in the nutrition, gleaning through the facts and fiction. Talking, listening, feedback and encouragement. Whatever it takes to keep you going. Not always the exact way, yet another way, we all press on. Beauty and perfection exist in the process. Anything else is chaos.

DISCOURAGEMENT AND LACK OF MOTIVATION

Building muscle and losing fat is a tough job for anyone. It's especially hard for those no longer driven by youth and naïve expectations or for those who have for too long indulged themselves and substituted athletic playfulness entirely with the pursuit of career and family obligations. Men and women confront their plight and discover it's hard — near impossible — to process the fitness goal, engage the unwilling spirit, revive endurance and perseverance when each day every step reveals no apparent progress, no change significant enough, the accumulated extra pounds successfully concealing the long un-stimulated muscles and any sign of improvement from view. How hard it is to keep going!

Photographer unknown

Cool but fuzzy shot of the Mr. Universe line up mingled with an assortment of rugged-looking contestants from around the world.

Sometimes I'm grouchy in the morning and have a dim view of life. I'm best left chained up in the backyard to a big tree on those days. Ask anyone. At times during those glorious golden days of bodybuilding history I hated my early morning descent into The Dungeon, knowing it would be three grim hours before I'd see daylight again, month after month with no letup for years, force-feeding, experimenting, guesswork and an occasional nod of approval from another inmate. Significance amongst few. I dragged my torn, be-splintered body out of that smelly gym only to stuff it with two twelve-ounce cans of chunk tuna, a pint of low-fat cottage cheese, sixteen ounces of lean ground beef, a gallon of non-fat milk and six eggs, before I again squeezed myself through those dark, foreboding doors the following morning to do it all over again.

I loved the thought of it always — training, weightlifting, whatever it was — before I knew what it was. And I loved it while I less than loved it on a day-to-day basis, when it whooped me and I ached and who cared — an unconditional love that binds. There comes a time when, believe it or not, something happens, sort of suddenly in slow motion, like taking with intense care a photograph of the same unchanging scene, time after time, in black and white and one day you pause, review the prints before discarding them and notice a dash of color — a fine, pale mix of crimson and yellow and green: You appear, you materialize. You close your eyes long enough to open them and see a separation, a line, a distinct sweep, mound or roundness of toned muscle in a place you never before this day had seen, you're sure of it, and, can it be … a desirable absence of loose flesh in another? This is all it takes, all that is required.

Forty-five years and more than 15,000 workouts have been logged and still I approach my training with a vague apprehension. Workouts are tough, both physically and mentally. They're supposed to be tough. As is common with most bodybuilders, powerlifters and weightlifters, I expect a great deal of myself and find it hard to accept less than one-hundred percent (give or take a percent or two) on the gym floor.

This one-hundred-percent pressure on ourselves is good, providing it's applied with intelligence and tender-loving care. However, unrealistic demands and expectations can lead to pre-workout anxiety, reluctance to train and poor performance.

In my own training when I'm in a treacherous valley, it sometimes goes like this: First, I check out the territory. I consider the scheduled workout, its appeal and whether I'm bored, burnt or bothered. I pretend I can walk out anytime I please, though leaving is simply not an option. I scan the gym floor, my internal monologue consisting of brittle words of challenge, perseverance and courage.

Inevitably, I begin my workout with the midsection — crunches, leg raises and rope tucks. These movements work the abdominals and torso; they stretch and warm the entire body in addition to raising the heart rate and providing precious time to sort out the thoughts of the day. These actions clear the mind and provide harmony for the more concentrated weight training exercises. In this way I ease into my training, gauge my body's capacity for work, gain a sense of accomplishment and build up training momentum.

And it works. The mind is cleared, and the body's warm. I'm set in motion, and the blood is looking for places to go. No time to lose, I pick a favorite exercise, one that's fun and never fails. A sure thing quickens my pace, usually works a favored bodypart and is self-inspiring.

As momentum and assurance build, I relax and ease into a complete training program. Here I may agreeably abbreviate my routine by decreasing the number of sets and reps. I look to stimulate the body and gain a comfortable pump and burn. Subtle and less punishing, this workout is lighter and more enjoyable. It renews lagging interest in the gym.

NEGATIVE CONDITIONS

What is it that causes us to be down when, according to our mental diary, we should be up and aspiring?

There are a variety of subtle conditions we respond to, and any combination of them contributes to our state-of-being. To shed light on the dilemma, consider the following factors when you struggle with a slump:

• Nutritional menu — too fatty, too little protein, too much sugar, too many unusual foods that confuse the body chemistry, destroy energy and eventually retard muscle growth

• Level of training — excessive overload training, too long without sufficient layoff

• Low-grade body infection — flu, tooth disorder, minor food poisoning that causes nearly imperceptible body ache, congestion, minor headache and defeat

• Minor injury — diminishing total voluntary output

• Stress — subtle distractions that erode basic physical, emotional and spiritual structure

• Negativity —the attitude of submission in relation to the natural phenomenon of "being down" without an obvious explanation

Awareness of these insidious human weaknesses may provide the God-given strength to fight and overcome them.

NAUSEA AFTER A WORKOUT

Do you sometimes feel nauseous fifteen minutes after a workout? There are several possible reasons. Low blood sugar or hypoglycemia engenders discomfort, light-headedness and a tingling muscular slump. This is common and dangerous yet can be quickly treated by rest and the restoration of blood sugar — the immediate ingestion of protein and high glycemic carbs.

The state of being deconditioned accounts for our early submission to exercise overload resulting in rapid breathing, muscular fatigue and dizziness. An un-tuned system is incapable of attaining an optimum performance level and the accompanying endorphins that subdue pain and heighten well-being. Yet, we've seen this happen to elite Olympians when they thrust themselves into the outer orbits of performance.

The real culprits here are the metabolic wastes that pack the system resulting in nasty low blood pH and toxin overload. The body, like any energy-generating factory, produces prodigious amounts of toxins and must eliminate them entirely and efficiently — or fail.

The solutions may be easy. Hydrate — drink oceans of water, thirsty or not. Dilute and wash away the junk. Accept a fifteen-minute, post-workout low as your system detoxifies. Your discomfort is an indicator of a killer workout.

Restore and refuel your body with first-class protein and carbs. Then sit back and grow like an orchid amongst the briar.

PACKED CITY

You walk into the gym and it's packed. Gyms are like that; for no apparent reason an off time can be mobbed simply by coincidence of a secret holiday or your bad luck.

Scan the scene and without missing a beat, find an unused, inconspicuous spread of floor space and commence with your crunches and leg raises back-to-back. Give yourself this block of time to adjust to your presence, the pressure, the sights and sounds. It's going to be a good workout. Dig in and be tough until the abs and heart are satisfied, you're warm and the muscles are stretched. Your options should be clear at this point.

Stand, smile and nod where you please and must but don't engage in conversation — you're on a mission. Grab onto an appropriate projection and pull slowly and progressively from side to side to work a stretch and pump into your lats and prepare your wrists, grip and biceps for their forthcoming jobs. Your body continues to move as you continue to locate your space. There's a bench and there's a pair of dumbbells; you're in. A little light, but they'll work well for a switch in pace and focus.

You perform a set of flat bench presses for slower reps with a one to two second pause at the midway point to maximize exertion. With meticulous form you strive for ten reps instead of six to eight. Put one dumbbell under your bench and with the other smoothly continue on to a set of stiff-arm pullovers to complement the work of the newly accented dumbbell presses.

This A-1 combo will keep you busy and productive for fifteen minutes as you scope out your next square footage. How about the same bench but switching to a bent bar for standing curls coupled with lying triceps extensions? Here again, with supersetting actions and a small plate change between sets, you're progressively occupied for another fifteen minutes: focused reps, high and tight with curious variations on every other rep or so for play and learning and growing.

You're loose now, well-invested, assured and heightened. Don't lose stride, don't ever lose stride. What do you want to do? Chins and dips, leg extensions and curls, squats, one-arm dumbbell rows? Look, listen, locate and lock on.

ABANDONED WORKOUT ROUTINES

Unless a new routine feels just plain wrong or is undesirable for legitimate reasons, four weeks from my experience is the minimum input for a training commitment. It takes that long to determine the weights to be used, establish continuity and pace and recognize the workout's overall effects.

Laree practicing with heavy shadows to produce drama in the photograph.

Once fixed in place, practice and press on to understand the workout, to finesse, tweak and dial it in, to hammer it and mold it. This takes extensive time, six to eight weeks or more, with fair adjustments along the way.

Too often we abandon a good workout before it has fully served us, before we are fully saturated by it. Our eyes are diverted, looking elsewhere for another way before we have applied honest discipline by persisting, squeezing, taking the necessary one step back before taking the exotic two steps forward. Tough times. It's here that I suspect the mean sticking points are surpassed — overpowered — and maximum adaptation is achieved. This is the critical point of development.

I AIN'T GOT NO TIME AND I AIN'T GOT NOBODY

I'm bad. I'm quick to commend the attributes of an exercise lifestyle and condemn those who can't collect the three or four hours a week it takes to go to the gym and do the deed. Fact is, the gym is often across town, packed and there's no parking. Personal schedules, today in their complexity, rival those of an air traffic controller: no space, no time, near collisions daily and other undetermined variables. How well would I do were I not a gym owner planted in place each day?

Another obstacle with which I've never been faced is lack of support and understanding. What could it possibly be like not to have your partner absolutely adore your madness? One more rep, Babe. Protein, protein, protein.

Is it a lonely trip for you? Is there no way to persuade your mate to join you in your life-building pursuit, no way to inspire, to encourage, to inveigle? I'm sorry, I truly am, for them and for you. Don't give up, you mustn't. Your persistence, unless patronizing, domineering or otherwise negative, will surely strengthen you and tend to impress and gradually guide them. I've seen this happen and not in isolated relationships. The good exercise and eating habits reflect an inner might and clear-mindedness. Why compromise these enviable traits? And with what would they be replaced?

Will, humility and planning, without selfishness, allow you to lead through your training. Enhance your partner's life as you enhance your own. You're not alone, you're together.

Compromise builds strong worlds. Early morning training, lunchtime workouts, solid pace multi-set routines that fit in tight places, basic home workouts alternated with more complete gym workouts, aerobics and crunches at home and the weights (the Real Deal) at the gym, spirited nonstop training verses snail training. Saturday morning or Sunday afternoon at the gym and the worse TV night of the week. There's a way if you will.

About your home-based eating ... don't let go. Follow your scheme of protein, carbs and fats as talked about in these pages for health and life and forever. Just put on your plate whatever works. Be the gentle shepherd, not the innocent sheep.

CHANGES

Changes are a constant. They are a paradox, a seasoning, a sweetener and a bitter poison. They are a fact of life. Your training partner drops out of the picture, your job changes, your schedule changes, you move. The timing is never right and you're always caught off guard. This is when your training displays its noble head and the resilience you've acquired from its honing is put into affect. A pause to consider your forthcoming move is wise, but hesitation is time lost, a dark cloud in a clear blue sky. Disruption unchecked and submission to circumstances present vulnerability and erosion is quick to appear. Act now.

Outline on paper a routine that is entertaining, forgiving and mixed with your favorite movements. Meet your new training partner — yourself — in a new place, at a different time. You're alone with yourself, the best dang companion in town. Don't set up goals beyond the hearty completion of a program that stimulates the body and challenges the muscles like a bear hug around a good old friend. Fix yourself in place with an easy hand and encourage the environment to adjust and grow as you grow.

New town, new gym, Yellow Pages and calls, visits and trial passes, antennae and radar and prayer. Be prompt and determined but not desperate to find a new gym, a new refuge. Everything you ever wanted

Laree Draper

The good ole' boys at Joe Gold's gym in Venice, Calif., 1990. Brother Dave, Sandman Joe, Zabo Sunshine, Steely Eddie and Iron Lou.

might be down the street from your new digs. Bet they give you a key and a nifty training partner.

PAIN AND INJURY

Pain and injury, though not our chosen friends, serve us well as masterful teachers. We are bound to treat these miseries with ice and rest, and unless the case is of major proportions, as little training time off as possible. Through training, blood laden with life-giving oxygen and nutrients will flood the damaged tissue to accelerate the healing process.

Aerobic exercise at this time is especially good for us. The stimulation provided will lift our spirits while it raises the core temperature of the body preparing the muscles and joints for more specific exercise. I find that warming up the injured area makes it more receptive to exercise allowing more range of motion with less pain or risk of further damage.

Pain is the signal and ultimately we guide ourselves through what exercises or portions of exercise we can perform. This takes the ten big ones: experimentation, focus, concentration, careful assessment, instincts, guts, will, perseverance, patience and courage. We use machines where we once used dumbbells, ten pounds where we once used a hundred, a partial movement repeated slowly around the pain, not through it or it sends its unmistakable instructive signal. To accommodate our need to press on, we invent new ways to position our bodies, arranging the resistance in a particular way to recruit the desired muscle without impacting the aggrieved area.

As we train, overtrain and push through plateaus, we're bound to stumble across some injuries. They come in all shapes and sizes, and range from muscle tears to tendintious. Failure to warm up, overload, improper movement and poor nutrition all contribute to injury, one of the masters of the training experience.

Pain demands our attention and causes us to totally focus on the damaged area. Using the focus of pain, learn to feel out the injury, feel its depths and discern its severity. Learn to separate the positive pain of deep muscular burn from the warning pain of abuse. Develop sensitivity toward the quality of pain, its varying levels and degrees.

An injury can be the result of accumulative tears not repairing, with one rep serving as the final overload. Any injury is a learning experience, and if you let it, will teach you its lessons. In wanting to work the muscle in spite of the painful limitation, you learn to really focus and not abuse the injured area. It reveals to you a degree of your perseverance, the ability and willingness to work through pain carefully and hopefully.

Certainly to a bodybuilder an injury means an immediate loss of hard-earned gains, but it also seems to be the only time I truly learn anything new about my body. I wish I could be as attentive during all my training as I am when I'm working an injured area.

An injury brings about a new appreciation for the muscle, and when you are healed and can lift full-bore, it offers a new thankfulness with less taken for granted. The new awareness for the muscle is never lost and remains as a reflection of your training forever.

ROTATOR CUFF — THE MOST COMMON INJURY

The shoulders are a major trouble spot, taking abuse at every turn. We overload them as we work the biceps, triceps, chest, lats, lower back and legs. They have no place to hide. Throw a ball, shoot a basket, tackle a speeding body, take a nose dive over the handlebars and the shoulders are there being pounded, wrenched, rotated and separated.

A spill off a hillside some years ago busted my clavicle and completely tore the right supra-spinatus, putting me in a cast with my right arm ninety degrees out to the side, supported by a preposterous inflated balloon. Lousy way to spend the summer. Surgery was six hours, recovery continues to this day. The doc — the best — said, "You do the rehab. I don't want anybody tearing out the stitches." Thanks, Doc.

This is what I did:

One week after surgery I was back in the gym, cast, balloon, sling, Velcro straps, zippers, and what-all. Twenty minutes on the LifeCycle was no problem.

Crunches and leg raises required some improvising, movement abbreviation, but where there's a will, there's a way. Fine. From there, the first day I did my legs: extensions, curls, heavy leg presses, seated calves. It all worked well. I quickly became familiar with the regional pain and managed to isolate it.

Days two and three, upper body days, things got, um, silly, absurd, frustrating and gruesome. But that didn't stop me, I'm an elevator with cables cut; ready or not, I'm comin' down. I continued my training in keeping with my developing theory to maintain body symmetry by working everything but that which was not workable. I started with light weights, left side only. I used substantial body rhythm to involve as much torso and relative muscles without excessive contraction of the muscles directly under repair.

I imagined — visualized — my right side being involved. I began to feel my way around, extending my isotonic and isometric contractions to the injury perimeter. Very critical process. Initially the slightest contraction was painful (big signal) and could undo what the master had skillfully reconstructed. But, hey, I'm fighting for my life here, fans of the underdog, and I have the brains of a flea.

To make a long story short, and to not further expose my neurotic obsessive behavior, in a month the cast was removed, the balloon deflated and I was on my own. I'm convinced the lopsided training helped me maintain mass, balance and total circulation. It certainly kept me occupied, hopeful and reasonably sane. My training was never halted, only compromised. It enabled me to begin my rotator cuff rehabilitation with a head start and with confidence.

INJURY REHABILITATION

Next came shoulder rehabilitation. The advice I offer is always qualified by the sentiment, if not the statement, "This is what I would do if I were you." Work through it all and you'll heal sooner. Why? Food for thought, my guesses:

- Systemic response

- Anabolic and anti-catabolic properties of circulation

- Healing nutrients and oxygen supplied by the blood

- Detoxification

- Endorphin and hormone production

- Tender-loving care factor

- Goals — motivation stimulus

- Maintenance of attitude

- Stemming of stress and submission

- Social interaction keeps one engaged, fulfilled, directed and attuned

- Psychology of proactive, positive steps toward recovery

Seriously, unless you have a concussion, you're bleeding or beyond reasonable mobility, there are no excuses, are there?

The first thing I did during this next phase was find the most private corner of the gym so it was me, alone. Selfish, undistracted, unselfconscious, focused. I supported my repaired right shoulder by holding it at the elbow, bent forward at the waist as if preparing to do a dumbbell row and slowly lowered the arm so it hung there by its own weight. Amazing — I imagined the internal stitching and reconstruction to be delicate and the shoulder not yet ready to be released from its nest. Thirty seconds of hanging with a small circular motion the size of a plate and it began to throb — one set down, four to go. Enough for one day.

Within a week I progressed from a five-pound plate to a ten-pound dumbbell and was doing five sets of twenty-five, clockwise and counterclockwise circles: gravity and me in full sight of wise-guy gym members offering me a spot if I needed it. Each evening at home I stood before a stucco wall, placed my hand against the textured finish and used my fingers to walk my hand up the wall much like the movement of a disturbed caterpillar bound for the ceiling. Tough stuff. My main focus was to get movement and range of motion as soon as possible, and prevent scar tissue from limiting my shoulder rotation without damaging it. Nonstop I wondered where the fine line between healthy therapy and damage would reside. Pain is the moderator. Five sets of finger walking as high as I could — higher, higher still. Instinct, intelligence, caution and risk are the balls one juggles like a frowning circus clown.

Next I grabbed a broomstick, over-grip as if ready to reverse curl and with stiff arms raised the bar before me, my strong arm leading and assisting in the action. I started and completed the movement with the broomstick parallel to the floor. Another four sets of eight to ten reps is sufficient, each successive set giving me greater height. It would be a long time before I'd be standing with arms straight overhead. Three weeks and it would get easier, greater volume of reps, more aggressive, more determined and the pain a factor defined, accepted and understood. No longer an enemy, diminishing now.

The first major exercise I was able to perform is the famous inner and outer rotation with a rubber band or ExerTube. You know the drill: Stand rigid with your arm by your side, bent at the elbow and rotate your hand inward, toward the body, and alternately rotate your hand away from the body. Four sets of twenty-five reps — left and right.

Bottom line: You break a leg, you train the top; you break an arm, you train the bottom. If you have the internal strength to look, you'll find something you can work left side or right.

STEROIDS

Speaking of internal strength, I often wonder if there would be the proliferation of bodybuilders today if the chemical enhancers weren't available to make the muscles grow faster and stronger, eliminating the time, toil and grief necessary for real muscular achievement.

Steroids change the body's hormonal action and improve the body's ability to use protein more efficiently for rapid tissue repair. However, these chemically induced activities provide a long list of side effects from hair loss to acne, from kidney failure to liver disease. In using steroids, the compromises are extraordinary and should be carefully considered. Yet the will — the ego — is so strong that the side effects are often dismissed. The self, matching today's lifestyle, looks only toward the favorable effects, and, hoping for the best, plunges headlong into careless drug use.

The risks involved with using anabolic and androgenic steroids do not stop with acne or hair loss. If you're a committed bodybuilder and enjoy an essence of independence in your life, you can surely plan to lose it. Steroids are insidious, and commonly cause psychological as well as physiological addiction. When you're on a chemical cycle, the weights go up easier, your muscles pump and so does your ego and enthusiasm. But when off the chemical cycle, and as the body normalizes, the reverse inevitably takes place. The lifter is left with depression and a hopelessness, which often leads to radical social behavior and the cessation of training entirely. This is a very sad and unhealthy situation indeed, and silently plagues many young bodybuilders today.

When taking any medications, a doctor's supervision through blood testing and monitoring of vital statistics is essential. Steroids are no longer legally prescribed to athletes to enhance their physical abilities; doctors are unable and unwilling to provide the necessary supervision. The black market is full of bogus drugs with suspicious ingredients and high price tags. What we have is an abundance of illegal toxins streaming through the bodybuilding and sports world, messing up athletes young and old.

It's curious to hear from all levels of bodybuilding — participants as well as spectators — that today's lineup of competitors all share a conspicuous sameness; except for the head and height, there is very little difference one from another, with exaggerated muscles no longer looking lifelike. Zabo, the daddy of Muscle Beach in the 50s and today the "Chief" of World Gym, Venice, calls them "StarWar bodies, living in a fantasy world."

I was ten years into my training, two hundred thirty-five pounds and already Mr. America before steroids came widely on the scene. I used them sparingly under a doctor's supervision and noticed marked improvement in my muscularity and separation. I also noticed a marked loss of improvement as I stopped taking them, and this was the big catch.

Young bodybuilders, if you're not taking them, don't. If you do, you'll wish you never did. They'll eat away at the foundations you're trying to build before you build them. As a pro, well, the weight's on your back and you know where the rack is.

At our local World Gyms, there are no obvious steroid users. A look, mentality and behavior betray the user and his distinct attitude separates him. Soon it becomes apparent that his goals and motivations are not in harmony with those around him and he chooses to move on down the line.

I have observed that drug use within the healthy gym atmosphere Laree, our partners and I choose to present is destructive. Even conversations about "roids" are unhealthy, opening the secure door and knocking over the can of worms. Steroid gossip engenders an associated grumbling, loose temper, discontent, and an envy and obsession not to be perpetuated.

I offer no advice on the matter as I know very little. I simply say, "Don't." It's complex, complicated and highly technical. It's reserved for the pros, and at that you have a better chance at playing in the World Series or the Super Bowl.

Are you a bodybuilder or do you just want the body? Do you love your training, your goals and your growth or do you just want the body, at any expense — except work, discipline and courage? You want the degree, but not the school and the education? I'll take the medal, thanks, just don't want to achieve it.

Think: What happens when you stop? You've got to stop sometime. It's a lonely road down. Emotions crash. Training often stops. Cold.

Who pays for it? Where do you get it? It's illegal and the docs say, "No." How much do you take and where do you draw the line? Side effects? Hormones?

My point: Get the drugs out of your mind. Soon. Whoever doesn't is looking at obsession and disappointment. They're looking down and not up. Get real.

AGING

Aging is a fact.
Getting old is a state of mind.

Think, observe, experiment, practice, learn and grow. Press on ... or retreat.

If you've been training since your teens or twenties and you're now over forty, you're hooked. Congratulations. You can't let go. You are a member of the elite. Don't listen to conventional wisdom that slaps you on the back like a cunning ole' salesman and tells you you're in for a change in your training and expectations. Son, it happens to everyone when they turn forty; that's the way it is.

The most deceptive enemy in the process of slowly advancing years is the foolishness of conventional wisdom. I expected and almost accepted that, regardless of my stubbornness and muscle-building lifestyle, the pasture was beneath my feet and it was time I learned to graze. In the past fifty years, some grim figure in our shadows, a mystery person, told us that serious training at any age stresses our muscles, which leaves slight tears, which in turn leaves scars eventually resulting in injuries; and the older we get and the longer we train, the more and greater the injuries we accumulate. Caution must be the order of our days as we pass forty. Decreasing muscle response, joint degeneration and diminishing skin elasticity also scavenge our fading years. The same crotchety source suggested we slow down, don't expect to make gains, settle for maintenance, join the "Book of the Month Club."

For a few dismal moments in my forties I submitted. The accumulated injuries of more than thirty years of bodybuilding surfaced during those glue-like days and I magnified them out of sadistic curiosity. The injuries were real and their persistence convinced me of simple truths; I could no longer train as fast as I had in the years past.

I required longer recovery time, my durability was not what it was and the fierce last reps needed scrutiny, lest I break. Yet, when dawn broke and the rubble departed, inspiration revealed an unerring spirit that could not be diminished. The journey wasn't over. I wasn't bound to circle the same old ground; withdrawing wasn't an option. Persuading myself I should simply be glad I'm alive and that, along with cumulative injuries, I should put wisdom to effect by accepting age gracefully is a cute and noble attitude. Give me the Peace Prize, thanks, but I prefer the good fight.

Now I see that just as the mere awareness of age can affect your ego and attitude, so can a more confident and determined attitude awaken you to the fact that the other side of forty, and fifty, sixty and seventy holds a valid promise for improving your physique.

As the Good Book says, be strong and courageous. Be hopeful. A good plan is to continue to be aggressive in your workouts with ample time for repair and recuperation, being aware of overtraining. Work on a weekly schedule of two days on, one off, followed by two days on, two off. Hit each bodypart one or two times per week with two exercises per muscle group, a 15, 12, 10, 8 rep sequence, mixing heavy, moderate and light weights. Push hard and determined on days one and two and back off days three and four, being more fluid and playful.

Consider supersets as gold. Experiment with slower tempo rep patterns for joint-safe, deep-muscle stimulation.

From all I've been able to gather, the maintenance process begins at the mid-fifties. Serious muscular growth for anyone fifty-five and above and already ten to fifteen years invested in hard training is doubtful. We can hope for some shape here and some size there, a cut or two someplace, but mostly we're done. Great workouts are ahead as we adjust to age, inevitable injury and limitations.

Photographer unknown
In the bowels of the Academy of Music in Brooklyn, N.Y., at some point between line-ups at the 1966 Mr. Universe Competition. I weighed 230 pounds and felt strong. The filming of *"Don't Make Waves"* was at its peak. I felt like I was running a race with the wind at my back.

I love my training more than ever, push it as hard as ever though the groove of any variety of movements and the weight I use is altered to accommodate my fifty-eight years of planet survival and forty-some of iron battle. As I proclaim regularly, we're all different. Some wonder types will defy gravity, hoist the tonnage and retain the youthful features longer. The word drifted north to Santa Cruz from Joe Gold's gym not long ago that fifty-five seems to be the mean number. There is thoughtful and philosophical discourse often among the originals of Joe's group who have traveled the road less-traveled. They know this stuff. I arrived at the number on my own.

Do not read the following paragraph if you don't have a wild and crazy sense of humor. Graphic description. The demons of aging we can expect as bodybuilders include (gulp) diminishing muscle mass and density, declining strength as we adapt to injury and overuse limitations, tight skin tone giving way to looseness, gathering skin and wrinkles (are we having fun yet?), loss of muscle and ligament tenacity, gradual joint enlargement, fading joint flexibility and slower recovery evident in general everyday achy-ness. Neat. Good-bye hair. I could go on, but why? Take good care of yourself.

Weighing 225 pounds before the Neveux lens I was lean enough to look almost skinny. Tuna and hard-boiled egg whites and thirty years of training.

Mike Neveux

A man or woman who is returning to the weights after an extended layoff, however, or starting to work out for the first time at fifty-five or sixty-five or seventy-five can expect wonderful muscle and strength improvement. It will extend the precious years with more energy, power and purpose.

I poke fun at the years as they pile up. To this day I've never been happier. 'Cept when I was younger.

SMOKING

Evidently twenty percent of the American population smokes cigarettes. That's one out of five, and I expect it's double in many other countries.

Driving home from the gym recently I noticed the occupants of a car that kept pace with me as we bucked the rush hour traffic. Mom and Dad, I assumed, with a cute little four-year old, busying herself with playful imaginings and chatterings, and a tyke snuggly battened down in a car seat. Both Mom and Dad in their twenties were smoking, the windows were closed and the air around them was a cloud. This is beyond ignorant. The kids had no choice; they were not even offered an open window. I wanted to follow and confront them, report them and retrieve the kids as if from the hands of captors. I did nothing; what can you do? They took an early off-ramp; I kept my eyes on the road and smoldered.

As tobacco has become a billion-dollar industry, so has the movement and business to stop smoking. Wrenching oneself from a smoking habit can be an awesome, almost frightening undertaking. It presents antagonizing temptation and requires extreme resolve, often bringing one to a hopelessness and self-reckoning that's grim.

I've had to eliminate a bad habit or two myself, er, more like they eliminated me. These are not the dearest of my lifelong memories. Thank God, smoking wasn't one of them. Cigarettes, it seems, dig in like rusty nails.

Once I declared war on my enemies, I recall that burrowing in those first three weeks — where life is saved — was the hardest. After that, the commitment superseded the need. The time invested and the territory reclaimed became more valuable than the habit.

The early days are the most critical and defining. They are also the meanest. Scratch your way through them any way you can. Imagine their defeat clearly yet casually. See yourself free of the dismal self-image of a smoker and sense the relief from its hideous grasp. No way is too cowardly or weak, insignificant or extravagant, high tech, outdated or outrageous. It is your precious life, after all. Precious and precarious, it's your responsibility.

As hopeful and as optimistic as we are, as equipped and capable, as swift and courageous, daily living is rugged. You need everything possible going for you. Don't hobble yourself, don't limit your struggling body's ability to breathe, grow, run, resist disease, aspire, create and inspire.

I'm like most everyone else I know: selfish, part-hypocrite, partly self-righteous, a little proud, a tiny bit humble. I try to be honest. As I write I do not mean any harm; I seek only good. May I ask a few brutal questions?

When did it occur to you that smoking was no longer cool or popular, enjoyable or satisfying? That it was instead unclean, smelly and destructive and should be scraped? Did you act on this, or is this your first decisive step? Another fair question, please: Does it bother you that some unkind and greedy bandits persuaded and provided you with such a delightful and soothing and murderous addiction? And that these same powerful thieves steal a high school kid's perception and stick a cool cigarette in his or her mouth? Thanks for the ball and chain; I needed that.

You've got to stop ... you've got to stop. This isn't a mantra, it's an appeal. Don't give the tobacco industry another nickel. Be a role model before kids who are kids, innocent and susceptible. Think of your body as your favorite person, loved and honored. Don't mar it, scar it, abuse it. Take care of yourself and those around you.

As you sit here with this book, you're in a muscle-building mindset. Have you recently reviewed the calamitous consequences of smoking tobacco? How it stunts muscle growth, exhausts B and C vitamins, and a variety of other vital nutrients? Arteries that transport and valves that pump blood deteriorate. Lungs that purify blood and deliver oxygen become blackened with disease and graying skin pallor surrounds stained teeth, decaying gums and blinking eyes.

Can we ever take a step back and really look at ourselves? Will we ever stop exchanging cliches and reading bumper stickers? Are we ever able to be silent and listen to our wisdom? I mostly dwell restlessly in some hazy gray-white zone that imitates life just gone by, hypnotized, brainwashed, reflexive. A sheep I am, one of the flock. Feed me, shelter me, comfort me. Unawareness is a dumb, drowsy place and when I notice its control I must vigorously shake myself loose.

Are you a smoker? Does this harangue make you uncomfortable? Or angry? Or guilty? You're not the only one. Quit. For good.

The most important and most difficult battle undertaken by any of us in my estimation is the one to give up smoking. Though I've never smoked I am not without understanding of the tight and hateful grip of addiction. It does come in all forms. I'm not a generous soul. I see a person smoking and think, "I'm glad I don't have that one," and I feel smug, a condition far worse than the condition I condemn. I promise to the parties concerned that I shall this day forth discipline myself to — without piousness or superiority or self-virtue, derelict creature that I am — favor the hounded person with a prayer to God.

SLUMPS & SEASONS

The hard-core bodybuilder, the beginner, the deconditioned, the athlete, young, old, male or female — as I write I often wonder to whom am I writing. Whoever you are, though the information I offer varies, the message is always the same: Exercise faithfully, positively, regularly, enthusiastically. Hit the gym, build muscle, eat right, lose fat, heighten cardio, kill stress.

Owning a gym and observing its members tells me a brief story of mankind. He is driven largely by guilt, fear and vanity. Throughout the year we see him come and go. Mid-January he (or she, of course, my Sisters of Steel) comes to the gym, or returns as the case may be, after the confusion dies down and it's time to deal with the neglect and the procrastination. He can no longer stand the guilt; he's stumbled. The fear of getting repulsively and irreparable out of shape is frightening. Back to the iron.

This goes on for a while, six to eight weeks until mid-March and he's gonzo again 'cause he's feeling pretty good, paid some dues and the winter is dark. Early spring he's back for more at the first sighting of sun and bare skin. Time to look cool, not like a fool. Start with the steel.

The spring lures us to the gym to prepare for the summertime and outdoor activities. And, ironically, just as we are about to respond to our eager input, the very goal itself displaces our purpose, our fitness preparation. The gym falls dispassionately to the wayside. Our faces and bodies are less frequently seen in our favorite gym in July and August and the establishment of a superlative habit is broken.

Be careful. This is common; this is foolish. A dedicated hour of weight training twice a week through the summer in the iron palace and you remain on target — responsible, disciplined and motivated. Do your aerobics and sports vigorously and playfully in the fields, beaches and mountains. You're safe. You're free. No doubts, guilt or lost muscle density. No ever-growing training gap — the enemy — no post-summer procrastination blues, no distressing four-week reconditioning challenge in the fall.

Alas, summer drops in and mankind drops out. Busy having outdoor fun, relaxing, vacationing and getting lazy, maybe baby. September rolls around and so does his belly. "If only I had worked out and watched what I ate," he remarks as he steps on the treadmill.

Ugh. A man can do only so much for so long. It's Thanksgiving, for Pete's sake, and the holidays only come once a year. Right? And December — it's such as confusing time of year.

The days pile up, one on another and soon we need a plan before we're lulled into winter hibernation and isolation. Winter arrives. If not today, unspeakably soon and it's a different creature. Good. You like skiing and bundling up, snowballs and the fireside. Cute. Me, too. Take heed, the shorter and colder days during which we reside furthest from the sun are harsh on the system. We tend to fade, lose ground or defect.

We need to adjust quickly, mentally and physically. You can do it; it needs to be done. Too often we find ourselves suddenly neck-deep in calories and bodyfat, inappropriate and irregular training, misplaced goals, bitter and guilty self-consciousness, low resistance and the ensuing vulnerability to flus, colds and viruses. Diminishing disciplines, increasing television bloat, pronounced pear-shapeness, attitude spats, lost friendships, newfound evil enemies, hysteria, nightmares, paranoia, schizophrenia and occasionally the mumps. And we were making such good progress.

Make a plan. Reinforce it. Write it down. Scroll "urgent" across the top. Post it on your icebox door and outhouse wall. Study it, memorize it, recite it. Quote it.

Your goal is to make progress in your bodybuilding through each month of the year. Every month a silent and secret step forward. Another movement mastered, a new PR, a satisfying exercise combination practiced, a pound of fat gone, an ounce of muscle mass acquired, workout after successful workout. Mere maintenance or only a occasional slip backwards is not sufficient. A slip backwards is how we usually survive the off-season and find ourselves eventually tumbling backwards with ever-increasing momentum until we're out of control, disappointed and angry.

Put order in your workouts. Prepare for the psychology of the winter, its physical limitations, its tastes, noise and demands. Be ready for the altered atmosphere, attitudes and energies around you — at work, at home and at the gym. It's a different game, different rules, different scoreboard.

Have you noticed? With less skin showing we tend to fatten up. Less daylight and the on-coming nasty weather, we tend to be sedate, indoors and comfortably confined, less active and less motivated. We burn less fuel and eat more; there are holidays, parties, long nights, wet days, boredom, depression and developing bad habits with crumbling disciplines. Inertia.

I almost forgot. You know the man and woman you see at the gym all year, regular as a metronome? They're driven by love, the same force, I suspect, that drives you and me.

The seasons have a way of defining a person's life.

TRAINING PARTNERS AND MY DOG, SPOT

People. You can't live with them and you can't live without them. There are some trainees who absolutely cannot train without a training partner. They lose direction, pace, focus, courage and incentive. They fall apart. I have a friend who can lift a house but will hang out for hours until a training partner arrives who can spot him. He needs his weights handheld every set, every rep, up and down, off the rack and on the rack. Imprisonment. They're not weights, they're millstones. Some folks can't be pried loose from the bench in their garage and dragged to a gym, the presence of people a perturbing distraction. We probably need to adapt to training under a variety of conditions if we're to proceed, whether they show or don't, whether the gym is empty or full (although I prefer empty, not a great attitude for a gym owner).

Occasionally I'll have someone stand nearby in the squat and bench to prevent major crushing. Otherwise, I prefer to train unassisted. This has to do with focus, the accurate assessment of my full-on input, the elimination of distraction and the avoidance of dependency. If I'm unable to get the last rep, I put the weight away — rack it or properly dump it. This is rare, as I don't set myself up for failure. This occurs enough throughout the day without my deliberate help.

A spot when performing a 1RM (one rep max) is a good idea for safety and friendly support. Positioning a maximum weight from the rack in the bench press can severely overload the rotator cuff and cause a long-term injury. A spot poorly presented, of course, can be equally damaging. Know your spotter, know how to spot and don't cross signals. Are the circumstances imposing? Two spotters do the job best. A heavy squatter can use three, with a middle-man for minor rep assistance.

"Spotting" and "assistance" have their place in training early on to provide guidance, assurance and protection. Break free of assistance ASAP to mature in your performance of sound exercise, develop your form and gain a complete understanding of solo load-bearing exercise.

Though I've refrained from applying the technique of "assistance training," choosing to attain intensity levels independent of a partner, this overload methodology works. It will be of value as it's woven into your training pattern thoughtfully, knowing its purpose, your goals and then proceeding with caution. Practiced too often, this technique, developed to build strength and break plateaus, becomes ordinary and loses impact physically and psychologically. You stand the chance of becoming dependent upon a partner, your training may become rigid and there's the risk of tendon and joint overload, muscle tears and overtraining. When performing serious assistance training, be prepared for some extended repair and recuperation time. This is especially true of assistance training where the focus on negatives is accented.

You'll work out this personal aspect of your weightlifting smoothly along with all the other odds and ends. They simply fall in place.

Training partners are great while they last. Some last forever, some won't go away. Problems arise when setting partnerships in motion. There needs to be a personal connection, physical compatibility, goal alignment, matching zeal and timing. Good luck.

When one partner is lost or late, precious time marches on. Tough training is a psyche and misplaced time frustrates that valuable cerebral spark, leaving you dull and sluggish. I don't want to hear about the horse on the freeway or the baby you delivered in the elevator. I'm losing my pump here. Give me the gym, the weights and wide-open spaces.

I've had three very important training partners back in the '60s of Muscle Beach; they taught me and I taught them. Always there, great mutual support, necessary, fundamental, integral, hard-core and a blast. We pushed.

Arnold and I bounced around in the late '60s, America meets Europe; Zane and I paced each other in the early '70s. But we were all en route, alone or together; it was effective just to be in the same gym at the same time going about our own business.

"Come along" partners (spontaneous partnerships) work well now and again to pick up the spirits, change the pace and add a smile to the routine. Outside the gym doors, life is crowded and scattered about — downright hard to get authentic partnership together. Not impossible, just hard.

These days someone passes by my bench as I press and urges, "Come on, Draper," and I power out two more reps; next day my elbow hurts. Can't afford a training partner anymore. It's me, myself and I. What a wacky collection of characters that is.

TRAINING ON AND ON

We are none of us immune. Anyone at anytime will doubt, wonder, become uncertain or subtly negative. A wary nature is an essential of survival and an internal mechanism directing us toward success. In excess it can paralyze us or, at least, render life a harmless and uneventful occurrence. Suspicious, ever-questioning and procrastinating souls with wrinkled-up noses capture doubt and uncertainty, stuff and mount them over their mantle to be displayed as trophies of conquests never made. The wall upon which our trophy would hang is bare; we carry it with us, a warm and vigilant companion.

I think back, long and hard. At twelve I didn't ask, "What should I do?" Who could I ask? What should I ask for? I just did it. At seventeen I didn't ask what exercise builds this and what food builds that. Thank God, I just did it, harder. I don't ever remember asking much of anything. Never seemed that complicated. No one had to tell me it was hard work and took a long time. School was hard work and took a long time. Working after school to earn a few bucks was hard and took time. Why should lifting weights and building muscle be any different? You lift, you learn, you grow. That's life.

Today it's not so simple. How could it be and why should it be? The life-curve is different; it's more acute, active and occupied. Questions are no longer questions but riddles to be cleverly circulated. The absence of quickness and efficiency in a solution reduces it to a threat. Let's do it now, let's do it right, let's do it perfectly and at once ... before the other guy or gal. That's the message I've been getting lately. You can always tell when somebody's been watching too much CNN or reading *The Wall Street Journal.*

Building strong and healthy bodies need not be sought that way, as they cannot be achieved that way. It's a contradiction, in fact, isn't it? A hurried and anxious method of operation produces only injury, disappointment and stress, not the soundness of body, the fulfillment of accomplishment and the relief of tension that ought to be associated with hearty fitness.

Say you know all this. You've been around a few years and to be called well-seasoned is a compliment. Time is a peculiar, almost lovable mate that you've come to know and can't deny. Success and disappointment in their own relative way have come to visit, linger and leave. You are stronger because of them, you agree. You're a mature bodybuilder and the scenery appears to be changing. You still love to train, meet goals and reinvent yourself, but call it age or possibly just a slump, you now seem to be faced with questions that only an older bodybuilder can answer. Things like: Am I training hard enough or overtraining? If I push on myself to do one or two more reps is that good or am I overtraining? Sometimes I go to the gym and can train like a horse, strong and energetic. Sometimes I battle with, "Should I rest today or push myself? Why does my elbow joint hurt? Am I getting arthritis? What is the most effective way for me to train?" I used to do cardio activity everyday to help with bodyfat loss, energy increase and heart health. Am I overdoing it? It now seems to cut into my training energy where it never did before. I'm out of control.

The last paragraph includes a list of questions recently offered by an established bodybuilder approaching the broadening span of middle age; he's intelligent, realistic and persevering. His questions are legitimate and I ask them myself, frequently. I'm one of those coonskin-capped pioneers with a Bowie knife fixed in his teeth, clawing to broaden the span and push aging over the edge. Exhausting but I've got an enthusiastic audience cheering me on.

I will attempt to address these vivid issues in my typical "This is what I'd do if I were you" style. Of course, I need to take my afternoon snooze and my medications, and soak my feet and apply ice to my left shoulder, heat to my right shoulder (or is it the other way around?). I've got it written on large index cards somewhere.

Ah, here it is: answers to a selection of questions familiar to all of us. The questions are real, valid and daunting. They are particularly concerned with overtraining, training intensity and efficiency, overload, aerobics and muscle mass as the years pass and youth is replaced with middle age. Allow me to generalize, guess and pretend to the best of my recollection.

Press on as always. Each day I find will take us to another threshold. I don't embrace them; I beat them back. Overtraining is a predator on the prowl that will get us if we step into its territory and get us if we don't step close enough. I, therefore, hang on the ragged edges. This is one of my all-time favorite fingertip positions where I sort of blow in the winds and gusts, never knowing if I will be torn away or gain new territory. I take my chances. I'm not tough, cool, stupid, foolish (we're getting close) or desperate. I cannot train without intensity if I can train at all.

I sound like a madman — This is not good. Let me clarify (I'm interested in the clarification myself). I believe in maximizing the level of muscle-under-tension — modern lingo is TUL, time-under-load — within every workout, utilizing my intuition and logic to determine this baffling red-line. This is not achieved necessarily by the same method or pattern. That is, I don't use high reps consistently, though this is popular with me. I sometimes use near-max weight though far less often. I lately employ slow-tempo reps as joint problems are less aggravated and I've discovered an appeal for them as the body grows older. Too, static holds on later reps in different ranges of motion are gaining my interest for the same reason. I find them highly muscle-intense, satisfying and promising. A year ago I wouldn't let them on the gym floor.

Somewhere I've commented in half a dozen threadbare places that my training is not unlike my training of years ago, mostly supersetting, pyramiding to mix the reps, singles, doubles, triples staggered over three-week periods, three-on, one off, two-on, one off, training each muscle group two times every week done at a moderate pace. The alterations I am willing to make to the above semi-flexible parameters are beginning to reveal themselves day by day. My workouts have been fluid since I stepped out of competition thirty years ago; no less intense, just less rigid. Therefore, in that sense my training principles have not changed. I search each and every workout for the exercises, the combinations, the sets and reps, the pace and tempo, the methodology that will allow me to optimize intensity.

Maximum intensity may not be registered in every set, but it is in the overall workout. High intensity is sought in every rep, yet adjustments are made to accommodate joint overload, tendon inflammation and its prevention, muscle tear potential and exhaustion of muscle energy stores. I perceive the workout as the wringing out of a fresh sponge to leave no moisture, yet applying care not to shred its composition. Hence, my appreciation for cycles of volume mixed with heavy poundage and the recent employment of slow-tempo reps and static contractions.

How does this, the outline of my focused training approach, help you to answer the inscrutable questions related to overtraining and overload? My Bomber attack technique established early on has had me confronted with the overtraining dilemma for years and has thusly prepared me. You want to train like a horse, you've got to train like a smart horse. No saddle, no bridle — free. Each workout, with positive thought and high hopes, I warm up, assess my core disposition and proceed toward my most likely target. Put instinct and intuition on alert, feelers ready to approach the edge. Hit it.

There are safer and clearer prescriptions outlined by trainers, coaches and technicians but none more personally efficient and appealing than muscular finesse. What formulas of percentages prescribed for the workout of the day are more accurate than your own knowing? The development of this knowledge is to be part of our training; diligent practice, attention, trial and error and an unfailing trust in your achievement are the steps.

This is the way to get where you're going if where you're going is the top. Pull back appropriately to accommodate targets less ambitious but no less significant. Getting in shape is a superlative goal and should be approached with similar artful management.

When it's a question of one more rep or one more set, check the insertions, the duration of the concentric and eccentric motions, the pump and the amount of invested work of the muscle, based on a quick evaluation of sets x reps x weight. An approximation of this workout input compared to your last workout input, plus considerations of sleep, feeding and non-workout workloads should give you the clues to discern whether to move forward, stop or retreat. I'd say cut back on the reps and finish the sets, hold back on the weight and complete the sets with form and slower tempo. Get the prescribed sets and slow the pace. Other options are available by the modification of the variables. Your choice, chief.

A burdened and shoulder-weary depression might require that you forego your aerobic and midsection activity. Aggressive, direct action without delay will provide a psychological advantage and reserve energy stores for the muscle work ahead. Set yourself squarely before your taskmaster and apply yourself to the nudging of the weights. This is a test, a sounding of the ground, the locating of the wind as if by moistening your finger and holding it to the air. The first set of a light weight with a smile and slow reps with a stretch often open the creaking doors to a wonderful workout, a workout of grand proportions where inspiration plays host and personal records are sometimes set. If you discover resistance persists and a change in course fails, gather your things and head home for solace, food and rest. You're fine. You're growing. Be thankful.

Aerobic training has its place in conditioning, improving heart and respiratory health, energizing, detoxifying and warm-up. A conditioned muscle builder who participates in highly evolved volume training and is no slug on the gym floor can wisely put the activity on the shelf and reserve it for super conditioning or for those times when weight training due to injury, overtraining or burn out is not the practical scheme to follow. Extended aerobics, cross training combined with midsection and wind sprints are smart and tough alternate training styles to develop for overall body ability, flexibility, stamina and occasional variation.

Answers to specific questions require further information, conversation and time to understand. Don't let anything surprise you or short-circuit your plans. Of course, getting older is no one's favorite pastime and adjusting to the compromises is not eagerly done. Muscle recovery, strength and flexibility do not sky rocket with age, yet attitude and disposition will make up where the above falter.

Did I mention plenty of rest and good food? Bombs away.

Russ Warner

The channel of the world's largest recreational yacht harbor, Marina del Rey, California, before it was "the world's largest." Russ Warner and I played with the soft fall sunlight hoping to get a memory or two.

10

MEMORIES ARE THE STUFF

Memories are the stuff we're made of, along with muscle, bone and bright hopes. Ever find yourself staring off into the future, captured by the past, completely disconnected from the present? Moments: Our life is a series of distinct unforgettable moments connected one by one, a string of pearls and lead sinkers. With some we wrestle and try to defeat; others are cherished, nurtured and carefully recalled. Plenty are just an old hoot and carry us through the day like a clanking car on a crazy roller coaster ride. I'm guessing, but I think it is during these periods of drifting that growth hormone is released.

Writing this book has had me muse, ponder and reminisce. I have found myself an observer of a past that I hoped and gambled would interest you, give you insight and entertain. The book's end is near and some stories, relevant and irrelevant, remain. Toss them or pass them along were my call. I chose to include the nonsense for you to decide. What the heck.

NICE WORK IF YOU CAN GET IT
AND YOU CAN GET IT — JUST DON'T TRY

Hollywood isn't just around the corner. It's a convoluted place where "stars" are born and celebrities of film and television, rock n' roll work, congregate, celebrate, live n' play. Hollywood is famous and infamous, a stretch of boulevards that sparkle at night and attract the weirdest creatures known to man. It is alluring hillsides, scrappy and steep upon which stilted houses perch and shaded hideaways snuggle. Privacy, secrecy, mystery and the unknown reside as an odd family in need of no one but each other.

"Good evening ladies and gentlemen, boys and girls and you muscle worshipers. Welcome to *David the Gladiator*. Tonight's presentation ..." The words roll off my tongue as if I were again before the camera on Saturday night in 1963. "Tonight's presentation stars Reg Park, Steve Reeves and Brad Harris in ..."

DAVID THE
GLADIATOR
presenting
THE WORLD'S BIGGEST MOVIES!

SPECTACULAR!
STAGGERING!

★ HERCULES UNCHAINED

★ GLADIATOR OF ROME

★ SON OF SAMSON

★ GOLIATH AGAINST
THE GIANTS

to name a few . . .

COLOR
TV 9

EVERY SATURDAY NIGHT 8 ON TV 9

I had seen half a dozen movies and watched less than fifty fidgety hours of TV before I left the swampy shores of Secaucus, New Jersey, for the emerald and gold of Santa Monica, California. I was clueless, penniless, green as unpicked apples and dumb. I was also quiet and in my silence people thought I was, perhaps, cool. Wrong, but it got me through the first months during which time I grew wider and like a chameleon took on the colors of my surroundings.

I discovered something soon after my Muscle Beach arrival: acceptance and indoctrination. Nobody worked. Wes, the lovable gym keeper, responsibly delivered mail for the postal service. Mighty Merle was a manager at Sears and Ronnie "Lead-us" taught geometry at Venice High. The rest of the guys were dutiful members of the Screen Extras Guild. Their chosen profession required that they call the SEG hotline late each morning to inquire of possible "extra work" for the following day. Extra work constituted the presence of any background person needed to complete a scene being filmed for either motion picture or television. You know the roll — the soldier on the battlefield, the audience at the opera or the man and lady chatting on the street corner. If work prevails, they spend the day on the set playing cards and gabbing until their services are needed. This activity provided a neat day's pay and life was good. On an outstanding day you picked up a bit part, which calls for some action or speaking. "When the Captain arrives on the scene, get out of the police car and hand him the gun. Say to him, 'I found it in the bushes, Sir.'" Lights, camera, action. Heightened the fun and the wage considerably.

Bad days meant no work and you filed for unemployment and hung out at the beach and lifted weights. Some guys hung out the whole summer as filming typically slowed to a crawl. Nice work if you can get it.

These guys and gals had a trim network going and when work was coming up in the future they were tuned in. The prosperous seasons were a gift from heaven; an ongoing extra part on a TV series that ran for many seasons was diamond-studded and came only to the honored, privileged and blessed. Everybody I knew was a soldier on the '60s favorite, *Combat.* I think Zabo was a chief, my training partner was a spy and a few big blond dudes were enemy officers. I thought they had substantial occupations, Hollywood and all, and hoped I'd visit the place, and Disneyland, too, one day. Can't do everything at once. I gotta get huge. I gotta get a car.

Six months in sunny California and New Jersey faded to gray. One of my most-prized possessions is my East Coast history. You don't know the West unless you know the East. If you haven't spent time in New York City, you're simply guessing about the rest of the world. Who said that?

Anyway, one ordinary day word circulated through the gyms that the popular Los Angeles television station KHJ on Melrose in Hollywood was looking for a character to play the host of their upcoming Saturday prime-time evening show. The producers purchased a year's supply of male-hero films from the past — Victor Mature, Errol Flynn, Steve Reeves, those guys — and needed someone to introduce the flicks and visit with the audience at breaks throughout the presentation.

What ensued was a common Hollywood peculiarity, a cattle call, where everyone who in any way resembled the sought-after player shows up in flipflops and jeans carrying lunch in a paper bag. One by one you're sorted out by an assistant and his assistant until only a handful are surviving. I couldn't resist joining in the action.

Vince Gironda was sitting on a curb in front of the studio drinking a cup of coffee. He was called before the camera for a screen test while I milled about the remaining short list like a stray dog. Is that Reg Lewis over there with Ray Rutledge and Dick Sweet, my training partner? My name was announced and I was ushered onto a sound stage, placed before a marker and asked to read a handheld teleprompter that said, "Good evening, ladies and gentlemen, boys and girls, and you muscle worshippers. Welcome to *The Gladiator*. Tonight men with swords and shields will capture your hearts."

It must have been my New Joisey accent. You ever hear a frightened bodybuilder from Secaucus pronounce "girls" or "worshippers"? They drop the R's and kick 'em around da flaw. I got the part and they called the show "*David The Gladiator*." Highest Saturday night ratings. I got me a car.

Photographer unknown

Sword, helmet, breastplate, papier-mache rock and I'm ready for battle. Stand back, men. A gladiator's work is not for the faint of heart.

I'M THE BOMBER

I remember the first day I arrived in Sydney, Australia, after thirty-six hours of assorted travel time. The clothes you wear on global crossings become like pajamas shortly after dinner and everyone on board gets as comfortable as possible and very forgiving. Wrinkles are in and spots, stains and vague odors go unnoticed. You wallow in a timeless haze until the captain announces that arrival is in two hours. Hello. The flight's last leg is devoted to restoration and renewal as enlivened passengers break out their slick disembarkation finery.

"I'm sorry, sir, but there were no trousers with the jacket. They must have fallen off the rack when changing craft in Hawaii," explained the attendant in a cute Aussie accent. I stared at her with my mouth open failing to see the humor in the untimely joke. No joke? "I can see your lovely sport coat is crumpled and misshapen, sir. It had slipped under a stack of briefcases belonging to Counselor Morganchild who regularly accompanies the Ambassador on his trips abroad. I'm sure he'll be very upset."

I looked down and stared in disbelief and horror. I was wearing a sweatshirt cut off at the elbows: more room to stretch and be piggy. The hideous gold broad-corduroy pants cinched around my waist fit when I weighed two-fifty but now resembled a potato sack, partially filled with potatoes I might add. Is this depression I feel or is it lack of sleep, low carbs, decompression disease or jet lag? I was the last to descend the great aircraft stairway. The press, garlands of flowers, pretty beauty queens in swimsuits and high heels to greet Mr. America, on-the-spot daytime TV coverage ... I tried to go out the rear of the craft with the trash and empty food bins, but security caught me pushing a dolly without a proper name tag. I can beg. Please. I just want to help ... Saurie, mayte.

I did my rotten best and made some friends in spite of myself. Paul, the kind-hearted, street-wise promoter put his thick arm around my shoulders and said "We can do this, my man. Relax; go to hotel. I'll pick up your luggage and have it sent to your room. Two pieces, is it?" I apologized to my new friends and planned to meet them in the morning for a workout.

My room was a suite high above the harbor overlooking the Opera House. Where I was and what I was doing settled in as I gazed at the grand sight. Eat, unwind, unleash. No exercise for two days made me antsy. I kicked up into some handstand pushups to pump and burn the delts. Feels good, nothing like it. Coming down from my third set, having already ordered a steak from room service, I kicked an oversized end table with a smash, breaking a lamp … and my foot. I'm beginning to look like a bloody fool.

Somehow you get through the mess called life and get onto the next mess. I didn't see my luggage for three days. Bugger. "We think it's in Honolulu, sir, with your pants." Australians are great. They didn't throw me to the crocs.

Morning appeared and I reluctantly got up and hobbled to the window. Thoughts of disaster evaporated as I watched the rising sun decorate the waterways and high rises with sparkling diamonds and shimmering gold. The right foot was jammed, busted and swollen, but repair would come with time only, the friendly doctor assured me. No setting, no cast, no charge. These little white pills will get you through the weekend. A knock at the door was accompanied by Paul, his mates — now mine — and breakfast. "After food we'll get you some clothes and hit the uptown gym for a workout. Whattaya say, mate? "

While in another hemisphere and training in an unfamiliar gym, I was content to accept anything that resembled a workout; I was content to accept no workout at all. I have under the best of conditions a few minor discomforts to negotiate when training in a strange gym: self-consciousness, privacy, workout effectiveness and…um…ego. What if they recognize me and I have to maintain an image? I thought he was taller, younger, bigger and stronger. That's a drag. Worse yet, what if they don't recognize me? Hi, I'm The Bomber. The what? I'm the original Blond Bomber and I've been blasting the gyms around the world. Proud of it and I'm famous, too. Don't let the foot fool you. Can you imagine the misunderstandings and explanations just trying to get a pump? Search, hand cuff, interrogate…

I got past the front counter and stood at the edge of a comfortable, well-equipped, energetic but packed gym. Just the right size work area with all the tools, only there were people everywhere; some sort of weekend celebration had them all amped up. They weaved between the machines and gathered by the squat racks and water fountain. I spied a bench about to be vacated and casually limped to it, snagging a pair of matching 25s along the way; they were light but they were there.

The point now was to keep moving so no one asked to work in or borrow my puny-yet-precious dumbbells. Sitting on the end of the bench and looking downward to avoid eye contact, I scanned the scene to get

Jimmy Caruso

The Back Shot. Clean and simple, right? I don't think so. The day after the Mr. Universe contest in the steamy September of '66 I took a taxi to a run-down industrial section of New York City. On the fifth floor, the post contest photo studio was set up amidst upended crates, sagging cardboard boxes and abandoned metal desks and worktables. Jimmy Caruso, Joe Weider's foremost photographer in the early days, took the picture. He's a exacting technician who ran measuring tapes from his elaborate lighting system to his subject to achieve perfection in highlighting, shadows and background contrasts. While mild-mannered Jimmy fussed, adjusted and focused, Joe fidgeted, paced and repeatedly urged Jimmy to hurry along. I stood in absolutely one spot only, my attention on the task of keeping the backdrop and floor-covering clean. Clean never entered the four walls of this hovel, which had grimy windows painted shut, dust-laden spider webs suspended overhead and no running water. "Jimmy, don't take all day. It's getting late and the guy's getting tired." Joe's all heart. "Shoot the thing."

Truth is when Caruso took his position behind the camera and finally nodded, the Trainer of Champs leaned toward the lens and precisely coaxed me into the flexed stance, always making the most of what there was.

my bearings; the dumbbells hung by my side. A twelve-inch block lay near a column three feet to my left. I needed it to raise my bench and add some originality to the beginnings of what appeared to be a feeble workout. How do I get the block without leaving my post? I want that block.

I assumed a mildly transfixed expression and did a seated variation of rolling shoulder shrugs to warm up and position myself advantageously in the direction of the block. It had a cutout on the side that served as a handle. Shrugs completed, I placed the 25s on the floor and rolled them to within inches of the block, very carefully arranged my sore foot on the bench and proceeded to do a set of medium-grip pushups, dumbbells still in hand. On the last rep I released my left-hand grip and snatched the block like a lizard snatching an insect for dinner. I uprighted myself and planted the block under one end of the bench as if it had been forever attached. Now I am ready to blast.

Blasting with twenty-five pounders requires some improvising. I lie back on the incline, put my feet up on the bench and lowered the dumbbells toward the floor. From that position with my palms forward I raised the weights in a curling movement, a nice tight contraction at the chest and shoulders and a slow full extension down, pause and up. A set of ten and I press the dumbbells overhead, palms facing each other, to starting position number two. From the overhead position I lower both weights with concentration in a perfect triceps extension movement to burn and pump the back of the arms; ten reps and mission accomplished.

I slightly rearrange my extended arms allowing them to reach back and outward as I lower the weights in a fly movement to affect the pecs and lats at once. This action is difficult and done precisely with a three-count pause at its peak of extension followed by a slow return, pause and continuation for another ten reps. The timing is right to sit up, shift to the end of the bench, bend forward and allow the now-respectable twenty-fives to hang to the floor. My legs are together and I'm resting my torso on the thighs. The breaths are coming on strong and the pump is solidifying. The burn is being chased about the upper body like a scalded hound dog. I'm in heaven. I tug the dumbbells from a palm-counterpoised placement into a rear deltoid-slash-back movement and knock out ten mean reps.

I sit up calmly and place the weights on my thighs as I review the room lost to me for the past five minutes. It's looking a whole lot better after a pump, a burn and some sweat. No stopping. I shake my hands one by one as I resume my easy breathing. The dumbbell rack is still bare except for some cute pink things nobody'll go near. Fine by me. I've got my hands full. I start the process again: shrugs, curls, extensions, flys, bent-over laterals. A total of five delirious sets with minor pauses for minor adjustments and it's time to move on.

Is that an eighty-pounder that young man is about to unloose? If I coordinate this move just right I can replace the 25s, descend upon the big thing and drag it over here before the crowd notices. I can do this. Done.

Heavy compared to the twenty-fives, I prepare to do one-arm dumbbell rows for some full back work. Knee up on the bench is not my style but by employing the technique I retain possession of the object, as I require it for the stiff-arm pullovers that will follow in my favorite superset fashion. Five sets of six to eight reps. I'm all smiles.

Excuse me; are you finished with the Eighty? Oh, yeah. Sure, Pal. Help yourself. Anytime. I lie back on the bench, feet up and knock out twenty-five slow contractions in the ab-crunch followed by twenty-five leg raises followed by twenty-fve tucks off the end of the bench. Ten minutes of this act and I am done.

You guys hungry? Does anyone know where I can get some protein? I hear you have an ocean. Can I drive the Corvette?

NOCTURNAL PROWESS

Darkness fell quickly that winter evening in southern Africa. Reg and I set out on our fifty-mile journey through the countryside of Johannesburg to a village where physical culture was budding. No obstacles were foreseen; one makes a simple plan and simply executes it. Shortly into our trek, only ten miles out of town, our ride became an irregular bumping. The small vehicle affectionately nicknamed "Frenchy" rebelled, contorted and dragged us into a ditch. I, the designated driver, thinking it cool to be cruising the great Dark Continent with Reg Park, the lion and tiger of bodybuilding, was reduced to a struggling nitwit who found the nail that pierced the tire that pitched us into the precarious posture.

An early morning and engagements throughout the day promoting fitness to an uneducated audience left the two of us spent, somber and dull; show us the hoops and jump we will, but don't expect anything fancy or creative from this tattered pair. We groaned, worked our way free of the Renault, stood up and watched the car rise once relieved of our bodyweight.

No car phone; no AAA on-the-spot tow service, no highway patrol, no traffic on the two lane bi-way. Cozy. Reg, Hercules himself, looked at me. I, the Los Angeles Gladiator and Bomber from America tempted to defensively whine, "I didn't see the nail," looked at Reg. He flexed his enormous calves. I clenched my fists. We both shrugged our shoulders and grinned.

One of those flashlights the size of a pen hung from the key chain. It broke the darkness to reveal a spare tire, a lug wrench and no jack. Without a word we proceeded forward one step at a time, thinking that as each step was accomplished the next would be revealed and its execution enabled. The logic was that of the modern day muscleman, the only wisdom we understood: Action plus muscle equals solution.

We were partners and moved as one. Quickly we memorized our surroundings enabling us to pull the spare tire from the trunk and place it near its destination, the left rear rumpled wheel. Our hands as feelers and our eyes now focusing out of need and will, we removed all the lugs but one. An occasional dash of light from the magic pen renewed our perspective: tires, lugs, wrench and car position. Now the next step was clear. Take off the troublesome flat tire, put on the trouble-free round tire.

Darkness is empowering. The absence of options contributes to might. No need to make decisions conserves energy for the action alone. The mystery of the black beyond our reach stimulates adrenalin, which heightens the senses.

Reg grabbed the bumper and gave it a few warm-up tugs as he set his footing aright. You need to realize we had worked out very early that morning, 6 a.m., and heavy bench pressing was the subject. Our timing of "the spot" was impeccable. Ready? One, two, lift. The car went up, the wheel came off and was swept under the chassis as a support and down came the car. A dash of light renewed our view-point and positions. This time on the count of three I lifted the left rear engine-bearing corner of Frenchy as Big Reg jammed the good wheel on and fed it the lugs. He tightened them as I put the trunk in order. He insisted I drive and off we went, besmudged but no worse for the effort.

MY BUMPER, KNUCKLEHEAD

Nickel's Steak House is down a dark side street off Broadway. All streets off Broadway are dark compared to the brilliant and stunning excitement of the grandest intersection in the world. A bell from some-where sounded twelve times. Midnight in Manhattan is neither late nor early; it's just another hour of the day.

We plodded along, our trophies and gym bags in tow, as we casu-ally, almost aimlessly, returned to our hotel rooms. The steaks were exceptional, the day long and hard, the crowds a crazy blur and the announcement of our victories a bonanza one cannot presume. Our appearances at The Old Townhouse where Dan Lurie held his annual bodybuilding spectaculars in the '70s were complete and we were, for the moment, content.

The four of us — Boyer Coe, Ralph Kroger, Tony Schettino and me — crossed the narrow street diagonally under a street lamp that dumped its light on the dimmed storefronts and tightly parked cars below. What's with the guy in the tux standing in the shadows with the two women dressed to kill? No doubt the threesome wondered what was with the four guys the size of trucks comin' their way. No matter. They stood their ground looking dismayed and fretful. The end of their evening — or was it the beginning? — had taken a turn for the worse. The car belonging to them was a white snappy thing perfectly wedged between a Buick and a Chrysler.

We numbly stared as tuxman got behind the wheel and gunned the puny engine as if it were a Cat earth-mover about to crunch the two-ton obstacle piled before it and be on his merry way, pretty ladies and all. "Excuse me, sir," I said as I bent over and peaked in his win-dow. "We'll help you." He snarled and gave it his best shot, back and forth, another and another, until lady-in-red shrieked, "My bumper, you knucklehead." Tuxman, red as the lady's dress, relunctantly crawled out of the car and turned to us. His shoulders hung low and all the rage had drained from his blotchy and yielding face. The remnants of enthusiasm for a cause calling for muscle and might, plus a reserve of adrenalin to meet the task, gathered beneath our ruddy brows.

Powerlifters all, at one time or another, we assembled at the appropriate corners of the spiffy, yet immovable, vehicle. It's all the same, iron and steel, a grip where necessary, the back and legs and arms in synchronized tightness: the count, ready, one, two, lift, heave and down. Again, ready, one, two, lift, heave and down. In five consecutive shifts we had the little white darling in the middle of the street and pointing in the right direction. Ole Tux motioned to Red and Ms. Tipsy to climb in the liberated vehicle, relieved and awkwardly indebted, yet, suspicious of the perils of the evening before them. We didn't say much; what's to say? Thanks. You bet. No, we don't need a ride. Neat night. Bye. They bounded out of there like gazelle freed from a cage in the jungle.

We picked up our gear and resumed our jaunt in the general direction of home. Tony unwrapped his doggy bag and began to chew on the meaty bone of his leftovers.

"What time's your flight, Draper?"

SEQUINS AND PEARLS

It was the weekend before the Mr. America contest in 1965. My training was going well, as far as I could tell. Truth was I didn't yet know how to tell. I looked okay, but compared to what or whom? I was working hard, eating hard, braced with hard discipline and felt hard. My first months at Muscle Beach were a crash course and I established training methods I would follow forever; but I learned the essentials quickly and settled into private, unmitigated early-morning workouts. They were silent, undistracted and unrelenting: no compromise and no competition. How sweet it is.

Two years of isolated training and I wasn't sure who I had become. I moved with three different training partners at different stages and the reinforcement and friendship were priceless. They knew the Mr. A was on my mind and stood by my side; they were too close, however, to offer the critique and subjective counsel I now sought.

Backstage, Mr. A, 1965. As the contestants filed offstage after the pre-judging they were requested to step onto the box under the lights and pose for the staff photographer. The shots to catalogue the event were without fanfare or painstaking preparation. One, two, three; your name? Thank you. My, those look just like Bill Pearl's posing trunks.

Photographer unknown

Only an outsider could provide an evaluation and dare to place it in my hands. Who could I trust? I needed to know if I was ready for the competition in New York City only eight days away. I also needed a pair of posing trunks. Did I mention—procrastination was one of my specialties, followed by irresponsibility and dimwittedness? Nobody's perfect.

If you got on Washington Boulevard and followed it east for five miles you'd find yourself in East Los Angeles and standing in front of Bill Pearl's Gym. If you walked in the front door at 6 p.m. you'd find Bill, forearms pouring out of a cut-off sweatshirt, sitting behind a wood desk, chair tilted against the wall. If you arrived at 6 a.m. Bill Pearl was under a bar, bench pressing or squatting some absurd weight for a lot of reps. His training partners would be exuding energy, zeal and perspiration. For my first visit I chose the evening hour after a gentlemanly phone call to assure he would be there. Didn't need to go to East Los Angeles if he wasn't. Bill was the man I could and would trust with the deed of critical analysis; thumbs up or … er … thumbs down.

A legend at thirty-five, Mr. America, Mr. Universe — twice, served in the Navy, built and owned several gyms over the years, the man was known for his incredible power and ability to bend coins and tear license plates and phone books in half. "Hi, I'm Dave. Can you tell me if I have muscles? I don't know." "Sure, Dave. Why don't you come here tomorrow morning at six when my huge partners and I can stand you under the skylight and take a good look. Bring your posing trunks."

Me and my mouth. How could I say, "Never mind" or "I don't have posing trunks?" There are the tough times, Buster, when you can't go forward and you can't go back and you can't lie. The only thing left was the truth. I was right on time, my big grin and my big gym bag and my big feet. I found the skylight on my own but couldn't find my posing trunks. No problemo, Big D, you can borrow mine. Bill's generosity is also overwhelming. I didn't ask for music. Silence was loud enough.

I hit a few shots like Joe Weider, The Master Blaster, had taught me. Joe could pose a molting ostrich and he'd win "the overall" and "most muscular" hands down at any pro show on the globe. The gold metallic trunks offered by Bill fit perfectly and I felt pumped by the end of my routine. The guys were excited and full of suggestions, which further warmed me up and put the disabling self-consciousness to rest.

A few more run-throughs with additions and deletions, a change in timing and tempo, posture, facial expression and attitude adjustments and I was a different animal. You can win this thing, Draper. I'm tellin' ya.

MGM TOWN

The cattle call that served to locate Harry Hollard for *Don't Make Waves* was not unlike the *Gladiator* scenario two years prior. The word flooded the gyms like Gatorade and the muscular actors buoyed to the surface. This time the setting was the famous MGM Studios in Culver City, California, where silent films were made and Gable, Bogart and Monroe applied makeup, lunched and shouted, whispered and winked into the polished lenses.

The privilege was monumental — to enter the hallowed halls of the marvelously run-down studios that echoed of stardom and celebrity. No tourist could buy a ticket to this show. The hopefuls lined up to register their names in a less-than-orderly fashion. The distracted guards unwittingly gave me the opportunity to wander down the driveways between the massive studio walls, peer at their heights and pretend to be a part of their importance. I noted the blinking red warning lights at entry ways that indicated filming was under way: Silence, please … do not enter. The great and unseen powers were at work piecing together another lifetime full of wonders and more emotions than the ones we knew as our own, heroes and heroines more alive than the people with whom we worked, ate and slept. I couldn't help but feel lost, ordinary and alone. Jealous is an ugly word.

I moved on and hastened across an abandoned and dusty streetfront with plank walkways, hitching posts and wooden wagons still before old clapboard storefronts and a sheriff's office. Confused for a second I hesitated and glanced to the left and the right; long early morning shadows still formed and a breeze stirred an embroidered curtain in an open window above the Mercantile Shop. The strong smell of coffee wafted along the street and I imagined it came from the saloon or the hotel on the corner. Muted voices carried from a mingled distance and laughter gave a gaiety to the dark beyond the swinging doors of the parlor. Small chirping birds circled overhead and flapped their way to a sprawling oak tree beyond a white fenced cottage. A

Dick Tyler

Russ Warner, master photographer, comedian, generous soul and mentor, stands in the background as he often does. The man this side of the lens is another remarkable guy, Dick Tyler, remembered for his crack-up humor and right-on insight in presenting the California muscle scene of the '60s and '70s to the readers of Weider's muscle rags. I couldn't ask for two better men to stand by my side.

sudden roar broke the calm and antiquity of the make-believe world. I spun to confront a diesel tractor-trailer bearing down Main Street with a plush mobile home in tow that had "Director" written in bold letters above the front door.

I waved as they rumbled by me, just another prop man or electrician earning his wage. A Boeing 727 appeared briefly overhead in the near skies as it readied for landing at the Los Angeles International Airport only two miles away. I grabbed the wooden and metal spokes of an old wagon wheel and tugged to stretch my lats and flex my grip. The sound of a bullhorn in the distance seemed to be giving orders to dutiful wannabe actors — something about the next bus to back lot three. With pause and reluctance I returned to the group, wondering where I was going.

I remember sitting on a vast green and grassy slop where the camera on a dolly and a boom mike were positioned. It was sunny, warm and casual. One by one the performers that made the final cut were given their one minute before the directors, producers and assorted attendants. We were requested to walk up the lawn hand in hand with a Sharon Tate look-alike to a mark five feet from the camera, face each other, speak clumsy sweet nothings, turn and walk away. I thought for sure Larry Scott would get the part as he was a confident and capable guy who already worked in a beach party movie and was occasionally

Reg Lewis adjusting my back on the Muscle Beach set during the filming of *Don't Make Waves*. Tony Curtis looks on with suspicion and cunning. Chet Yorton reads his horoscope with confidence and Sharon Tate bounces on the trampoline like a child.

Photographer unknown

Photographer unknown

The first day of shooting *Don't Make Waves*. I had Mr. Curtis at a disadvantage, him having lost his pants and all, and immediately took control by muttering. Claudia Cardinale melted. Chester Yorton and Ann Elder back me up like true beach buddies do.

seen doing strings of cartwheels and back flips in good form across the manicured lawn. Mr. California, after all. Hollywood is full of surprises. The greatest part about being chosen for a co-starring role in a feature film is being chosen. The second part is working.

This ever happen to you? You recall incidents in your life when you were much younger and wish you could do them over again, not to make major changes, but to tidy them up a little? Born in the east coast vacuum, I was slow to appreciate the things that were happening to me in the brave new world.

Working side by side with Tony Curtis, who couldn't have been more impressive, generous, fun and easy, was a privilege diluted by my stunted self-esteem. Tony got through to me and easily revealed his own insecurity, which we all share, when his words before the camera would not come. He stood with me out of camera and said, "Sometimes I can remember my lines, but they vanish when the director calls for action. I step off the set, close my eyes and in the blackness of my mind I'm able to relax and go back to work in thirty seconds. It happens to everybody."

He genuinely laughed when he tried to lift a refrigerator that I'd been carrying around the set for most of the day. The crew dared him to move it to the background and it didn't budge. He believed they nailed it to the floor to provoke his competitive nature, expecting him

There's a cameraman on the set at all times shooting stills for publicity, production, cataloguing, future advertising and promotion. He or she becomes invisible and moves about the commotion gathering the material. While the director and film crew prepare the next shot, the actors relax, stand ready or rehearse. Sharon Tate practices her leap from the trampoline into my arms for the upcoming scene. We'd only met and barely knew the difference between a hobbyhorse and a trampoline. Nerves were no problem and I was impressed that she trusted me. Tony and Ann Elder look on, catch rays and wait for direction.

Photographer unknown

to move it or die. He called their bluff early on and I, on cue, walked over, grabbed it and carried it up a short flight of stairs, between scenes slapstick. The old refrigerator trick is always good for a few laughs. Just don't ask me to tell a joke.

My, what a big chest you have, thinks Tony Curtis, playing Carlo Cofield in MGM's production *of Don't Make Waves*. My, what a big belly you have I think as I write the caption for you, my friends. Pictured here I weigh 245 pounds, the early days of filming, spring of 1966. By the summer's end as the filming was being completed I weighed a muscular 235 to win the Mr. Universe.

Photographer unknown

Photographer unknown

We wrapped up filming *Don't Make Waves* at Paradise Cove in Malibu. A mock up of a battered hillside home that slid onto the beach during a treacherous California storm released the forlorn and frazzled survivors. Sharon and I do tricks.

Sharon Tate was younger than I and a few solid steps ahead. We became friends like kids in school. I carried her books. She was wrapped up with Roman Polanski and I was married. She felt unthreatened and we could pal around and travel together when promotions required our

Photographer unknown

The last day I reported to make-up at 6 a.m. and the last day I hung the plastic shark's tooth around my neck. All done. Sharon Tate is pushing me around like an overgrown rag doll. I'm tough.

presence. She held onto my arm and wouldn't let go as our four-passenger aircraft worked its way through a storm on a flight to Charlotte for a preview of *Don't Make Waves*. I treasure more than anything the late evening I saw Sharon at Los Angeles International Airport a few years later. She was with friends and dressed in black. She squealed my name and came running over to give me a big hug. We passed in the night like lost friends.

Did you know that Claudia Cardinale lives in a villa in Rome and has a sister who is a world famous photographer? We sat together in director chairs in the darkness of a soundstage the size of a football field. The day's filming was complete and the entire set was closed down early for a holiday weekend. A three-man skeleton crew prepared to pick up two unfinished scenes, one with Ms Cardinale and one with me. We yawned and talked about nothing, as there was nothing to talk about. But we did the awkward thing without awkwardness and it became a pleasure to be simple, unpretentious and ordinary. The next day we were scheduled to take a handful of publicity shots outside the same sound stage. She said she looked forward to it, presented her brief scene to the camera in one take and was gone. I was yet to climb behind the wheel of my bus and suffer the loss of my beloved Malibu. Adventure in the daily life.

MEMORIES OF MUSCLE BEACH

There's a picture that appears in the muscle mags and a book or two that sneaks up on me occasionally and causes me to shudder. I'm twenty-two, two-hundred and fifty pounds and a brand-new resident of Santa Monica, California. I'm a donut covered with powdered white confectioner's sugar and I stand conspicuously like a grinning duffer on the hallowed sands of Muscle Beach. I'm in trunks yet. 'Scuz me. How did I know there was film in the camera?

It was late Saturday morning in mid-July and that picture was just the beginning. I was making friends and getting comfortable in my new world; like a mutt in a new home, tail wagging, chasing balls, yelping … I was ready to play. I wandered across the crowded beach to the water's edge and gazed beyond the surf and splashing kids to the tips of tiny sails racing in the distance. The rugged pier that stretched offshore stood fifty yards to my right and the majestic blue Pacific reached for my knees with each vigorous wave.

I grew up on a lake and the sports in which I competed included swimming. Water was not my problem. It was the ocean I had not yet embraced. The restless and mighty waves fascinated me and what was lurking beneath the surface gripped my imagination. Something about sharks caused me to pause and consider the weight of my courage and fear. My courage sank like a rock, yet fear, powerful as it was, could not defeat my pride. I dove into the churning, seductive white waters and joined in the revelry.

The thrust of the waves and the tug of the undertow captured my attention and soon I was lost in play, my physical yearnings peaked and dared. I flopped and floundered yielding to the sea, for in spite of its mass and muscle it was, today, a gentle bully. One good thrust and one good tug sent me upended into deep waters. I rode the swell above the crowd with a grand view of the undulating, watery, people-packed beaches. Suddenly, the swell dropped me into a deep trough where all but the ominous sea walls vanished. My feet hit the sandy bottom briefly and up again I rose. MAYDAY … MAYDAY … Head for dry land, full speed. Negotiate the rise and fall of this formidable joy ride and head for shore, post haste.

Up and down, again and again, my adrenaline in pursuit. I rolled with the next big, wet, smothering cushion and hoped it would take me to the beach. My feet once more touched the ocean floor as I drifted toward the towering pier and its breakwater protection. The exaggerated sea levels diminished, my short-lived rip-tide consumption left me both energized and weary; most certainly humbled.

The great blue ocean, the vast, inscrutable and wonderful sea, was not yet done with me. I thanked God as I recognized a hazy onlooker, Panic, and his assortment of devices to bring one before his Maker. Clever rascal, I thought, as I continued to grope for shore. I was in reach of the innocent and playful children now, their screams, laughter and wiggling bodies a fantastic delight. We're in heaven for a day. I wanted to hug them, lift them and toss them like my Uncle Johnny did at the lake. Life was never more fun.

Up and down with smaller breaking waves, I struggled with confidence and renewed energy … my foot stepped on something slick … something large and smooth. A swell lifted me up and forward and, at last, I stood waste deep in the foaming release of the big waters. What did I kick? What was that bulky slithering object? I stood frozen. I was safe. I cast my eyes in its direction and wondered if it was alive. Did I encounter a shark? Was it a bather? I scanned the surface looking for movement and saw only families of carefree swimmers. Seconds later I was back at the spot amidst the swells, breakers and undertow; looking, searching, prodding, again within the gaze of Panic … get ye behind me … There, hovering beneath my kicking feet was a large figure of a man looking up, looking still. Down I went to grab the hulk and drag him to the surface. I fought frantically as he slid with the ocean's movements and slipped repeatedly from my arms, my bear hug of insignificant might. We looked like and sounded like all the rest of the mid-summer frolickers, only he was silent. He made it to the water's edge where I dropped him. My lungs ached as I lay on the wet sand like miserable debris. I saw stars and thought wildly. The man, his lungs didn't ache. No stars, no thoughts.

Lifeguards added oxygen and electricity, two hours too late. Nobody knew him. He jumped off the pier early that morning, so they say. Probably around the same time I was posing for that dumb picture.

TRAVELS WITH ZANE

Embarrassment. We nearly give up life, liberty and limb to avoid this wrenching exposure of our raw and delicate ego. Also known as humiliation, this cruelest of feelings I endure regularly and find extraordinarily educational. Kind of like a training injury; gets your attention, causes you to focus and guides you on to repair and rehabilitation. Hopefully, makes you a stronger person. Hmmph.

I have one such memory that's clear and still causes me to shake. We met at the Paris Central Train Station at 7 a.m. one downcast autumn morning to continue our tour of Europe. It was a busy midweek workday and Europeans use the rails like we use our precious cars to get around; up-town, cross-town, and out of the country. Frank Zane, his dear wife Christine and I were destined to arrive in Brugge, Belgium by early afternoon. Our 8:30 a.m. express was packed with solemn commuters subject to another day of mundane travel, newspapers folded, Thermos bottles underarm, briefcases in hand.

As if in a black-and-white scene from life we ever so slowly lurched forward. The collective metal of seventeen passenger cars and freight carriers creaked, groaned and stretched. I looked across endless acres of track, side by side and intertwined, a scattering of switching poles and signal towers, distant corrugated factories, bleak and gray. There were engines of crushing size and power moving incredible mass and solid iron and impossibly thick wheels and axles of steel. Smoke and steam idly drifted and belched from the leaky, Gothic landscape.

Frank looked uneasy, Christine smiled agreeably (everything about Christine is agreeable), and I sought to capture the moment. The London Mr. Universe was behind us, a rather sloppy performance on my part. I got a late start, grabbed the wrong bottle and wound up smearing wheat germ oil on myself backstage. Thick, gooey stuff like glue that smelled rancid and got a lot of attention. Barely survived that night and that's not even the embarrassment. Frank won the amateur Mr. Universe, Arnold the pro Mr. U. and I came in third after Reg Park. I was using lighter fluid to remove the organic oil as the celebrations begin. Don't come near me with that match. Don't worry, Draper, I wouldn't come near you with a ten-foot pole.

Next day I made a quick return to Ohio for an Olympia sortie with Arnold and Sergio, another hysterical blitz. And now, here I am with the Zanes for a brisk tour of Europe, just to say we did, and back to New York City for the Mr. Universe, Mr. America and Mr. World competitions. Give me the "here and now," win or lose. I began to settle down and see what I could see. Soon we'd be traversing the romantic countryside of France: sights and sounds of a very different place, perspectives of very different people.

Frank raised his window suddenly and stuck his head out as if he knew where we were and where we were going. The clanging, shiny and angular abstract of tracks told me nothing. Frank declared we were on the wrong train, going in the wrong direction. Christine's smile broke into something like laughter and my sweet reverie bristled to alarm. We conferred like The Three Stooges as our fellow commuters mildly looked on. Entertaining, those Americans. A troublesome, yet comical, lot. They act as if their pants are on fire. Wish they'd stay home. The train picked up speed, the clacking increased and the dense railway yard thinned out.

Frank, a.k.a. Mr. Universe, leaped over me, hit the center aisle and in two strides reached the box marked, "Emergency Only." He shattered its glass covering with the tiny hammer and pulled the handle with the thrust of a heavy one-arm lat row. The train screeched as if tortured, all wheels locked and inestimable tons of mechanized iron slid forever to a pronounced halt. The side door automatically unlatched and partially opened. Our escape.

We dragged the door open. At a time like this you pretend nobody else exists, just you and your two invincible buddies. If only we could stop time, step out of the picture and watch from a safe place as the action resumed. All three of us looked down at once to discover we were six feet from the tracks and five hundred yards from the station. The commotion behind us was building and beginning to organize. As if catapulted by an unseen force, Frank and I were airborne with Christine close behind, still genuinely enjoying herself.

Heads were out the windows, hundreds of them. Necks straining, expressions of shock, fright, confusion, anger and relief. Hundreds of animated faces shouting and glaring at us. With no composure, no grace, no brains, we grabbed our luggage and made a run for it. A sad and desperate trio staggering as we hauled suitcases and gym bags over slick tracks and railroad ties with conductors, security police and a half dozen furious passengers in hot pursuit. Tell me I'm dreamin'. I don't think so. Frank did it. It was him. I'm a hostage.

We were beat and broken and not up to the long conspicuous walk back to the platforms. The conductors were prompt and serious. So were the police. A rather sizeable crowd had gathered by the time we reached the concrete loading ramps of the station. Nobody asked for an autograph or a most muscular pose. There was an interrogation through an interpreter, phone calls, paperwork, apologies, a fine (no snack) and we were in Brugge by early evening. Gentle old Europe of cobblestone streets and tiny backyards where gates hang crooked on rusting hinges.

We received awards there for our contributions to physical culture. My award was engraved on a six-inch brass plate (I stashed it in my shirt); Frank's was a gold cup on black marble standing eighteen inches tall. I should have pulled the emergency cord. You see, it's that kind of directness, determination and oneness of purpose that enables one to win Mr. Olympia three times in a row.

A TRIBUTE TO ARTIE ZELLER

Gathered in a bright and airy room overlooking a central square in Venice was a collection of the Muscle Beach and Golden Age originals. Lou Ferrigno and Arnold were two of the youngest of about a hundred who came together to honor the memory of Artie Zeller, a beautiful guy who told the story of bodybuilding to everyone, everywhere, through his photography. You know his work; it's your favorite black-and-white candid pictures that depict the age of bodybuilding before it rolled over.

Everyone knew each other, everyone genuinely embraced, everyone a character with history and miles. There was great food, refreshments and excited conversations. Point-and-shoot cameras were constantly being produced and engaged.

Now here's the man I've been talking about: your friend and mine, Artie Zeller. See that black object in the man's hand? That's no mere camera; it's a magic box. He was trying to get away from me but I wouldn't let him. For five big ones, guess who took the picture.

Art Zeller

Artie turned his camera into the sun one evening in '67. The coast of Malibu was still and dreamy and we gave way to its charm.

Eventually John Balik of IronMan spoke and set in motion a series of spontaneous eulogies from an emotional congregation. Arnold told of Artie's mentoring — had us rolling on the floor with his Zeller imitations and stories. They spent a lot of time together and were tight.

Joe Weider was beside himself and Gregory Hines couldn't keep back the tears. Mostly, we laughed, and nodded, and agreed we were a family that had captured a priceless moment in time.

Artie Zeller was a true friend. I loved the guy and miss him. He was, indeed, a most unforgettable character, an original, un-duplicatable. His life was defined by his love for his wife, Josie, his camera and his far-reaching friendships of the bodybuilding world — a curious world that spanned half a century. Artie's first years as a bodybuilder were spent pumping iron with Marvin Eder on Coney Island in the crazy New York City territory. He particularly loved Santa Monica and Venice Beach, his haunts during most of these fascinating years.

Artie's wonder and keen insight bore holes in the social landscape in which he dwelled. He didn't miss a tone or shade of the life that surrounded him. Look at his black and white photography and understand. You don't see a paper photo; you see a story and feel a mood and hear voices and are compelled to listen. They're a moment, still yet continuing. His honest composition takes you there and you don't care to leave.

What is a man without his sense of humor? Artie considered every issue carefully and had strong and bright convictions. At the same time he found comic in most everything, never silly, sometimes cynical, but mostly laughably funny.

His favorite stories centered on his photo shoots, Joe Weider and the beloved bodybuilders. There's the one where a splotch of us were positioned before Artie's precise lens on Venice Beach — muscular, tan and perfectly lit by the fading day's-end sun. Joe Weider was directing activities with great passion, "Artie, Artie, shoot the picture," Joe said. "I'm out of film," replied Zeller. "Artie, I don't care, shoot it anyway," Joe yelped, jumping and flailing his arms.

Artie's camera clicked and all was quiet.

UNDER THE PIER

I picked up on the '60s drift and began building oversized furniture out of pier wood to pay the mortgage. We ate but spent no long weekends in the South of France with the jet set. Hard physical work appealed to me (loved it) and was a habit since my childhood years when delivering heavy boxes of groceries to the fifth story tenants of Hoboken, N.J.

Muscles for display only was to me irrational, the peak of vanity, a frightening conceit. Use that power and mass to overcome. Apply the strength gained for practical purpose; better yet, to build and create.

It was New Year's Eve thirty years ago and I needed wood. It was a dismal day, almost rainy, perfect for working under the moist and muffled pier. The structure was hundreds of yards by hundreds of yards, a vast aged-wood and rusting-metal emporium. Once a grand and popular amusement park, Pacific Ocean Park (POP) was deserted and scheduled for dismantling in the mid-70s. It housed staggering vagrants sharing wine and mattresses in one or two dark pockets and the remainder was mine as I kept to the shadows.

Equipped with my battered handsaw, I slowly began to wander about the magnificent underside of POP. Everything I needed was there in abundance, including the echoing rhythm of the surf, the salty, wet air and a distinct sense of awareness that tingled with fear. It was dark, crisscrossed with timber bracing, illusionary, maze-like and off limits. Once I tripped over a body, another time I was followed to its depths by a pair of hairy muscular legs. Stories for another time. After carefully selecting each piece, I gathered my wood at the pier's edge. No easy task, 5x7s and 3x12s — twelve-feet long, wet and slippery — cut, dragged, stacked and guarded. All after a tough early-morning New Year's Eve workout.

Across the sand two hundred yards away sat my beat-up station wagon, built for the task. I sat atop the aging Douglas Fir and assessed my treasure. One day soon this stack would become a massive four-poster bed, two tables to match and a chest of drawers. Burned, distressed and finely smoothed. Brass, leather and rusty metal would be affixed for a subtle touch. It would be cut, fitted, carved, drilled, bolted, pushed and pulled, and turned over and over again until, with all its mistakes, it was just right.

Hungry, thirsty and getting chilly as the last of the year's sun went down, I prepared for the hardest part of the day, hauling my booty to the wagon. You see, it's all a workout. Reps counted while cutting off the planks. Sets counted as they're lugged, sorted and piled. And now, the intense powerlifting match across the deep sand. Technique ... lean planks at a forty-five degree angle against a piling, largest board on the bottom and stacked with sure balance. Now, as if squatting or deadlifting, approach the pulpy weight, tight-bodied, with focus, accomplishment and psychological might. By feel and instinct locate the center of gravity with your strongest shoulder. Three deep breaths … LIFT … Steady … one step at a time, another and another till the feat is done.

Crossing the beach that evening was rich and exhilarating. I ached, panted and grimaced. I strained until I could go no further — the backside of my battered and listing workhorse, the White Voyager, and sent the wood down with a thud. Ah. Champagne for the soul and cheer to the spirit. Let the years never cease.

GEORGE BUTLER—GOING BACK

Going back twenty-five years to rummage through my mind can be a musty experience. Not every thought I turn over is a precious and delicate item of nostalgia or a rusting, rugged tool used to forge a splendid future. Dim recollections, they are more like sagging, threadbare, spring-popping mattresses and worn-out, tight-legged bell-bottoms: often embarrassing, uncomfortable and tiresome. The '70s were for me lusterless and without grand imagination. Not necessarily bad years, they just happened.

What went on in the land of bodybuilding, I'm not sure. I carried on my merry weightlifting with internal enthusiasm and fulfillment like a fly-cast fisherman in a secret cove on his favorite lake up north. I missed the Olympias, the Mentzer-Schwarzenegger Battle and the whole muscle population explosion. It's as if I had peacefully slept.

One day amidst those sleepy times, Artie Zeller came to my house in Playa Del Rey for a friendly visit, as he often did to break up his day. He brought with him a very nice young man, George Butler; both were carrying large, professional cameras. I was working on a chandelier of beams, chain and rusted iron the size of a Volkswagen. The torch was blazing and tools were scattered everywhere in my workplace. I looked like … well … a madman; broken goggles, shredded jeans, barefooted and generally dirty. I had taken up heavy barbell curls and push-presses for the summer and was busting out of a tie-dyed tank top This pleasant scene was further enhanced by my bearing a lingering symptom of mild acetylene poisoning; a slack, slightly paralyzed jaw. Cute. Conversation was one-sided. I listened and uttered grunts as we sat around that enlightening afternoon. George Butler, a smooth gentleman, the Pumping Iron film master and me, Bomber gone bonkers.

You can't live and die by these horrific faux pas. They are indelible and cringing yet so outrageous as to be too good to be bad. To this day I smile upon the event and am flattered by the visit. You can't kill pride. And for all these years I think the good fellow thinks I'm a nut. The story has just begun.

Pumping Iron, the film that breathed super life into bodybuilding and set it amongst the constellations, celebrated its twenty-fifth anniversary in spring 2000. The writer, producer and director, George Butler, was at the Arnold Classic, also celebrating its twenty-fifth year in Columbus. A gathering of the film's stars — Franco, Lou, Arnold, Ed Corney, Mike Katz — were being interviewed for an HBO special as part of the film's re-release in the summer in conjunction with Arnold's big show—a staggering co-incidence in the year 2000. Further coincidence, as a spokesman for World Gym, I was there also and wondered if I would bump into George. Now that I could speak I could, no doubt, put my entire foot in my mouth.

Friday late morning as a World Gym convention breakfast was winding down I was invited to the stage to welcome the gym owners to the seminars that were to follow. As I approached the microphone a special acknowledgement was made to a celebrity in the audience: Pumping Iron's own, George Butler. Evidence of his reverence was clear. I slurped out a few heart-felt words ... hi, nice, good, happy, er, swell, so-long ... and casually made toward the famous exit, where George stood beaming with both hands extended. One looking on might think we were long-lost friends. As indeed, we were.

The obvious next thing long-lost friends must do is to get to know each other. As we were off in different directions for the day, we arranged an appointment for a forty-five minute interview later that evening. The interview went on for nearly two hours during which we recorded historical gaps and recent enterprises. No mention was made of the elaborate hanging lamp of burned beam and rusted metal or the clown that hung it twenty-five years ago. Upon parting George put his hand to his heart and said, "You bury me or I'll bury you." Friends for life.

STEVE REEVES

A door closed that I expected would remain open forever. Steve Reeves died and I didn't know him. I stood behind him backstage at an extravagant Dan Lurie contest in Manhattan off Times Square; he was being awarded a medal of honor and I was pumping up for the evening's exhibitions. I declined, that night, offers to meet the man, the star, the legend of Hercules. He was tall, stately and handsomely dressed. What was he doing here? — I thought, the occasion too slight for his presence. I was an oily, smelly and gritty gym rat, a slovenly and garish image in comparison. I was, also, busy. Another time, I thought. The Golden Fleece slipped through my fingers.

I missed Steve Reeves on the silver screen, as well. Though he gave majestic form to the meager goals I sought, he appeared to me on posters only. Movie-going was out of reach during my childhood. The beauty and heroics of this Hercules, however, could not be chained. I ached to look like him and knew I couldn't. It wasn't till after winning the Mr. America that I saw the man again; television portrayed him amidst commercials on a seventeen-inch RCA. There was no hiding the handsomest of men who possessed muscular grace beyond compare.

Not many people I hung with or talked to knew Reeves. The Muscle Beach originals — Zabo, Joe Gold, Chuck Collras, Armand Tanny — knew him, yet gave me small insight into his life. Rich tales about every real and imagined character that walked the sands of Muscle Beach or served hard time in The Dungeon were shared and relived by the players, as the curtain closed on that burnished era. No stories, no observations, not a clue.

In '63 I dropped out of the sky like a lost bell-tower pigeon from Jersey. Russ Warner picked me up in Santa Monica and saw to the restoration and re-direction of my wings. A jewel, Russ took the classic and most-prized photographs of Steve Reeves, standing atop the world and seeking the heavens. No one comes close to Reeves in stirring the heart by way of muscle and might, balance and striking feature, bearing and countenance. Curious. Russ, in all his vividness and vitality, gave me no notion of the man, Steve Reeves.

I ask and can answer only one question: Who, after all these years, comes close? No one. One doesn't take perfection, should one perceive it, and improve upon it. You can only admire it and feel very, very good.

ARNOLD SCHWARZENEGGER, THE GREAT

It was not infrequently suggested that I open a gym, do what I like to do and live happily ever after. Why did I know there was more to it than that? The dumb idea was never remotely entertained, not even for

The following photographs are of a collection dear to the hearts of a core of muscle builders who think of the late '60s as the Golden Era of Bodybuilding. As Russ Warner captured the spirit of the Muscle Beach Days, so Artie Zeller embraced the muscle life of the '60s.

The work out for the evening is done but not complete without a conference of four. Mid-summer has us relaxed as we approach the eight-week marker. Serge Jacobs is the non-competing stabilizer from Holland who encourages us and offers an objective eye. Arnold and I plan with Frank our individual forthcoming strategies. Frank's 205. There's time …

Art Zeller

a second. Enter one ear, exit the other. Goodbye. One couldn't separate me from my training and the gym, but I cannot say it was a swell
love affair that had me enthralled and blinded to other stimuli in life. I
was not soaked in passion for barbells; my grip on the dumbbells was
not a tender and longing embrace. I walked into the gym, nodded to
anyone who was there and got to work, post haste. Crunches, leg raises;
you know the routine. When the deed was done, I was gone. See ya.

One day a gym in town closed down and someone said, "Let's
reopen it." I felt a little tug. Sounds simple. I mentioned it to Laree, my
good friend, and the next day she prepared a business proposal. The
following year we were married and had a World Gym in Santa Cruz.
October was the month, '89 the year and we endured the earthquake
that knocked central California silly.

Arnold watched the progress and said, "Dave, when you do a grand
opening let me know. I will help." The gym was open for business but
the detail work was not complete till February the following year. Lynn,

Best bars for squatting are bent bars. The weight settles down across the back
and doesn't roll around looking for trouble. There's always a curious on-looker
ready to make a comment. "Zabo. Who let's these guys in here?"

Art Zeller

Art Zeller

Another day in the journey, another pump, another gallon of water, another lesson learned. You toss the thoughts out there and talk them over: resolve a problem, share an insight, make a plan and laugh at the nonsense. "See ya tonight, man. Chest and back." Like protein, it helps the muscles grow.

Arnold's secretary, called one Thursday afternoon to let me know "Arnold has Friday a week from tomorrow free if you can put something together." The great news for a grand opening could not have had better timing. We were dazed and stumbling seven days a week, sunrise to sunset, the tunnel with no end, not even an oncoming train in sight.

We leaped as if charged with electricity. In seven days the tasks, which had taken on the rigidness of road kill, were completed. The word was out and newspapers and TV suddenly took interest in our project and plans. Press releases were distributed and thirty-second spots on pop radio could be heard at prime times throughout the week. Over a thousand people showed up with special passes that allowed entrance to the rather spectacular affair. Santa Cruz enjoys good food and the caterers were excited to oblige. The World Gym of seven-thousand square feet was pleasantly over-run with extraordinarily well-behaved people.

Art Zeller

Franco can't be seen but he's in the far corner of the gym loading up a bar for deadlifts and this could take all day. Remember, Zeller is the man stealthily roving about the gym with chuckling remarks and a face anointed with contentment. That's Big Mike Katz on the cables and Christine Zane's husband, Frank, with his back this way. The Oak is firmly rooted. No music but the orchestration was stunning.

There's a busy yet small airport in neighboring Watsonville that has seen a jet or two in its past. Arnold and his entourage landed there, on time, no hitch, with the California Highway Patrol on hand to escort the white limousine convoy that we provided. Very cool driving up Route 1, two limos flanked by two motorcycle escorts, a police car at the rear: What did the people think? Arnold and I talked about old times and skiing during the thirty-minute drive. More than once I felt like scrambling through the sunroof, shouting and waving at every-body. I fought the urge.

The crowd was still forming when we arrived at twilight. Arnold knew the work before him and immediately assumed his roll. He pen-etrated the throng and began making his way through the gym, shaking hands, signing autographs, embracing the girls as the cameras clicked and engaged in honest conversation with every opportunity. At one point he choreographed a group picture starring the local Special

Olympics Team who had gathered at the lifting platform in their colors and gear.

The hungry news media had a picnic. Conan the Barbarian, with Grace Jones hanging on his arm, was laughing and playing and eating and drinking, live in Santa Cruz. The Terminator was stomping around in their backyard. Seven-time Mr. Olympia leaned against a squat rack and talked into their cameras about muscles, politics and being a dad.

Never stalled for long, the big friendly guy made his way up the staircase to the loft where the aerobic equipment spread out and another hundred people jammed for a birds-eye view of the action. The heat was building and the natives were getting restless; they began to grab at him and I knew the end was near. I joined Arnold, now with Joe Gold, to act as the host and his right guard, Joe on his left. We made our way to the steel railing and looked down at the ebullient fun-makers, a mass of mild and congenial rioters. I chose to speak to them, thank them and introduce them to the evening's mystery guest. But

Pumping Iron, the bottom line.

Art Zeller

how could I expect to gain their attention? How could I dare interrupt the frolic?

Er ... Excuse me, everybody ... there was instant and absolute silence. Oops. Now look what I did. I handed the mike to Arnold and he did the rest: ludicrous old stories about our travels together had the mob roaring, training advice had young men making mental notes and bold encouragement gave us pins and needles.

Twenty minutes later he was ducking his head into the white limousine declaring, "I'll be back" to the delight of fans. The jet was already warming up.

The last of the night's workout, donkey calf raises. They are like squats to the calves.

Art Zeller

11

RARE OLD MAGAZINE COVERS
Including Early Editions of
Blimp Illustrated and *It's a Whale's World*

We've come to the end, nearly. All has been said and done. Well, almost. The twenty-seven pages to follow display the magazine covers upon which I appeared largely through the '60s and '70s. Why doesn't that seem like such a very long time ago? Another century, after all.

When the website, davedraper.com, was in formation in January of 1999, Laree and I began the gathering and organizing of photographs to fill the pages and give the site dimension. One month from commencing the project we had before the visitor fifty pages of information and pictures. I had estimated in my sieve-like mind that there were six or seven magazine cover shots we could count on to help bloat the thin offering, a more is better philosophy.

The site grew and the reader base grew and friendly participation was reflected in the generous contribution of long-buried blasts from the past. Old articles, private collections and memories, magazines from other countries and eventually we amassed a total of twenty-seven covershots.

There now floats in the mysterious vastness of the web an excess of six hundred pages of the davedraper.com e-works and somewhere around seven thousand pages viewed daily. And how did I miss all those covershots? Dunno. Tried?

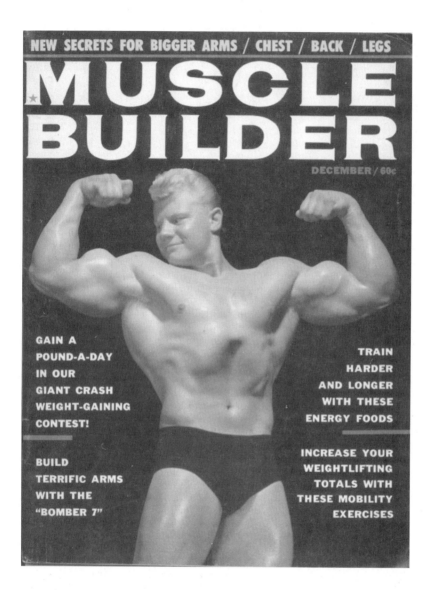

Muscle Builder, December, 1963

THE MAGAZINE CHAMPIONS BELIEVE IN

MUSCLE
BUILDER

INCORPORATING MUSCLE POWER

JULY/50¢

Exposed: THE MUSCLE CRAZE THAT'S RUINING CHAMPIONS

Reported by Joe Weider
Trainer of Champions

"HOW I USED THE TOP
MUSCLE-BUILDING TECHNIQUE
TO BUILD MY 19" ARMS"
Reported by Freddy Ortiz, Mr. Universe

"HERE'S THE TOP MUSCLE-BUILDING
TECHNIQUE THAT MADE ME A
CHAMPION"
Reported by Reg Park, Mr. Universe

THE MUSCLE-BUILDING WISDOM
OF BILL PEARL (Mr. Universe)

BUILDING A MAN-SIZED CHEST
Reported by Larry Scott, Mr. America

HAROLD POOLE'S MR. UNIVERSE
POWERHOUSE DIET SECRETS REVEALED

REPORTS ON: ★ Weightlifting ★ Gossip
★ Exercises that build mighty Arms / Chests
/ Shoulders / Legs

Muscle Builder, July, 1964

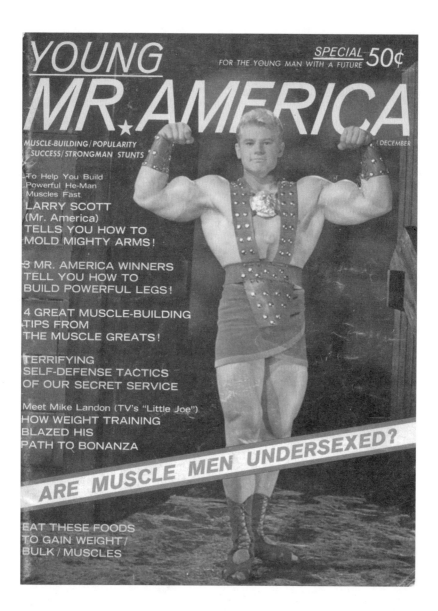

Mr. America, December, 1964

Mr. America, January, 1965

Muscle Builder, August, 1965

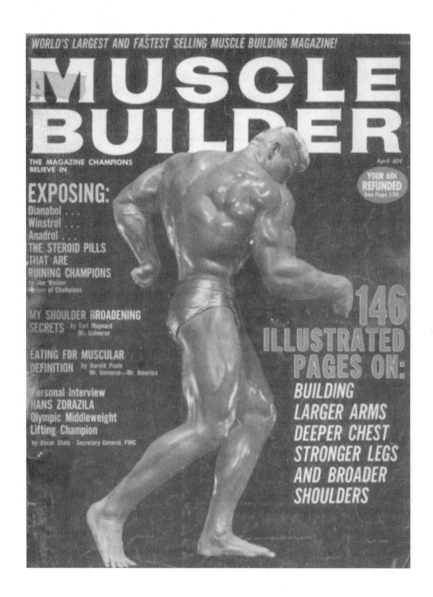

Muscle Builder, April, 1966

Mr. America, September-October, 1966

Mr. America, November, 1966

Mr. America, July, 1967

Mr. America, October, 1967

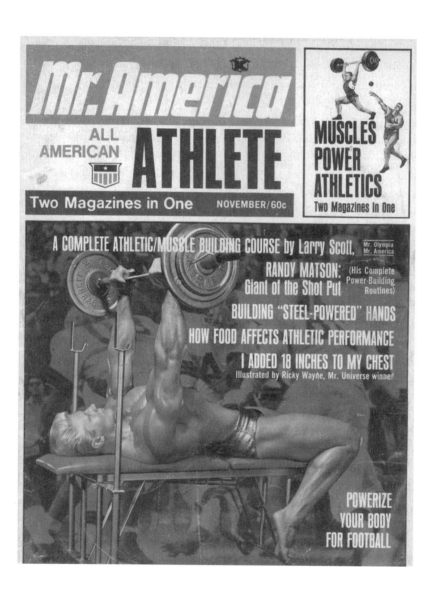

Mr. America, November, 1967

Muscle Builder, November, 1967

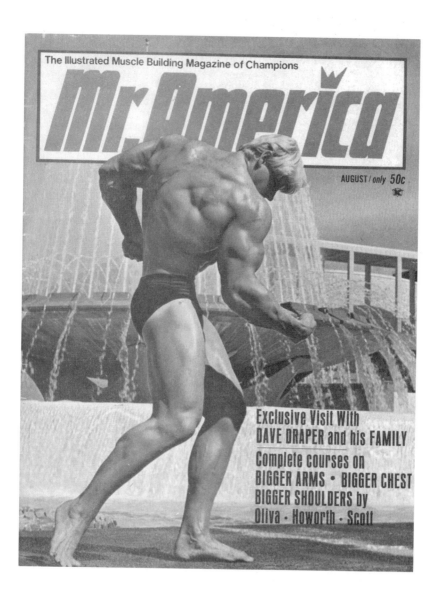

Mr. America, August, 1968

Muscle Builder, September, 1968

Muscle Builder, October, 1968

MAY 1969 60¢

Mr. AMERICA
THE FITNESS MAGAZINE FOR VIRILE MEN

HOW TO SLIM DOWN FOREVER!

LARGER ARMS FOR YOU by Arnold Schwarzenegger "Mr. America"

BUILD A VIGOROUS BODY AS ATHLETES DO

RESORTS WHERE THE GIRLS ARE

THE ATHLETIC LOOK IN FASHIONS

In This Issue

A COMPLETE FITNESS COURSE
fully illustrated

Is it true what they say about
VITAMIN E
THE VIRILITY VITAMIN

Mr. America, May, 1969

JUNE 1969 75c

Mr. AMERICA

THE FITNESS MAGAZINE FOR VIRILE MEN

THE ASTRONAUTS' KEEP FIT PROGRAM

BILL TOOMEY—How The Decathlon Star Made It

ENLARGE YOUR CHEST—HERE'S HOW

DESSERTS THAT SLIM

SURFING CAN BE SEXY

In This Issue

FOODS
THAT
INCREASE
VIRILITY

THE FLAT, SEXY WAIST...
AND HOW TO GET IT

Mr. America, June, 1969

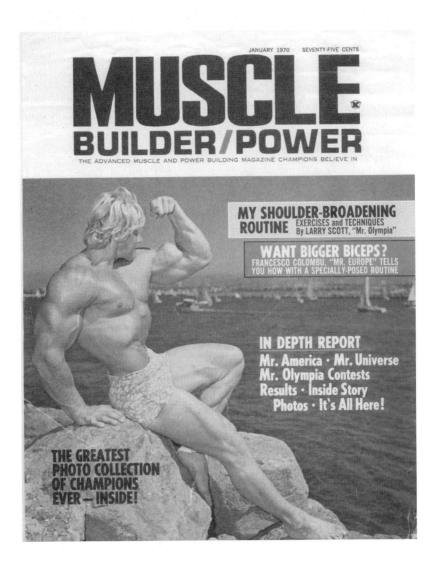

Muscle Builder, January, 1970

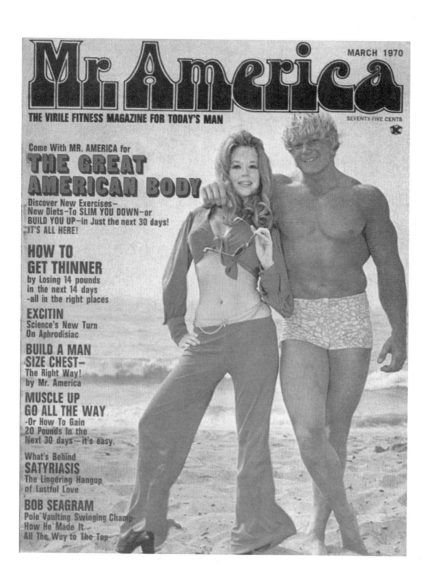

Mr. America, March, 1970

Mr. America, April, 1970

Mr. America, July-August, 1970

Muscle Builder, July-August 1970

Peak, September, 1970

THE OFFICIAL NABBA JOURNAL

health and

Incorporating
MAN'S WORLD

strength

THE DAVE DRAPER STORY JAN 1971 **20**p (4/-)

Health & Strength, January, 1971

Peak, June, 1971

Muscle Builder, September, 1971

THE ADVANCED MUSCLE AND POWER BUILDING MAGAZINE
CHAMPIONS BELIEVE IN
MUSCLE
25p
K 48632
JULY / $1.00
ARNOLD SCHWARZENEGGER'S NEW DIMENSIONS
COMPLETE CHEST BUILDING COURSE
PHOTOS-LATEST TECHNIQUES AND PRINCIPLES
A COMPLETE ILLUSTRATED COURSE
SERGE NUBRET IS OLYMPIA-MAD
AND THAT'S BAD FOR ARNOLD!
A DARK SHADOW OVER ARNOLD
REPORTS RICKY WAYNE
WATCHING KEN WALLER ("MR. AMERICA")
SLIM AND MUSCULARIZE HIS WAIST
A FULL ILLUSTRATED COURSE
POWERIZE YOUR WORKOUTS!
TRAINING HARDER AND LONGER MADE EASY
FABULOUS PHOTOS-COMPLETE REPORT
BAGHDAD'S MR. UNIVERSE
(MEET NEW FACES—SURPRISE RESULTS!)
A NEW STAR IS BORN
DON HOWARD—THE TULSA GIANT
(HE TELLS HOW HE GOT THAT WAY)
WHY BLAST YOUR MUSCLES?
PROVOCATIVE THOUGHTS BY
AMERICA'S MOST FABULOUS STAR
LARRY SCOTT, "MR. AMERICA"
ASK THE CHAMP
ARNOLD TELLS YOU
HOW THE SUPER-STARS MAKE IT!
SOLVING YOUR TRAINING PROBLEMS
FRANCO COLUMBU SOLVES THEM FOR YOU
DAVE DRAPER
WEIDER TRAINED CHAMPION

Muscle Builder, July, 1973

12

STOKING THE TRAINING FIRE

> Woke up this mornin'
> Couldn't find my shoes
> My baby done left me
> And I got the trainin' blues.

Do the haunting words of this sad refrain echo in your mind? Has lifting heavy metal lost its thrill? Do you gag at the thought of bench pressing? Do you find the gym depressing and its members a bunch of twits?

Welcome to BBA, Bodybuilders Anonymous. Stand up, state your name and repeat, "I am a bodybuilder and I have lost my will to train." This is a common and treatable disease, not to be ashamed of or denied. There are ten steps we must consider if we are to overcome this malady and put our training in good order. Let's work together, one day at a time.

1 — The first step in recovering your muscle-building spirit is to review your early training goals. Question: Why are you training in the first place? The desires, the passions, the anticipated rewards we originally formed are remarkable and we need to never lose sight of them. They are the essential catalyst of our formation, the spark that makes us go. They set us in motion, keep us in motion. Our goals, like DNA, ultimately account for our uniqueness and significance.

2 — Reassessing every now and then is healthy and a sure sign of growth. Adjust your early impressions and objectives at this point in time. Who wants barn-door lats, cannonball delts and washboard abs, anyway? Sounds a little silly, come to think of it. I'm not suggesting your set your sights low to assure that you don't miss the mark. Set them high. Just don't set yourself up for disappointment.

Bodybuilders tend to be tough on themselves once they've become regularly invested. This is good if it's drive: You'll grow. This is bad if it's driven: You'll burn out.

3 — Our training edge can't be expected to maintain its sharpness; life is a tough gruel through which it must cut. We have only so much time, energy, focus and discipline. Something's gotta give. Job, family and responsibilities, though often filled with joy and satisfaction, devour us.

Life is big and can bully us. Our training will take a hit once in a while. Be strong, don't submit, accept daily living. If you fall, pick yourself up. Adjust your exercise schedule to suit the times, the struggles, the detours. Remember, the gym and the workouts prepare us for the grind. It's during these days that your training pays off in toughness, endurance and perseverance. How does anybody get through the week without training, the great stabilizer?

4 — After starting exercise, stopping and starting again, you've come to realize you need it. You feel better, much better, when you're on than when you're off. You know the list of endless benefits. You're happier with yourself and about yourself when you eat right and work out. You're more comfortable, less stressed, more competent and confident. Of course, you feel less guilty because you're taking care of yourself as compared to neglecting yourself. What a relief. You lift more with less effort in half the time. Your flesh flexes rather than jiggles and there's less where there should be less. Energy and endurance are like buried treasure discovered, keys to doors once locked. Your doctor remarks approvingly about your blood pressure and the checker at the market asks where you work out. Yes!

Laree Draper

Laree and I planned to resurrect my dismantled image — put Humpty Dumpty back together again — in 1987. We had nothing better to do and were sort of unemployed. She loaded her camera bag and we took 205 pictures of me, yours truly, Dave, and after careful editing only this one remained. We were off to a bad start. This lonely photograph launched a few projects where we applied and honed our persistence. It eventually adorned the cover of our first self-publishing effort, *Get Serious*, a 75-page encyclopedia filled with crackers and crumbs. As the captain of an early bombing mission once said, "A bad start is better than no start at all. Let's see if we can make this thing fly, Bombers."

5 — Alas, there's a constant element in daily living about which we stumble. It moves silently and forever and pauses for no one, not for an instant. Neither you nor I have enough; it's time. I listen to people at the gym who are overweight, under-muscled and deconditioned. They tire easily and settle for a small portion of life.

Without energy, they are without enthusiasm, creativity and the joy of living. "You can fix this," I say. They nod reluctantly and say, "I don't have the time."

Mike Neveux

Mike Neveux, cameraman extraordinaire of IronMan Magazine, just happened to be passing by as I was trying on my new World Gym outfit. If only I knew he was photographing me. I could have flexed my lats.

What could possibly be more important? You're twenty-five, or is it forty? And your youth, vitality and zeal threaten to leave you like a receding tide. Is it your job, family and obligations? To whom or to what are you more responsible than you, your health, longevity and quality of life?

What must we do to recover our misplaced training? The corporate term is "prioritize." We must make time — regular, unrushed, focused and devoted training time. Under these conditions only will we respond to our training: build muscle, burn fat, learn, fulfill and enjoy. Squeeze it in when and where you can and you feel half-empty and frustrated. Make time to train.

There are a hundred reasons and a thousand excuses why we can't make it to the gym. If you believe them, they're all valid. Believe this: Stop exercising and things well never get better. They'll only get worse.

6 — This should be a universal command: Do not allow a gap in your training. You cruise, you lose. A day becomes a week; a week becomes a month. Layoffs? Sure, when absolutely necessary, but regard your exercise and menu as part of your life, like your house, your work, eating, sleeping, friendships, good habits and opinions. Spare yourself from training darkness. Don't let a training gap spread over you like an evening fog. It's so hard to find your way home.

7 — Here's another good question: Be honest — Are you new at this? Have you figured it out yet? Listen, this is not complicated stuff. Getting in shape is tough; make no mistake. It takes a lot of patience, discipline and long hours of hard work. But it isn't complex. If you go hunting for secrets, believe the incredible hype and prefer anatomical, biochemical and physiological research to lifting weights and eating good food, then you've got "complicated" and you're off in the wrong direction, more like outer space. Get into the basics of hard training and sound, high-protein eating and stay there.

Superset. Hit heavy workouts. Everybody's worried about overtraining. Sheesh. Push it, blast it, no tiptoeing through the fields of metal. Train with confidence and enthusiasm — the only way to train. If you perceive exercise and hard work as dull and dubious, they will be. Fact is, they are fun, exciting and fulfilling. Your perception may be broken and your confidence not established. Tune them up. Pain, strain, gain.

Sorry, got a little carried away there. Just stay focused on the good old basics should you peruse the worldwide junkyard of information. There are no secret methods, no secret ingredients except enthusiasm and confidence. The seventh step in training resuscitation: Keep it simple, orderly, clear. Practice form and focus. Load, aim, fire, hit the target.

8 — This step is thin yet integral and has to do with moods, urges, rhythms, seasons, vibrations ... that stuff. Sometimes everything is right and nothing is wrong, yet you have the training blues. As long as you're not given to defeat or negativity, ride it out. Don't miss your workouts, don't lay off, don't be cynical, don't complain. Just wait. Be patient. Persist. The fire will come back and you will unknowingly kindle it.

9 — Inspiration, that majestic charge that stirs us, comes when we're loose, open and honest, faithful and hopeful. Inspiration is everywhere. It isn't a thing to pursue; inspiration pursues us. Somewhere in the words above is the ninth training fix — an ether of sorts. Breathe deeply.

10 — Finally, share the good fight with a pal who understands. "Misery loves company" should not be the theme of your relationship. Pity parties are for losers. But kicking things around in the light of good company reveals resolution, clarity and substance. It's like cleaning out your junk drawer and putting it in order.

SMALL JARS

The years under and over the weights, buying and selling them and building gyms filled with them, cleaning around them and standing behind the counter expounding upon their indispensability have given me a thimbleful of insight, which I store in a jar. Writing articles for the magazines, a column for a newspaper and a weekly email newsletter for the davedraper.com website over the years have added another splash to the jar. Walking the gym floors, working, instructing, policing and playing, training others and myself and always observing have filled that jar considerably. I'm not boasting, of course. You see, I've got a small jar.

The point? I've noted, as we are different, so are we very much the same. The gifted are gifted, the brilliant are brilliant and the seemingly ordinary simply carry on. In every instance their lives could measurably be rewarded by a spirited and intelligent participation in the exercise of which we speak in these pages; nutritious eating to serve our bodies, discipline to guide our walk, perseverance to reinforce our determination, patience through which we understand, commitment by which we achieve, motivation that is self-inspired and the exercise of hope by which we continue.

Let's turn up the heat and bring the smelting pot to a boil. You can't leave until you extract something of value, a defining truth or singular fact, the lone answer or mysterious missing clue, one more bit of information to make the way clear or that glint of insight that settles it all. For someone who denies the promise of information and insists on the deed, I sure display a lot of words. The barbells, the dumbbells, the cables and machines, the diets, the practice and the planning, all shape and strengthen the body. Their work does not stop there. It's only begun.

Though it's obvious I've run out of things to say, let me toss out a closing surmise. If you are not already an inveterate musclehead, consider having read this book a significant step in the general direction. Fix a small jar-sized plan in your mind and allow it to breathe and grow and spill over. It's not what you know but what you do that counts.

You'll see.

This page intentionally left blank

RESOURCE APPENDIX
in alphabetical order

BOOKS

General Training Books

A Practical Approach to Strength Training
Matt Brzycki
ISBN: 1570280185

Anabolic Muscle Mass: The Secrets of
Anabolic Reinforcement Without Steroids
Dennis B. Weis
ISBN: 1552100006

Arnold: The Education of a Bodybuilder
Arnold Schwarzenegger, Douglas Kent Hall
ISBN: 0671797484

Barrel Lift, The
Steve Justa
ISBN: Not Available
www.ironmind.com

Beyond Brawn: The Insider's Encyclopedia
on How to Build Muscle & Might
Stuart McRobert
ISBN: 9963616062

Bigger Faster Stronger:
50 Ways to Build Muscle
Dave Tuttle
ISBN: 0895299518

Body Flex, Body Magic
Anja Langer, Bill Reynolds
ISBN: 0809239302

Body for Life:
12 Weeks to Mental & Physical Strength
Bill Phillips, Michael D'Orso
ISBN: 0060193395

Bodybuilding 101: Everything You Need to
Know to Get the Body You Want
Robert Wolff
ISBN: 0809227843

Building the Classic Physique:
The Natural Way
Steve Reeves, John Little, Armand Tanny
ISBN: 1885096100

Challenge Yourself:
Leanness, Fitness & Health At Any Age
Clarence Bass
ISBN: 0960971475

Complete Book of Butt and Legs, The
Kurt Brungardt, Mike & Brett Brungardt
ISBN: 0679754814

Complete Keys to Progress, The
John McCallum
ISBN: 0926888013

Composite Guide to Strongman
Competition, The
Mike Bonner
ISBN: 0791058689

Cory Everson's Lifebalance: The Complete
Mind/Body Program for a Leaner Body
Cory Everson, Greta Blackburn
ISBN: 0399524444

Cory Everson's Fat-Free & Fit: A Complete
Program for Fitness, Exercise & Healthy Living
Cory Everson, Carole Jacobs
ISBN: 0399518584

Designing Resistance Training Programs
Steven J. Fleck, William J. Kraemer
ISBN: 0873225082

Essentials of Strength Training
and Conditioning
Thomas R. Baechle (Editor), Roger W. Earle
ISBN: 0736000895

Fabulously Fit Forever
Frank Zane
ISBN: 1560251379

Facts & Fallacies of Fitness
Mel C. Siff
ISBN: 18681838

Flawless: The Ten-Week, Total-Image
Method for Transforming Your Physique
Bob Paris
ISBN: 0446394068

Frank Zane: Mind, Body, Spirit
Frank Zane
ISBN: 1560251123

Get Buffed!
Ian King
ISBN: Not Available
kingsports@b022.aone.net.au

Getting Stronger:
Weight Training for Men and Women
Bill Pearl, D. Moran
ISBN: 0936070048

Hardcore Bodybuilding:
A Scientific Approach
Frederick C. Hatfield, Tom Platz
ISBN: 0809237288

High Performance Bodybuilding
John Parrillo
ISBN: 0399517715

Insider's Tell-All Handbook
on Weight-Training Technique
Stuart McRobert
ISBN: 9963616097

Ironman's
Ultimate Bodybuilding Encyclopedia
Peter Sisco (Editor)
ISBN: 0809228114

Ironman's
Ultimate Guide to Building Muscle Mass
Peter Sisco (Editor)
ISBN: 0809228130

Ironman's
Ultimate Guide to Natural Bodybuilding
Peter Sisco (Editor)
ISBN: 0809228149

Ironmind: Stronger Minds, Stronger Bodies
Randall J. Strossen
ISBN: 0926888021

Keys to the Inner Universe:
World's Best Built Man
Bill Pearl
ISBN: 0962991007

Lean for Life:
Stay Motivated & Lean Forever
Clarence Bass
ISBN: 0960971459

Lee Haney's Ultimate Bodybuilding
Lee Haney, Jim Rosenthal
ISBN: 0312093225

Loaded Guns
Larry Scott
ISBN: 0963147900

Lou Ferrigno's Guide to Personal Power,
Bodybuilding & Fitness
Lou Ferrigno
ISBN: 0809231255

Lower Body Solution
Laura Dayton
ISBN: 0966275225

Mastery of Hand Strength
John Brookfield
ISBN: 092688803X

Maximize Your Training: Insights from Top
Strength & Fitness Professionals
Matt Brzycki (Editor)
ISBN: 0844283177

Monarch of Muscledom – John C. Grimek
David Gentle
Mail order: $25.00 cash only, no checks
C/O Mark Shaw
384, Ashby Road
Coalville, Leicester LE67 3LE, England

Muscle Mechanics
Everett Aaberg
ISBN: 0880117966

Muscletown USA: Bob Hoffman
The Manly Culture of York Barbell
John D. Fair
ISBN: 0271018550

Not Just Pumping Iron:
On the Psychology of Lifting Weights
Edward W.L. Smith
ISBN: 0398055440

Of Stones & Strength
Steve Jeck, Peter Martin
ISBN: 0926888056

Optimum Power Program, The:
Your Personal Guide to Athletic Power
Michael Colgan
ISBN: 1896817009

New Encyclopedia of
Modern Bodybuilding, The
Arnold Schwarzenegger, Bill Dobbins
ISBN: 0684857219

Periodization
Tudor O Bompa
ISBN: 0880118512

Periodization Breakthrough:
The Ultimate Training System
Steven J. Fleck Ph.D., William J. Kraemer Ph.D.
ISBN: 1889462004

Periodization Training for Sports
Tudor O. Bompa
ISBN: 0880118407

Physical Culture and the Body Beautiful:
Purposive Exercise in the Lives of American
Women 1800-1870
Jan Todd
ISBN: 0865545618

Poliquin Principles, The: Successful
Methods for Strength & Mass Development
Charles Poliquin
ISBN: 0966275209

Power Factor Specialization: Abs & Legs
Peter Sisco, John Little
ISBN: 0809228270

Power Factor Specialization: Chest & Arms
Peter Sisco, John Little
ISBN: 0809228297

Power Factor Specialization:
Shoulders & Back
Peter Sisco, John Little
ISBN: 0809228289

Power Factor Training: A Scientific
Approach to Building Lean Muscle Mass
Peter Sisco, John Little
ISBN: 0809230712

Power to the People: Russian Strength
Training Secrets for Every American
Pavel Tsatsouline
ISBN: 0938045199

Program Design for Personal Trainers :
Bridging Theory into Application
Douglas Brooks
ISBN: 0736000798

Quantum Strength & Power Training:
Gaining the Winning Edge
Pat O'Shea
ISBN: 0964869802

Remembering Muscle Beach: Where Hard
Bodies Began—Photographs & Memories
Harold Zinkin, Bonnie Hearn
ISBN: 1883318017

Resistance Training Instruction
Everett Aaberg
ISBN: 0880118016

Rock, Iron, Steel: The Book Of Strength
Steve Justa
ISBN: 0926888072

Sandow the Magnificent: Eugen Sandow
and the Beginnings of Bodybuilding
David L. Chapman
ISBN: 0252020332

Science and Practice of Strength Training
Vladimir M. Zatsiorsky
ISBN: 0873224744

Serious Strength Training
Tudor O. Bompa, Lorenzo J. Cornacchia
ISBN: 0880118342

Sons Of Samson, Volume 2 Profiles
David Webster
ISBM: 0926888064

Static Contraction Training: How to Gain
Up to 25 Pounds of Pure Muscle Mass
Peter Sisco, John Little
ISBN: 0809229072

Steve Reeves—Worlds to Conquer,
An Authorized Biography
Chris LeClaire
ISBN: 0967675413

Strength Training for Seniors: Instructor Guide
for Developing Safe & Effective Programs
Wayne L Westcott, Thomas R Baechle
ISBN: 0873229525

Strength Training for Young Athletes
William J. Kraemer, Steven J. Fleck
ISBN: 0873223969

Stronger Abs & Back: 165 Exercises to Build
Your Center of Power
Greg Brittenham, Dean Brittenham
ISBN: 0880115580

Strongman Competition
Mike Bonner
ISBN: 0791058778

Successful Long-Term Weight Training
Steven J. Fleck, Cecil Colwin
ISBN: 1570281947

Super Slow: The Ultimate Exercise Protocol
Ken Hutchins
ISBN: 0963319906

Super Squats: How to Gain 30 Pounds of
Muscle in 6 Weeks
Randall J. Strossen
ISBN: 0926888005

Supertraining
Mel C. Siff, Yuri V. Verkhoshansky
ISBN: 1874856656

Target Bodybuilding
Per A. Tesch
ISBN: 0880119381

Teenage Bodybuilding
Ed Gaut
ISBN: 0964094525

Thinking Big
Skip LaCour
ISBN: Not Available
www.skiplacour.com/thinking.htm

Winning the Arms Race
Charles Poliquin
ISBN: 097019790X

Olympic Weightlifting Books

An Introduction to Olympic-Style
Weightlifting
John M. Cissik
ISBN: 0070434883

Weightlifting Encyclopedia, The:
A Guide to World Class Performance
Arthur J. Drechsler
ISBN: 0965917924

Powerlifting Books

Power: A Scientific Approach
Frederick C. Hatfield
ISBN: 0809244330

Powerlifting
Barney R. Groves
ISBN: 0880119780

Powerlifting Basics, Texas-Style
Paul Kelso
ISBN: 0926888048

Abdominal Training Books

Awesome Abs: The Gut Busting
Selection for Men & Women
Paul Chek
ISBN: 1552100022

Beyond Crunches
Pavel Tsatsouline
ISBN: 0938045172

Complete Book of Abs, The
Kurt Brungardt
ISBN: 0375751432

Flexibility Books

Beyond Stretching:
Russian Flexibility Breakthroughs
Pavel Tsatsouline
ISBN: 0938045180

Sport Stretch
Michael J. Alter
ISBN: 0880118237

Stretching (20th Anniversary Edition)
Bob Anderson, Jean Anderson
ISBN: 0936070226

Stretching Scientifically:
A Guide to Flexibility Training
Thomas Kurz
ISBN: 0940149303

Supple Body, The:
The Way to Fitness, Strength & Flexibility
Sara Black, Antonia Deutsch, Liliana
Djurovic
ISBN: 0028604415

Vital Health Books

The Heart Disease Breakthrough: The
10-Step Program That Can Save Your Life
Thomas Yannios, M.D.
ISBN: 0471353094

Nutrition
Diet Manipulation Books

Amino Acids and Proteins for the Athlete:
The Anabolic Edge
Mauro Di Pasquale
ISBN: 0849381932

Back to Protein: The Low Carb/No Carb
Meat Cookbook
Barbara Hartsock Doyen
ISBN: 0871319128

Bowes & Church's
Food Values of Portions Commonly Used
Jean Pennington, Anna De Planter Bowes,
Helen N Church
ISBN: 0397554354

Carbohydrate Dieter's Diary, The
Corinne T. Netzer
ISBN: 0440508525

Complete Book of Food Counts, The
Corinne T. Netzer
ISBN: 0440225639

Complete Book of
Vitamin and Mineral Counts, The
Corinne T. Netzer
ISBN: 0440223350

Complete Guide to Food for Sports
Performance, The: A Guide to Peak
Nutrition for Your Sport
Louise Burke
ISBN: 1863739165

Complete Guide to
Vitamins, Minerals & Herbs
Art Ulene, M.D.
ISBN: 1583330046

Creatine: The Power Supplement
Melvin H. Williams, Richard B. Kreider, J.
David Branch
ISBN: 073600162

Dynamic Nutrition for Maximum
Performance: A Complete Nutritional
Guide for Peak Sports Performance
Daniel Gastelu, Fred Hatfield
ISBN: 0895297566

Ergogenics Edge, The:
Pushing the Limits of Sports Performance
Melvin H. Williams
ISBN: 0880115459

Everyday Low Carb Cookery -
Revised Edition
Alex Haas
ISBN: 0965754812

Everything You Need to Know
About Fat Loss
Chris Aceto
ISBN: 0966916824

Fats That Heal, Fats That Kill: Guide to Fats,
Oils, Cholesterol & Human Health
Udo Erasmus
ISBN: 0920470386

Ironman's
Ultimate Guide to Bodybuilding Nutrition
Peter Sisco
ISBN: 0809228122

Ketogenic Cookbook, The
Dennis Brake, Cynthia Brake
ISBN: 1886559996

Ketogenic Diet, The: A Complete Guide
for the Dieter & Practitioner
Lyle McDonald
ISBN: 0967145600

Living Low-Carb: The Complete Guide to
Long-Term Low-Carb Dieting
Fran McCullough
ISBN: 0316557684

Low-Carb Cookbook, The: Complete
Guide to the Healthy Low-Carbohydrate
Lifestyle with over 250 Delicious Recipes
Fran McCullough, Michael & Mary Eades
ISBN: 0786862734

Manly Weight Loss: For Men Who Hate
Aerobics & Carrot-Stick Diets
Charles Poliquin, L. L. Dayton
ISBN: 0966275217

Metabolic Diet, The
Mauro DiPasquale
ISBN: 0967989604

Metabolic Typing Diet, The: Customize
Your Diet to Your Own Unique & Ever
Changing Nutritional Needs
William Linz Wolcott, Trish Fahey
ISBN: 038549691

Metabolism at a Glance
J. G. Salway
ISBN: 0632052740

Muscle Meals
John Romano
ISBN: 1889462012

Nancy Clark's Sports Nutrition Guidebook
Nancy Clark
ISBN: 0873227301

Natural Hormonal Enhancement
Rob Faigin
ISBN: Not Available
http://www.extique.com/

Nature's Sports Pharmacy: A Natural
Approach to Peak Athletic Performance
Frederick C. Hatfield
ISBN: 0809232219

Neanderthin: Eat Like a Caveman to
Achieve a Lean, Strong, Healthy Body
Ray V. Audette
ISBN: 0312243383

Nutrition Almanac (4th Ed)
Gayla J. Kirschmann, John D. Kirschmann
ISBN: 0070349223

Nutrition for Health, Fitness & Sport
Melvin H. Williams
ISBN: 0697295109

Nutrition for Serious Athletes
Dan Benardot
ISBN: 0880118334

Peak Performance:
Training & Nutritional Strategies for Sport
John Hawley, Louise Burke
ISBN: 1864484691

Priming the Anabolic Environment:
A Prastical, Scientific Guide to the Art &
Science of Building Muscles
William D. Brink
ISBN: 1552100030

Protein Power: The High-Protein/Low
Carbohydrate Way to Lose Weight, Feel Fit
& Boost Your Health-in Just Weeks!
Michael R. Eades, Mary Dan Eades
ISBN: 0553574752

Realities of Nutrition
Ronald M. Deutsch, Judi Morrill
ISBN: 0923521259

Right Protein for Muscle & Strength, The
Michael Colgan
ISBN: 1896817092

Sliced—State-Of-The-Art Nutrition for
Building Lean Body Mass
Bill Reynolds, Negrita Jayde
ISBN: 0809241161

Sports & Exercise Nutrition
William D. McArdle, Frank IKatch, Victor Katch
ISBN: 0683304496

Super T: The Complete Guide to Creating
an Effective, Safe & Natural Testosterone
Supplement Program for Men and Women
Karlis C. Ullis, M.D.
ISBN: 0684863359

Supercut:
Nutrition for the Ultimate Physique
Joyce L. Vedral, Bill Reynolds
ISBN: 0809253879

Ultimate Sports Nutrition
Frederick C. Hatfield
ISBN: 0809248875

Ultimate Sports Nutrition Handbook, The
Ellen Coleman, Suzanne Nelson Steen
ISBN: 0923521348

Understanding Body Building Nutrition & Training: Practical Answers to Common Bodybuilding Challenges
Chris Aceto
ISBN: 0966916832

Related Training Books

Explosive Power & Strength:
Complex Training for Maximum Results
Donald A. Chu
ISBN: 0873226437

Jumping into Plyometrics
Donald A. Chu
ISBN: 0880118466

Isokinetics in Human Performance
Lee E. Brown (Editor)
ISBN: 0736000054

Mental Edge, The: Maximize Your Sports Potential With the Mind/Body Connection
Ken Baum, Richard Trubo, Karch Kiraly
ISBN: 0399524819

New Toughness Training for Sports, The: Mental, Emotional & Physical Conditioning
James E. Leohr
ISBN: 0452269989

Power Training for Sport:
Plyometrics for Maximum Power Development
Tudor O. Bompa
ISBN: 0889626294

Precision Heart Rate Training
Ed Burke (Editor)
ISBN: 0880117702

Sports Medicine — Rehabilitation Books

7 Minute Rotator Cuff Solution
G. Robinson, Horrigan
ISBN: 0944831257

Athletic Taping & Bracing
David H. Perrin
ISBN: 0873225023

Jock Doc's Body Repair Kit, The: The New Sports Medicine for Recovery & Increased Performance
Andrew Feldman
ISBN: 0312199058

Rehabilitation Techniques
in Sports Medicine
William E. Prentice (Editor)
ISBN: 0072894709

Shoulder Injuries & Weight Training:
Reducing Your Risk
Cynthia L. Humphreys
ISBN: 1552100138

Sports Massage for Peak Performance
Gregory Pike
ISBN: 0060951672

Sports Medicine Bible, The: Prevent, Detect & Treat Your Sports Injuries Through the Latest Medical Techniques
Lyle J. Micheli, Mark D. Jenkins
ISBN: 0062731432

Reference Books

ACSM's Exercise Management for Persons With Chronic Diseases & Disabilities
American College of Sports Medicine, J. Larry Durstine (Editor)
ISBN: 0873227980

ACSM's Resource Manual for Guidelines for Exercise Testing & Prescription
American College of Sports Medicine, Jeffrey L. Roitman
ISBN: 0683000268

Biomechanics in Sport: Performance Improvement & Injury Prevention
(Encyclopaedia of Sports Medicine)
Vladimir M. Zatsiorsky
ISBN: 0632053925

Bodyworker's Muscle Reference Guide, The
Craig McLaughlin
ISBN: 0965567923

Exercise, Nutrition & Weight Control
Perspectives in Exercise Science & Sports Medicine, Vol 11
David R. Lamb (Editor)
ISBN: 1884125700

Exercise Physiology: Exercise,
Performance, and Clinical Applications
Robert A. Robergs, Scott O. Roberts
ISBN: 0815172419

Exercise Physiology:
Energy, Nutrition & Human Performance
William D. McArdle, Frank Katch, Victor Katch
ISBN: 0683057316

Exercise Physiology:
Human Bioenergetics & Its Applications
George A. Brooks (Editor), Thomas D.
Fahey, Timothy P. White, Baldwin
ISBN: 0767410246

Kinematics of Human Motion
Vladimir M. Zatsiorsky
ISBN: 0880116765

Kinesiology of Exercise: A Safe & Effective
Way to Improve Athletic Performance
Michael Yessis
ISBN: 0940279363

Legends of Health & Fitness
Mitchell Lane Publishers
ISBN: 1584150521

Musclemag International's North American
Bodybuilding & Fitness Directory: Find
What You're Looking For!
Mark Shaw (Compiler)
ISBN: 1552100189

Physiology of Sport and Exercise
Jack H. Wilmore, David L. Costill
ISBN: 0736000844

Science & Practice of Strength Training
Vladimir M. Zatsiorsky
ISBN: 0873224744

Out of Print Books
Worth the Search

3 More Reps (original publication)
Posedown: Muscletalk with the Champs
(revised version)
George Snyder, Rick Wayne

Arms and Shoulders Above the Rest
Rick Wayne

Bev Francis' Power Bodybuilding
Bev Francis

Big Arm Book (Big Chest Book, etc), 1930s
Bob Hoffman

Big: Bulkbuilding Instructional Guide
Ellington Darden

Blood and Guts
Dorian Yates

Body Beautiful
Oscar Heidenstam

Bodybuilding: An Illustrated History
David Webster

Bodymen, The
Rick Wayne

Best That's In You, The
Strongman, The
Bonomo books (any and all)
Joe Bonomo

Complete Guide to Weight Training &
Sports Conditioning for Young Athletes
Frederick C Hatfield

Defying Gravity:
How to Win at Weightlifting
Bill Starr

Developing Grip Strength
David Gentle, David Webster

Hepburn's Law
Doug Hepburn

How to Mold Series (any and all)
George Jowett

Jack LaLanne
Way To Vibrant Good Health, The
Jack Lalanne

Mind Pump:
The Psychology of Bodybuilding
Tom Kubistant

Muscle Wars: The Behind-the-Scenes
Story of Competitive Bodybuilding
Rick Wayne

New High-Intensity Bodybuilding
Ellington Darden

Pro-Style Bodybuilding
Tom Platz, Bill Reynolds

Pumping Iron
Charles Gaines, George Butler

Raw Muscle!
Dennis B Weis, Robert Kennedy

Revitalize Your Life After 50: Improve Your
Looks, Your Health & Your Sex Life
Jack Lalanne

Secrets of Strength and Development
Bob Hoffman

Stack It:
The Ultimate New Strategy for Mass
Robert Kennedy

Super Athletes, The
A Record of the Limits of Human Strength,
Speed & Stamina
David P. Willoughby

Thomas Inch's Book of Strength
Thomas Inch

Ultimate Physique, The
Bill Richardson, David Webster

Underground Body Opus:
Militant Weight Loss & Recomposition
Daniel Duchaine

Unleashing the Wild Physique
Vince Gironda, Robert Kennedy

Journals & Newsletters

Email Newsletters

Dave's Weekly Email Newsletter
http://davedraper.com/draper-newsletter.html

ThinkMuscle Email Newsletter
http://www.thinkmuscle.com/

Sports Journal, The
http://www.thesportjournal.org/

Print Newsletters

Ageless Athletes
610 N. Main Street Suite 221
Blacksburg, VA 24060
$24 U.S. or $30 outside the U.S

All-Round Weightlifting Strength Journal
(IAWA)
Bill Clark
3906 Grace Ellen Drive
Columbia, Mo. 65202
$12.00 US/4 issues

Assoc. of Oldetime Barbell & Strongmen
AOBS
4959 Viceroy St., Suite 203
Cape Coral, FL 33904
$20.00

Dinosaur Files
8801 Hunter's Lake Drive #511
Tampa, Florida 33647
12 issues/$50 US; $55 outside the U.S

Fitt Quarterly
1180 Cassells Street, Suite 102
North Bay, ON   P1B 4B6
CANADA
$6.95/year or $9.95/2 years

Hardgainer
CS Publishing Ltd
P O Box 20390
CY-2151, Nicosia, Cyprus
6 issues/US $29.95, check or money order
(not a postal money order) or £18.95
private cheque or postal order in the UK

Hard Training Newsletter
(formerly known as the HIT Newsletter)
Edited by Dr. Ken E. Leistner
Hard Training
P.O. Box 19446,
Cincinnati OH 45219
US $15.00/4 issues

Iron Game History
Todd-McLean Collection
Dept of Kinesiology, Rm 107
Anna Hiss Gym/A2000
The University of Texas
Austin, TX 78712
$25 U.S. or $35 outside the U.S

Iron Master Newsletter
Osmo Kilha
199 SE 10th Court
Hermiston, Oregon 97838
(541) 667-8123
3 issues/$25.00

MILO Strongman
P.O. Box 1228
Nevada City, CA 95959, USA
(530) 265-6725
4 issues/ US: $39.95, Canada or Mexico:
$45.95, $59.95 all other countries

Parrillo's Performance Press
4690K Interstate Drive
Cincinnati, OH 45246
(800) 344-3404
12 issues/$19.95; $29.95 in Canada &
Mexico;$49.95 other countries

Powerlifting USA
Mike Lambert
Lock Box 3238-C
Camarillo, CA 93011
(800) 448-POWER
$31.95 U.S. or $42 outside the U.S

Steele Jungle
Max Furek
57 Jeanette Street
Mocanaqua, PA 18655
(717) 542-7946
4 issues/$10.00

Strongman Memorabilia, Muscular
Memorabilia
William E. Moore
P O Box 20732
Tuscaloosa, AL 35402
Rates vary, average $6.00 per year

Weightlifting News
Published by Lift & Run
112 East High St.
Balliston Spa, NY 12020
$34.95 in the US, $39.95 in Canada and
$49.95 in other countries

Weightlifter's Newsletter
Denis Reno
30 Cambria Road
West Newton, MA 02165
$24 US, Canada $26, Europe $32 and the
rest of the world $37

X-ercise Files Magazine
Brian Johnston
4040 Del Rey Avenue #7
Marina Del Rey, CA 90292
(310) 301-8481
4 issues/$19.95

Worldwide

Amicale des Anciens Culturistes Enseign
Ants et Pratiquants (AACEP)
Jean Long
AACEP
Rue de Varennes 50, 36210
Chabris, France

Associazone Italiana Culturismo
Biagio Filizola
C.P. 15, 84073
SAPRI (Sa), Italy

Health & Strength
Roy Edwards
H&S
Pant Cottage, Pant Lane
Austwick, Via Lancaster, LA2 8BH, England

Musclemob Newsletter
Steve Gardener
72, Bell Green
Lower Sydenham, London, SE26 4PZ,
England

Muscle News Tabloid magazine
Muscle News
10 Alpha Court
Denton, M34 3RB, England

Strand Puller Newsletter
Jim Bartlett
88, Schofield Street
Hathershaw, Oldham, Lancs OL8 2QJ
England

Strength Athletes Newsletter
Mark Shaw
384, Ashby Road
Coalville, Leicester LE67 3LE, England

Strength Journal (IAWA), UK edition
Frank Allen
11, Orchard Road
Birstall, Leicester, LE4 4GB, England

Journals

Exercise Protocol Journal
IART
2545 Trout Lake Road
P.O. Box 24016
North Bay, Ontario, CANADA P1B 9S1
www.ep-mag.com/
www.i-a-r-t.com/

Journal of Athletic Training
NATA-JAT
2952 Stemmons Freeway
Dallas, TX 75247
$32 in US; $40 outside US
www.journalofathletictraining.org/

Journal of Nutrition
American Society for Nutritional Sciences
9650 Rockville Pike
Bethesda, MD 20814

Journal of Strength and Conditioning
Research
William J. Kraemer, PhD, CSCS
The Human Performance Laboratory
Ball State University
Muncie, IN 47306

NSCA Strength and Conditioning Journal
955 N. Union Blvd.
Colorado Springs, CO 80909

Strength and Conditioning Journal
P.O. Box 1897
Lawrence, KS 66044-8897
6 issues/$88.00

Certifications

ACSM American College of Sports
Medicine
401 W. Michigan Street
Indianapolis, IN 46202-3233
(317) 637-9200
www.acsm.org/

American Council on Exercise
5820 Oberlin Drive, Suite 102
San Diego, CA 92121-3787
(800) 825-3636
www.acefitness.com/

IART
2545 Trout Lake Road
P.O. Box 24016
North Bay, Ontario CANADA P1B 9S1
(705) 476-6058
www.i-a-r-t.com/

ISSA
International Sports Sciences Association
035 Santa Barbara Street
Santa Barbara, CA 93101
(800)892-4772
www.issaonline.com/

National Strength and Conditioning
Association:
1955 N. Union Blvd.
Colorado Springs, CO 80909
(800) 815-6826
www.nsca-lift.org/menu.asp

Associations and Federations

See Website Category for Specific Lifting Federations

ACSM American College of Sports
Medicine
401 W. Michigan Street
Indianapolis, IN 46202
(317) 637-9200
www.acsm.org/

AFPA American Fitness Professionals &
Associates
PO Box 214
Ship Bottom, NJ 08008
(609) 978-7583
www.afpafitness.com/

IDEA The Health and Fitness Source
6190 Cornerstone Court East # 204
San Diego, CA 92121-3773
(800) 999-4332
www.ideafit.com/

IHRSA International Health, Racquet &
Sportsclub Association
263 Summer Street
Boston, MA 02210
(617) 951-0055
www.ihrsa.org/

NATA National Athletic Trainer's Association
2952 Stemmons Freeway
Dallas Tx, 75247
(214) 637-6282
www.nata.org/

NFPT National Personal Fitness Trainer
PO Box 4579
Lafayette, IN 47903-4579
(800) 729-6378
www.nfpt.com/

NGA National Gym Association
PO Box 970579
Coconut Creek, FL 33097-0579
(716) 692-6150
www.nationalgym.com/

NSCA National Strength & Conditioning
Association
1955 N. Union Blvd.
Colorado Springs, CO 80909
(800) 815-6826
www.nsca-lift.org/menu.asp

USSA The United States Sports Academy
One Academy Drive
Daphne, Alabama 36526-7055
(334) 626-3303
www.sport.ussa.edu/

Muscle Memorabilia

Muscle Memory—The Internet Bodybuilding Database
Preserving the History of Bodybuilding
This database contains over 30,000 entries and can be sorted by year, contest title, contestant's name or even by letters in alphabetical order for when you're not sure of the name. You'll also find a listing of all the muscle magazines known to be printed, all the movies featuring bodybuilders sorted either by movie title, year or bodybuilder's name and a nice selection of very old magazine article reprints. Save your steps; most of your competitive bodybuilder questions will be answered right here.
www.musclememory.com/

AOBS Assoc. of Oldetime Barbell &
Strongmen
4959 Viceroy Street, Suite 203
Cape Coral, FL 33904

eBay
Auction:memorabilia, books or magazines
www.ebay.com/

Archives Rare Bodybuilding Books
David Landau
(305) 932-9878

GMV Video Productions Ltd
Wayne Gallasch
P.O. Box 10164
Gouger St. Adelaide,
S.Australia 5000. Australia.
www.gmv.com.au

Iron Men on The Net, 1920-1980
www.creative.net/~adworx/index.shtml

Strength Training Library
William F Hinbern
32430 Cloverdale
Farmington, MI 48336-4008
(248)477-2739

Strongman Memorabilia
Muscular Memorabilia
William E. Moore
P O Box 20732
Tuscaloosa, AL 35402

Weight Game History
Howard Havener
11031 Wooldridge Dr.
Manassas, VA 22111.
Please send $1.00 for listing

Todd-McClean Physical Culture Collection
Dept of Kinesiology, Rm 107
Anna Hiss Gym/A2000
The University of Texas
Austin, TX 78712
www.edb.utexas.edu/faculty/jtodd/index.html

Equipment Websites

CYBEX International
www.ecybex.com/

Eleiko Equipment USA
www.dynamic-eleiko.com/

Eleiko Equipment EUROPE
www.eleikosport.com/

EZGrip—Bar gripping tool
www.4ezgrip.com/

Hammer Strength
www.hammerstrength.com/

Ironmind
Buffalo Bar, Apollon's Axle (Thick bar)
Captains of Crush grippers and other
training tools
www.ironmind.com/main/index.asp

Ivanko Barbell Company
www.ivanko.com/

Manta Ray/Sting Ray Squat Assistance
www.adfit.com/

PDA—Piedmont Design Associates
Fractional Plates & Shrug bar
www.fractionalplates.com/

Pendulum Fitness
www.pendulumfitness.com/

PlateMate
www.theplatemate.com/

PowerBlock dumbbell system
www.powerblocks.com/

Shoulder Horn Rotator Cuff Repair
www.shoulderhorn.com/

Southern Xercise Tru-Squat
www.southernxercise.com/

Titan Sport Powerlifting Gear
www.titansupport.com/

Trap Bar
www.gerardtrapbar.com/

York Barbell Company
www.yorkbarbell.com/

Online Discussion Groups & Bulletin Board Forums

Dave Draper's IronOnline (IOL)
www.egroups.com/group/IronOnline

Crain's Muscle World Powerlifting Forum
http://members.boardhost.com/
powerforum/?1387

Fred Hatfield's Dr Squat Training Forum
www.drsquat.com/

GarageGym Bulletin Board
http://server2.ezboard.com/
bgaragegymironpageforum

GoHeavy Bulletin Board Forums
www.goheavy.com/forums/

Hardgainer
www.hardgainer.com/roundtable.html

HIT Digest
www.egroups.com/group/Hitdigest

Low Carb Diet & Exercise List
http://solid.net/~homerc/

Strength-Digest
www.deepsquatter.com/strength/list.htm

USA Powerlifting Bulletin Board Forum
www.powerlifting.ca/cgi-bin/usapl.cgi

Weights List
www.weightsnet.com/weights/

Training and Nutrition Websites

Nutrition & Diet Related Websites

BrinkZone-Supplement Expert Will Brink
www.brinkzone.com/home.html

Dave's Gourmet Albacore Tuna
www.davesalbacore.com/

Paleolithic Diet Page
www.paleodiet.com/

USDA Nutrient Database
www.nal.usda.gov/fnic/foodcomp/

Weight Commander Diet Software
www.interaccess.com/weightcmdr

Bodybuilding Specific Websites

ABA/INBA/PNBA Bodybuilding Assocations
Amateur Bodybuilding Association
International Natural Bodybuilding Assoc
Professional Natural Bodybuilding Assoc
www.naturalbodybuilding.com/

ANBC
American Natural Bodybuilding Conference
www.anbc.org/

IFBB International Federation of Bodybuilders
www.ifbb.com/

NABBA National Amateur Bodybuilders Assoc
WFF World Fitness Federation
www.nabba.com/
www.nabba-international.com/

NABF North American Bodybuilding Fed
www.nabfusa.com/

NPC National Physique Committee
www.npcnewsonline.com/
www.getbig.com/info/npc.htm

Olympic Lifting Federations & Training Websites

Gallery of Olympic Weightlifters
www.geocities.com/Colosseum/Field/7342/

International Olympic Committee
www.olympic.org/

International Weightlifting Database
www.iat.uni-leipzig.de/weight.htm

International Weightlifting Federation
www.iwf.net/

Olympic Lifting Basics
www.olympus.net/personal/cablebar/

Olympic Lifting On The Web
www.lifttilyadie.com/w8lift.htm

Strength Online Olympic Lifting
www.deepsquatter.com/strength/
archives/olympic/

The Weightlifting Encyclopedia
www.wlinfo.com/

USAWA United States All-Round Weighlifting
IAWA International All-Round Weightlifting
www.usawa.com/

United States Olympic Committee
www.olympic-usa.org/

USA Masters Weightlifting
www.mastersweightlifting.org/

USA Weightlifting Federation
www.usaweightlifting.org/

Powerlifting Federation & Training Websites

ADFPA/USA American Drug Free
Powerlifting Association
www.adfpa.com/
www.usapowerlifting.com/

American Powerlifting Association
www.home.xnet.com/~frantz/

Canadian Powerlifting Union
www.powerlifting.ca/

Critical Bench—Bench Pressing Power
www.criticalbench.com/

European Powerlifting Federation
www.europower.org/

International Powerlifting Federation
www.worldsport.com/

NASA Natural Athlete Strength Association
www.nasa-sports.com/

Pan-American Powerlifting Federation
www.panampl.com/

Powerlifting.com
www.powerlifting.com/

Rickey Dale Crain's Muscle World
www.crainsmuscleworld.com/

Strength Online Powerlifting Instructional
www.deepsquatter.com/strength/
archives/tommc/

USAPL USA Powerlifting-formerly ADFPA
www.usapowerlifting.com/

USPF United States Powerlifting Federation
www.uspf.com/

WDFPF World Drug Free Powerlifting Fed
www.geocities.com/~wdfpf/

Westside Barbell Club
www.deepsquatter.com/westside/main.htm

WNPF World Natural Powerlifting Fed
hometown.aol.com/wnpf/index.htm

Strongman Federations & Competition Websites

American Federation of Strength Athletes
www.full-strength.com/

International Federation of
Strength Athletes
www.ifsaworld.com/

IronSport Gym
www.ironsport.com/

National Strength Athletics Association
www.strength-athletics.com/

North American Strongman Society
www.home.swbell.net/wwillyh/index.html

Power Building Strongman
www.mcshane-enterprises.com/PB/

Scottish American Athletic Association
www.saaa-net.org/

Strong As Steel
www.strongassteel.net/

Strongest Man Alive
www.strongestmanalive.com/

World's Strongest Man
www.strongestman.com/

Iron Game Memory Websites

Brian's Drive-In Theatre—Draper Memories
www.members.tripod.com/%7EBrianJ1/
davedraper.html

Charles Atlas
www.charlesatlas.com/

Muscle Memory
www.musclememory.com/

Schwarzenegger By Butler Photography
www.schwarzeneggerbybutler.com/

Sandow
Historic Photographs of Early Bodybuilders
www.geocities.com/SoHo/Museum/6496/

The Betty Zone
Harold Forsko's Tribute to Betty Weider
www.bettyweider.com/

Research Reference Websites

Ask the Dietitian
www.dietitian.com/

Berkeley Heart Lab Advance Lipid Testing
www.berkeleyheartlab.com/services.html

Consumer Health Misinformation
www.quackwatch.com/

Glycemic Index List
www.mendosa.com/gilists.htm

Harcourt International Journal Publications
www.harcourt-international.com/

Human Kinetics Publications
www.hkusa.com/

Journal of Performance Enhancement &
Jrnl of Performance Supplement Review
http://members.tripod.com/mprevost/

Kinesiology Forum
www.kines.uiuc.edu/kinesforum/

Medical Journals Online
www.freemedicaljournals.com/

Medline Medical & Scientific Research
www.medscape.com/

National Library of Medicine
Consumer Health Database
www.nlm.nih.gov/medlineplus/

Nutrient Data Laboratory
Food Composition Products
www.nal.usda.gov/fnic/foodcomp/Data/
index.html

Skeletal Muscles of the Human Body
www.ptcentral.com/muscles/

SportDiscus Directory
www.sportdiscus.com/

Sports Science Research
www.sportsci.org/

UMLS Metathesaurus
www.igm.nlm.nih.gov/

Training Websites

Dave Draper's IronOnline
www.davedraper.com/

Abdominal Training FAQ Page
www.timbomb.net/ab/ab.faq.html

Ageless Athletes
www.ageless-athletes.com/

American Bodybuilding
www.getbig.com/

American Strength Legends
www.mcshane-enterprises.com/ASL/

Baye.Net High Intensity Training
www.baye.net/

Bodybuilding Competition FAQ Page
//nps.ticz.com/bbcfaq.htm

Clarence Bass' Ripped
www.cbass.com/index.htm

Charles Poliquin
www.charlespoliquin.net

Charles Staley's Myo Dynamics
www.myodynamics.com/

Cyberpump—Home of HIT
www.cyberpump.com/

Deepsquatter Strength Online
www.deepsquatter.com/

Dictionary of Lifting Terms and Techniques
www.trygve.com/weightsglossary.html

Dinosaur Training (Brooks Kubik)
www.dinosaurtraining.com/index.shtml

Dr. Squat (Fred Hatfield)
www.drsquat.com/index.htm

East Coast Muscle Competition Site
www.eastcoastmuscle.com/

Ellington Darden's Classic-X
www.classicx.com/

Exercise Demonstrations & Calculators
www.biofitness.com/manual.html

Exercise Instruction & Structural Kinesiology
www.planetkc.com/exrx/Exercise.html

Explosive Athlete
www.explosiveathlete.com/

Grip Training
www.leikestova.org/solan/grip/index.html

International Association of Resistance
Trainers (HIT)
www.i-a-r-t.com/

Internet Bodybuilding Search Engine
www.searchbodybuilding.com/

Iron Magazine Online
www.ironmag.com/

Mass Machine (Skip LaCour)
www.skiplacour.com/

Mesomorphosis.com
www.mesomorphosis.com/

Musclehedz Cartoons (John Gleneicki)
www.musclehedz.net/

Muscle Monthly
www.musclemonthly.com/

Physique-Engineering Technologies
www.physique-engineering.com/

Quality Mass Gain (Sandeep De)
www.deepsquatter.com/strength/archives/
misc/sandeep.htm

Repetrope Muscle Videos
www.repetrope.com/

Sports Training with Dr. Michael Yessis
www.dryessis.com/

SuperSlow Exercise Guide
www.superslow.com/

WeighTrainer
www.stas.net/weightrainer/main.html

WeightsNet
www.weightsnet.com/

Weighty Matters Archive Page
staff.washington.edu/griffin/weights.html

Women's Weightlifting (Krista's)
www.stumptuous.com/weights.html

This page intentionally left blank

Index